Cold War Football

A gargantuan battle for hearts and minds, the Cold War is the supreme example of a 'people's war'. But what did the 'people's game' have to do with it? From Dynamo Moscow's stormy tour of Britain in 1945 to the inaugural Women's World Cup in 1991, Tony Shaw and Alan McDougall chart the clash between capitalism and communism in ten iconic football matches. They take us across Europe, Asia, South America and Africa to uncover football's part in bolstering democracies and dictatorships and in the struggle for influence in the developing world. They show how these matches offered a rare opportunity to see what life was like on 'the other side' of the Iron Curtain, making friends of enemies but also fuelling revolution. Featuring legendary players, goals and on- and off-field controversies, this is a fascinating history of how the Cold War shaped football and how football shaped the Cold War.

Tony Shaw is Professor of Contemporary History at the University of Hertfordshire. His books include *Eden, Suez and the Mass Media* (1996), *Cinematic Cold War: The American and Soviet Struggle for Hearts and Minds* (2010) and *Hollywood and Israel: A History* (2022).

Alan McDougall is Professor of History at the University of Guelph. His books include *The People's Game: Football, State and Society in East Germany* (2014), *Contested Fields: A Global History of Modern Football* (2020) and *Dreams and Songs to Sing: A People's History of Liverpool FC from Shankly to Klopp* (2025).

TONY SHAW AND ALAN McDOUGALL

COLD WAR FOOTBALL

A HISTORY IN TEN MATCHES

Shaftesbury Road, Cambridge CB2 8EA, United Kingdom

One Liberty Plaza, 20th Floor, New York, NY 10006, USA

477 Williamstown Road, Port Melbourne, VIC 3207, Australia

314–321, 3rd Floor, Plot 3, Splendor Forum, Jasola District Centre,
New Delhi – 110025, India

Cambridge University Press is part of Cambridge University Press & Assessment,
a department of the University of Cambridge.

We share the University's mission to contribute to society through the pursuit of
education, learning and research at the highest international levels of excellence.

www.cambridge.org
Information on this title: www.cambridge.org/9781009456128

DOI: 10.1017/9781009456098

© Tony Shaw and Alan McDougall 2026

First published 2026

A catalogue record for this publication is available from the British Library

Library of Congress Cataloging-in-Publication Data
NAMES: Shaw, Tony, 1965– author | McDougall, Alan author
TITLE: Cold War football : a history in ten matches / Tony Shaw.
DESCRIPTION: New York, NY : Cambridge University Press, 2026. | Includes bibliographical
references and index.
IDENTIFIERS: LCCN 2026000671 | ISBN 9781009456128 hardback | ISBN 9781009456142
paperback | ISBN 9781009456098 epub
SUBJECTS: LCSH: Soccer – Political aspects | Soccer matches – History – 20th century | Cold
War – Influence | Sports and state – History – 20th century
CLASSIFICATION: LCC GV943.9.P65 S57 2026
LC record available at https://lccn.loc.gov/2026000671

ISBN 978-1-009-45612-8 Hardback

CONTENTS

INTRODUCTION

It's 1979: a big year for the Cold War. When the United States and Communist China finally normalise relations. When Moscow and Washington sign their first nuclear arms-reduction treaty. When the Iranian revolution ousts the pro-Western shah in favour of Ayatollah Khomeini's theocracy. When the Marxist Sandinistas topple the pro-American Somoza regime in Nicaragua. And when, in December, the Soviet Union invades Afghanistan, triggering the 'new' Cold War of the 1980s.

In Europe in 1979, the Cold War drags on. The continent's now been divided for more than three decades into two strange sub-universes. The capitalist West stands for freedom, democracy and wealth. The communist East stands for social justice, mutual cooperation and ideological duty. Neither side is perfect. Urban terrorists are killing and maiming in Ireland, Italy and West Germany. Families are desperately escaping East Germany in hot-air balloons. Amidst the tensions and troubles, two football encounters breach the Iron Curtain. With very different results.

In March, the top team in East Germany's Oberliga, Dynamo Berlin, play a friendly against FC Kaiserslautern in Rhineland-Palatinate, across the border in West Germany. Travelling back after the game, a member of Dynamo's squad, Lutz Eigendorf, disappears at a rest stop and defects to the West. Eigendorf (see Figure 0.1) is no ordinary East German player. He's a product of an elite sports school in Berlin, a former soldier and a candidate member of the ruling Socialist

Figure 0.1 Dynamo Berlin's Lutz Eigendorf (left) and Stahl Brandenburg's Gerhard Kraschina, at the Sportforum Hohenschönhausen, East Berlin, 22 November 1975. © Gert Kilian/ullstein bild via Getty Images.

Unity Party. He plays for the East German national side and is so highly thought of he's been dubbed the Beckenbauer of the East.

Erich Mielke, Dynamo's chief patron and the cut-throat boss of the Stasi, East Germany's secret police, wants vengeance. Eigendorf's wife divorces her traitorous husband, having fallen for a 'Romeo' agent planted by the Stasi. In West Germany, Stasi spies relentlessly shadow Eigendorf, sending Berlin detailed reports on his love affairs and faltering career in the Bundesliga with Kaiserslautern and Eintracht Braunschweig. In Braunschweig in March 1983, Eigendorf dies after wrapping his sports car round a tree in suspicious circumstances. The police and coroners blame alcohol. Others blame Mielke. Today, the jury is still out.[1]

Six months after Lutz Eigendorf's defection, in September and October 1979, another East German team, FC Magdeburg, play a team from the West, home and away in the first round of the European Cup Winners' Cup. Their opponents are Wrexham AFC, the Welsh club that will be bought in 2021 by the Hollywood stars Ryan Reynolds and Rob

McElhenney. Despite Magdeburg having defeated the mighty AC Milan to win the Cup in 1974, neither they nor Wrexham are famous, especially for serving up first-class entertainment. But both games are crackers. Wrexham edge the first leg in Wales 3–2. Magdeburg win the return leg 5–2, after two dodgy penalty decisions and calamitous Wrexham defending in extra-time.

During the two matches, players and fans get chatting: about life, politics and, mainly, football. From nothing, the clubs forge an unlikely, barrier-breaking friendship. The bond will outlive the Berlin Wall, and last for decades. In January 2018, two hundred Magdeburg fans touring Britain with their team visit Wrexham's Racecourse Ground. After beers in the bar, they cheer on the Welsh team's 4–0 drubbing of Torquay United. 'From Prussia with Love', runs the headline in Wrexham's local rag the following day.[2]

Football has always been deeply intertwined with politics. As the world's most popular sport, how could it be otherwise? Recent events only confirm this. Just look at the footballers taking the knee before matches to demonstrate their opposition to racism. Or the global debate about sexism triggered by Spanish football boss Luis Rubiales' kissing of Jenni Hermoso after the 2023 Women's World Cup final. Or the allegations Saudi Arabia will cynically use its hosting of the 2034 World Cup to sportswash its human rights reputation.[3]

Football's bloody links with war in particular go back a long way. To the poignant Christmas truce game between British and German soldiers on the Western Front in December 1914. To the Death Match between a bunch of Ukrainian bakers and their Nazi occupiers in Kyiv in August 1942. To the Football War fought between Honduras and El Salvador in July 1969. And to the Yugoslav Wars of the 1990s, in which Croatia's president Franjo Tuđman, tweaking the famous Clausewitz dictum, declared that 'football is merely the continuation of the war by other means'.[4]

This is the first book to unveil football's role during the defining ideological conflict of the twentieth century, the Cold War. A gargantuan battle for hearts and minds fought across the globe between 1945 and 1991, the Cold War is the supreme example of a 'people's war'. Politicians and military commanders might have appeared to be the conflict's key players, but we now know that it was the millions of ordinary citizens who held the most power. This explains the massive propaganda campaigns that governments conducted, designed to court their own and their enemy's citizens. The result – a giant philosophical, technological and cultural struggle for supremacy – was unparalleled in scale and ingenuity. The contest involved everything from the Beatles and Solzhenitsyn to Picasso, Disney, Gagarin and McDonald's. And it impacted on what virtually everyone heard, tasted, read, laughed and cried about, watched and played.[5]

As the 'people's game', football was inextricably bound up in the cultural Cold War. But how exactly? The stories of the two matches from 1979 briefly outlined above give us a good clue. Football could, those matches suggest, make friends out of enemies during the Cold War and even spark murder. Our book shows that football did both these things – and a whole lot more. Football forecast, maybe even helped start, the Cold War. It generated fear, hatred, derision and suspicion. It contributed to revolutions and heightened racism. It poked fun at religious and authority figures. It offered a rare opportunity to see what life was like on 'the other side' of the Curtain. It bolstered democracies and colonial dictatorships. It served as a substitute or outlet for military conflict. It anticipated the collapse of the Berlin Wall. And it presaged the geopolitical tensions we live with today. In short, football's impact during the Cold War was as vibrant, contradictory and absorbing as the game itself.

Simultaneously, the Cold War also impacted on and even changed football. By using football as a tool to win over large parts of the developing world to their side, the conflict's chief protagonists helped the sport to grow geographically. By competing against their Cold War rivals or enemies, countries introduced new ways of thinking about the game, revolutionising it tactically. By investing so much in football for political ends, governments popularised the sport and, possibly, improved the quality of the game. Conversely, by exploiting football for nefarious Cold War purposes, politicians may have put people off playing or watching the game. In some places, weaponising the sport possibly killed its appeal. Take Dynamo Berlin as a case in point. After Lutz Eigendorf's defection, the club, thanks to Erich Mielke's patronage, won the Oberliga ten years on the trot. As a result, league attendances plummeted, even at Dynamo.[6]

Cold War Football captures these dual dynamics by bringing to life ten carefully selected matches. Each match centres on a key political theme, and ties football to important stages of, or moments in, the Cold War. Chronologically, the matches bridge the whole conflict, from

Dynamo Moscow's hilariously combustible encounter against Arsenal in a foggy London in November 1945, to China's historic victory over Norway in the opening match of the inaugural Women's World Cup in Guangzhou in November 1991. Some of the matches – such as the 1954 World Cup final between Hungary and West Germany and the World Cup quarter-final in 1966 between Portugal and North Korea – are iconic and given a Cold War twist. Others – like the friendly game between Ireland and Yugoslavia in 1955 and the fiery derby between Steaua Bucharest and Dinamo Bucharest in 1988 – will be brand-new to most readers. The matches take the reader around the world, from Spain's fascist dictatorship to the megalomaniac terror of Mobutu Sese Seku's Zaire. They combine stories about clubs and national teams, and men's and women's football, and they roam across Europe, Asia, South America and Africa.

Cold War Football is richly researched. Drawing on the archives of powerful international football organisations, foreign ministries, secret intelligence services and even religious figures, as well as film footage and players' memoirs, this is no ordinary book about football. These original sources allow us to hear the voices of the players, managers, politicians and spectators involved in the matches. They also enable us to get *behind the scenes* of our matches and, in doing so, get answers to questions that football fans have been asking for decades. Were, for instance, Arsenal cheating when they fielded 'wizard winger' Stanley Matthews as a ringer against Dynamo Moscow in 1945? Did the North Korean dictator Kim Il Sung sentence his players to the gulags after Portugal kicked them out of the 1966 World Cup? What really caused the Soviet Union not to show up for their crucial World Cup-qualifying match against Chile in Santiago in 1973, and how come the match went ahead anyway?

As well as going behind the scenes, *Cold War Football* also takes us *on to the pitch*. Each of our ten matches is forensically examined, with vivid coverage of glorious goals and haunting misses, peevish fouls and ludicrous mishaps, and controversial decisions and crowd trouble. Our aim is to bring out the real drama of the action, to reveal things many readers will have never seen. We also want to revisit legendary on-field moments, moves and miscarriages of justice: to look, for example, at whether suspect British refereeing and West German drug-taking robbed Hungary's Magical Magyars of the World Cup in 1954. Or how Spain won the 1964 Euros with what has been described as 'one of the all-time great headers'. Or why Zaire defender Mwepu Ilunga infamously ran out of his team's wall to hoof the ball up field at a Brazilian free kick in the 1974 World Cup finals. A serious book with important things to say about football at war, *Cold War Football*'s tales of shorts-dropping Romanian defenders and Korean-chanting Teessiders capture the comical side of its subject.

Cold War Football reveals, ultimately, just how important and eclectic a role football played in international affairs after 1945. In Francisco Franco, Lavrenty Beria, Nikita Khrushchev, Augusto Pinochet, Nicolae Ceauşescu, Josip Broz Tito and Henry Kissinger, the book features some of the most venerated and despised political figures of modern times. In Pelé, Franz Beckenbauer, Luis Suárez, Ferenc Puskás, Lev Yashin, Dragan Džajić and Eusébio, it boasts some of the greatest names in football history. *Cold War Football* uncovers both the enthralling and ugly sides of the beautiful game. We hope you enjoy reading it as much as we enjoyed writing it.

1 THE FOG OF WAR
Arsenal vs. Dynamo Moscow, London, November 1945

November 1945. Adolf Hitler has been dead six months and World War Two is finally over. What better way to celebrate victory and promote lasting British–Soviet unity than a football match in London between the pride of England, Arsenal, and the league champions of the USSR, Dynamo Moscow? Football is the biggest sport in both countries, yet the two teams have never met. The football bigwigs in Britain and the Soviet Union support the idea. So do their governments, or sort of. Unfortunately, things don't quite turn out as expected.

The trouble starts long before a ball has been kicked. On arrival at their menacing-looking digs in London's Wellington Barracks, the Dynamos initially refuse to get out of their bus for fear they've been cruelly tricked and are being imprisoned. Days later, Arsenal's boss George Allison likens a meeting with Dynamo's manager Mikhail Yakushin to being interrogated by the NKVD, the Soviet secret police. When Arsenal then announce they've selected a number of 'guest' players for the match, including England's 'wizard of dribble' Stanley Matthews, the Soviets cry foul. Right-wingers in Fleet Street don't see a problem. They argue Matthews' inclusion will make the game a proper contest between British individuality and Soviet collectivism. And anyway, how can Dynamo complain? The referee will be a Russian.

The game itself is a fiasco. That afternoon, the North London fog is so thick barely anyone, including players and officials, can see anything. Amid the haze, each side accuses the other of all sorts of wrongdoing. Arsenal allege Dynamo have taken advantage of the gloom and the Soviet substitute rule by playing periods of the game with twelve men. Dynamo accuse George Allison of trying to get the match abandoned after they've taken the lead, so he doesn't lose the hefty sum he's staked on an Arsenal victory. Towards the end of the game, a row breaks out over a nasty clash between two players, resulting in a black eye and a heavily disputed disallowed goal. Dynamo win the so-called friendly 4–3. Afterwards, the writer George Orwell pours scorn on the match and the 'orgies of hatred' engendered by such encounters, coining his famous phrase that international sport is 'war minus the shooting'.[1]

Was Orwell right? Had the author of *Animal Farm* exposed the stupidity of organising a high-profile football match between British and Soviet teams when relations between the two countries were on a knife edge? Had the game terribly backfired, spoiling not soothing relations between the wartime Grand Alliance partners? Had the match, when coupled with the three other games Dynamo Moscow played on their headline-grabbing tour of Britain that November, even added to the international tensions that triggered the Cold War? Just a month earlier, Orwell had been among the very first to warn of an impending 'cold war'.[2] Perhaps the great polemicist was ahead of the game, in more ways than one.

The 'farce in the fog', as several commentators described the Arsenal–Dynamo Moscow game in November 1945, is an apt place to begin our exploration of Cold War football.[3] Set amid that 'phoney' phase of the conflict, before events like the Berlin Blockade made it a grim reality, 'one of the most exciting games 54,000 people have never seen'[4] is an important marker of the underlying tensions between the emerging East and West. The match shows how football was weaponised from the very start of the Cold War in a variety of ways by both sides. It demonstrates football's ability to both entertain and proselytise. And it illustrates how football could generate animosity and affection at critical points in the East–West conflict. The Dynamos played a free-flowing style of football that took the British, long regarded as the masters of the game, by storm in late 1945 and won the team thousands of new fans. Whether the Soviets' revolutionary approach to the game translated into increased British support for the Soviet way of life is questionable. But there's no doubting, from sporting and political perspectives, which side won what might be called the Cold War's first football battle.

From a footballing point of view, Britain and the Soviet Union had been engaged in a cold war of sorts long before 1945. Immediately after the Bolshevik Revolution, fearing foreign 'contamination', the Soviet government largely cut itself off from 'bourgeois' international sport. In the late 1920s, the Kremlin did allow an amateur British team run by the socialist Workers' Sports Federation to tour the Soviet Union (where it lost heavily), and Arsenal were reportedly invited to undertake a similar tour in the mid-1930s, only for the trip to fall through.[5] By the end of the thirties, despite official claims that all sports in the USSR were strictly amateur, the Soviet football authorities had created a de facto professional league and grown less isolationist. Soviet club teams played a number of European clubs home and away, but not one of them set foot on British turf. The British government refused Soviet teams visas on the grounds that their visits were designed to spread communist propaganda rather than sporting goodwill. By way of contrast, teams from Nazi Germany were welcomed, most famously in 1935 at Tottenham Hotspur's White Hart Lane, where a swastika flew over the main stand. In 1938, just four months before the notorious Munich agreement, an England side even gave the Nazi salute in front of 110,000 spectators at the Olympiastadion in Berlin.[6]

Germany's invasion of the Soviet Union in 1941 created a marriage of convenience between London and Moscow, and it is therefore why Hitler, no football fan, should take principal credit for Dynamo Moscow's tour of Britain in November 1945. The summer and autumn of 1945 hadn't been kind to relations between the Führer's three chief vanquishers. Arguments had broken out over the Americans' reluctance to share its nuclear secrets, over the Soviets' occupation of Eastern Europe and over Britain's renewed imperial machinations. Despite this, a cold war by no means looked inevitable. The British public's respect for 'Uncle Joe' Stalin and the Soviets' immense sacrifices under Nazi occupation was widespread, and many British newspapers were heavily critical of Washington's so-called atomic diplomacy. The Arsenal–Dynamo Moscow game coincided with the opening of the Nazi war crimes trials in Nuremberg – strong evidence, surely, of the importance of continued allied solidarity.[7]

The main instigator of the Dynamo Moscow tour was the inimitable Stanley Rous. A distinguished football referee, codifier of the game's rules, and secretary of the English Football Association from 1934 to 1962 (he became FIFA president in 1961), Rous always maintained that politics had no part to play in sport. In 1944, Rous put the idea of a British–Soviet club match to the Soviet ambassador to London. A year later, in October 1945, with the complications of war over, Rous sealed outline arrangements for the November Dynamo Moscow tour, following discussions with Soviet sports officials at a match between Chelsea and West Ham at Stamford Bridge. The appetite for a high-level encounter between British and Soviet football teams had been whetted in September, when a Red Army side had soundly beaten a British garrison team 3–0 in Berlin. Miffed by this defeat, the British military scheduled a rematch for mid-October, this time stacking their team with a clutch of Arsenal players who were still in uniform. At the last minute, the Red Army team pulled out of the fixture, citing 'demobilisation' issues. This wouldn't be the last time the Soviet football authorities used such avoidance tactics against teams from the West in the years ahead.[8]

Though it pretended to have no interest in the Dynamo Moscow tour, Clement Attlee's new, vehemently anti-communist Labour government took it very seriously. Many Foreign Office officials were sceptical of the tour's barrier-breaking potential, but junior minister and former Olympic runner, Philip Noel-Baker, a Quaker, was all for it, arguing that football matches offered a wonderful route to breaking down the Soviet Union's seclusion. From Moscow, the Foreign Office's foremost expert on Soviet affairs, Frank Roberts, declared the tour 'a real opportunity to promote closer Anglo-Soviet relations' but also emphasised its propaganda dimensions. Britain needed to flex its great-power muscles at this critical juncture, Roberts stressed, and to use the matches against Dynamo to show that it was still 'the world leader' in football. The embassy in Moscow subsequently sent the Football Association detailed reports on Dynamo's playing record, tactics and players. These even included information on how individual players took penalty kicks.[9]

Joseph Stalin's regime also saw the Dynamo Moscow tour as a means of bolstering allied friendship, but its real aim was to use it to launch the Soviet Union as a major force in world sport. The Soviet Union's success in defeating Nazism brought with it a determination to flex its own 'superpower' muscles, culturally as well as diplomatically.

Soviet football enjoyed a golden era of popularity in the 1940s – Dynamo's biggest home matches regularly attracted upwards of 90,000 spectators – and was now deemed ready for export. A series of matches against high-class opposition in Britain, the country which had invented the modern game and stood at the centre of world football's 'bourgeois fortress', was a mouth-watering prospect – especially if Soviet football came out on top. Success of this sort would lift Soviet spirits after the miseries of war and advertise communism's progress across the globe.[10]

From the Kremlin's perspective, Dynamo Moscow were the perfect fit as the first Soviet sports ambassadors to Britain. The club could trace its origins to the Charnock brothers from Blackburn, football-loving engineers with interests in the Russian cotton industry in the decades before World War One who were hired by the Morozov textile mill outside Moscow to teach its employees a healthy leisure activity. More importantly, Dynamo had won the first two Soviet Championships in 1936 and 1937 and another pair of national titles in 1940 and 1945. The club was the preserve of the Soviet secret police. Unlike Stalin, Lavrenty Beria, the NKVD's malevolent boss, was an avid football fan. A Georgian whose first love was Dynamo Tbilisi, Beria stopped at nothing to secure Dynamo's – and by extension the secret police's – success. Threatening to shoot failing managers and imprisoning Nikolai Starostin, the founder of rivals Spartak Moscow, the trades union 'people's team' hated by the state authorities, was all in a day's work. In November 1945, Dynamo were the most disciplined and decorated football team in the Soviet Union, revered for their technical skills and innovative tactics. The Dynamo players that toured Britain were highly paid professionals posing as state amateurs, not NKVD operatives, but they knew what was expected of them and to whom they ultimately answered.[11]

The Dynamo Moscow party landed at Croydon Airport south of London, aboard their lend-lease Dakotas, on 4 November 1945. They would stay for a month, playing four matches. A problem arose immediately. The Dynamos had given Stanley Rous only three hours' notice of their arrival and the FA couldn't find them enough hotel rooms in war-damaged London. Space was found for the tourists at a gloomy Wellington Barracks near Buckingham Palace for the night. On arrival, the players were so frightened by the 'feudal' conditions and scenes of staff loudly berating new recruits, they smelt a capitalist gulag. Rous acted quickly, and Sir Guy Bracewell-Smith, the chairman of Arsenal FC no less, came to the rescue, arranging for temporary accommodation in the ballroom of his Park Lane Hotel. Whether this act of generosity endeared the Soviets to Arsenal, for the time being at least, is unclear. In the press, a war of words broke out over the lodgings mess-up. Rous accused the Soviets of fussiness. The Dynamos' manager, Mikhail Yakushin, with a tongue firmly in his cheek perhaps, said that he sympathised with the accommodation shortage in London as it was 'like that in Stalingrad and Kiev too'. A letter-writer in the communist *Daily Worker* was 'disgusted': 'If it had been [Rudolf] Hess, our enemy, he would have been found a castle'.[12]

After this inauspicious start, things got stickier following a series of meetings over the next few days between the Football Association and Dynamo officials about the tour's rules of engagement. Discussion centred on a list of fourteen conditions tabled by the tourists. The FA agreed to most of these. It accepted Dynamo's request that substitutes be permitted, in line with Soviet league rules, but only as replacement for injured players. The FA also took on board Dynamo's wish for the players to have as much privacy as possible, which fed Fleet Street suspicions the communists had something to hide. Two other conditions accepted by the FA were at the root of later controversies. These were that Dynamo only wished to play club sides, and that their opponents' teams would be chosen only from a list of players submitted days in advance. These conditions were clearly intended to limit, not unreasonably perhaps, the strength of Dynamo's opposition. The FA could not consent to the Dynamos' request to play all of their games on Saturdays, due to scheduled league fixtures. But it was happy, finally, to grant the Dynamos' most specific request, which was to play Britain's most famous team, Arsenal.[13]

Dynamo Moscow's first game was set for 13 November, against First Division side Chelsea. In between trips to a theatre and greyhound track (PR obviously trumped privacy on occasions), the Soviet team prepared assiduously, training on the match pitch and watching a film they'd shot of their opponents' recent game against Birmingham City. Over the years, Dynamo had perfected a style of play that many commentators today believe laid the foundations for the Netherlands' 'total football' of the 1970s. Devised by Yakushin's predecessor, Boris Arkadiev, the first great Soviet theorist of football, it was a radical variation on the so-called W-M (3–2–2–3) formation favoured in Britain and elsewhere. Dynamo adopted a 3–1–2–1–3 formation, in which players, especially the forwards, constantly interchanged positions. The team also favoured a short, swift passing game (*passo-votchka*, as it became known) over the more conventional long-ball-with-wingers approach. Dynamo's style was built around the team rather than key individuals, which fit with the communists' collective ethos. Most British people knew next to nothing about all of this, which, combined with the long-held assumption that British football was the best in the world, explains why London's *Evening Standard* predicted that Chelsea would 'sweep the Russians off their feet'.[14]

To say the match at Stamford Bridge, the first ever between first-class British and Soviet teams, was eagerly anticipated is something of an understatement. While 74,000 spectators paid to get in, it's estimated upwards of 100,000 people saw the game. Photographs show cloth-capped schoolboys spilling onto the pitch behind the goals. Newspaper reports tell us that countless spectators who couldn't get into the ground simply broke into neighbouring houses to watch the game from their rooftops. People were so keen to attend any international match soon after the war, and especially to get a look at the mysterious Soviet team (see Figure 1.1), a set of stadium gates was torn off its hinges.[15]

The monster crowd saw a pulsating match that ebbed and flowed and ended in a 3–3 draw (see Figure 1.2). Chelsea's new

Figure 1.1 Dynamo Moscow line up to play Chelsea at Stamford Bridge, London, 13 November 1945. © Russell Westwood/Popperfoto via Getty Images.

Figure 1.2 Dynamo Moscow and Chelsea in action at Stamford Bridge, 13 November 1945. © Central Press/Getty Images.

centre-forward, Tommy Lawton – signed, the Soviet press spuriously claimed, solely with the Dynamo fixture in mind – scored an excellent debut goal. But it was the Dynamos' intricate close passing, which offered such a contrast to Chelsea's reliance on chasing the long ball, combined with their flowing attacking moves that didn't rely on an obvious target-man, that most thrilled fans. Dynamo missed a penalty (perhaps the Foreign Office advice paid off) and should have won by a comfortable margin.

At the end of the match, thousands of people swarmed onto the pitch and tried to chair the Soviet players to the dressing room. That evening, despite language issues, the Chelsea and Dynamo players got along well at a dinner at the West End's Café Royal. The morning after, the British press showered the Dynamo team with praise. 'The greatest club side ever to visit this island', was the *Sketch*'s verdict. Charles Buchan, former Arsenal and England captain, thought the Soviets' teamwork, movement off the ball and clever positional play were nothing short of sensational. The mood in Moscow and among the Dynamo players and staff was more restrained. 'Our boys were visibly nervous in the first half', reported Moscow Radio. 'It is to be hoped that, armed with this experience', the report concluded, 'the Dynamos will not stop at a draw in future games'.[16]

A few days later, Dynamo journeyed to Wales to meet Cardiff City, one of the few clubs that could play the Soviets on a Saturday thanks to a gap in their league fixtures. Cardiff were a decent Third Division side with a crop of good, young players, but they were not expected to trouble the Dynamos too much; to take on the Soviets, the team had cancelled a friendly against lowly Chester City. The day before the game, the Dynamo players made goodwill visits to Cardiff docks and a nearby coal mine at Abercynon. The tourists looked far more relaxed in this heavily industrialised area than in London. The ubiquitous red flags with hammer-and-sickle, a sign of the power of the Communist Party in South Wales, probably put them further at ease.

The match at Ninian Park attracted 40,000 spectators, many having travelled from as far away as Liverpool and Manchester. In the ceremonials before kick-off, the Cardiff players presented their Soviet counterparts with miniature miners' lamps. Dynamo thanked the 'Velsh' by running up a cricket score, trouncing them 10–1. The scoreline represented the biggest ever defeat inflicted by foreigners on a British Football League team. Despite this, the teams left the field shaking hands and laughing together, proof that the game had been played in the best of spirits. In Moscow after the game, locals jokingly asked British residents whether they wanted to trade: 'We'll give you some footballers in return for the atom-bomb secret'.[17]

Those in Britain who thought that Dynamo's draw against Chelsea had been a fluke now clearly needed to think again. The mood in British football circles was one of delight mixed with obduracy. To some, like the *Daily Mail*'s football correspondent Geoffrey Simpson, the Dynamos' revolutionary, rhythmic way of playing the game showed the way to football's future. To others, the Dynamos were 'a machine' that, like everything to do with communism, relied too much on systematic thinking and didn't allow for self-expression. Put the Soviets up against the best British football could offer and the brilliance of homegrown individualists like Stanley Matthews, argued the former Arsenal star Alex James, and the result would surely be different. The scene was set for Dynamo's next game, the big one against Arsenal.[18]

Nicknamed 'the Bank of England team' for their record-breaking spending and gate receipts in the 1920s and 1930s, Arsenal were the very epitome of 'bourgeois' football. The Gunners dominated English football in the inter-war era, winning the league five times and the FA Cup twice. Under manager Herbert Chapman and skipper Charles Buchan in the mid-twenties, Arsenal had played a key role in tactically revolutionising British football, inventing the W-M formation, which created a stronger, three-man defence to counter changes to the offside law. In the mid-1930s, Chapman's successor, George Allison, made Arsenal the finest exponents of the style of play that emerged from that revolution and one which still held sway in British football in 1945.[19]

Days before the match against Dynamo Moscow, George Allison met with Mikhail Yakushin and Nikolai Latyshev in the FA's London headquarters at Lancaster Gate. One of the Dynamos' early, fourteen conditions had been that the referee they'd brought with them should officiate at least one of their games, and, after the Soviets' nomination, it had been agreed that Latyshev would handle the match against Arsenal. The FA apparently weren't aware that Latyshev, who'd go on to referee the World Cup final between Brazil and Czechoslovakia in Chile in 1962, was a former Dynamo player. According to Allison's later account of the meeting, published after the Cold War had really set in, Yakushin and Latyshev asked the Gunners' boss all sorts of 'intimate' and 'impertinent' questions, touching on his personal life and that of his players. The Soviets wanted to know where Allison lived, how he spent his time, what the players did in their spare time and how they trained. The probing went on for three hours and 'was more like a Secret Police quiz rather than a football parley'. Allison admitted to coming away from the meeting highly irritated, and presumably as keen as mustard to put one over on Dynamo.[20]

Though the Soviets, to put it kindly, might just have been trying to learn the finer points of British football from one of its best teachers, Allison's irascibility was understandable given the pressure he was under in trying to put together a team strong enough to beat the Dynamos. Allison had a two-fold problem. Arsenal's form had dipped considerably during World War Two, brought on by the retirement of legendary figures like striker Ted Drake and the untimely deaths of others such as Bill Dean. Added to this, a large number of Arsenal players, including top-notch defenders Eddie Hapgood and Leslie Compton, were still overseas on military duty. As a result, Allison did what the Gunners and other sides had been doing for years since the war had started: recruit guest players from other clubs.

Allison selected six guests who would start the Dynamo match. Among these were goalkeeper Wyn Griffiths, a relative novice who had played during the war as an amateur for Derby County; Ronnie Rooke, Second Division Fulham's aging, bow-legged centre-forward; and Fulham's popular full-back Joe Bacuzzi, who had played for Chelsea against Dynamo. The real headliners, though, were the 'two Stanleys', Mortensen and Matthews. Mortensen had nearly died in an RAF bomber crash before signing for Blackpool in 1941. After the war, his goalscoring feats would make him one of the stars of British football. Stanley Matthews, the thirty-year-old outside right borrowed from Stoke City, was widely regarded as England's greatest footballer. Allison's recruitment of Matthews was highly questionable. Arsenal had two available, younger right-wingers who could have filled that berth. News broke that Matthews' inclusion had been requested by 'higher authorities'. We can't be sure who exactly this was but, given the FA's denial that it was them and the Foreign Office's earlier comments about the political importance of maintaining British football's reputation against the Soviets, evidence points to someone in government.[21]

The Dynamos protested strongly about the inclusion of these ringers. A press statement issued by their captain, Mikhail Semichastny, effectively argued that Arsenal were cheating and that the British had broken the two agreed conditions about Dynamo only playing club sides and having the right to be informed of opposition line-ups well in advance. To all intents and purposes, Semichastny said, Dynamo would be facing an England XI. This wasn't true – for one thing, two of the team were Welsh – but even some British newspapers sympathised with the claim. Semichastny's assertion also made sense politically. Losing to an 'England' side might save the Dynamos from Comrade Beria's ire. If they won the game, the Dynamos could boast they were one of the best club sides in the world.[22]

Dynamo were in fact an extremely talented team, who would have the advantage over Arsenal of being a settled side. Their goal-keeper, Aleksei Khomich, was, as surviving tour newsreels show, supremely agile. Already nicknamed 'Tiger' by the British press for his bravery against Chelsea and Cardiff, Khomich would later mentor the Soviet Union's greatest-ever keeper, Lev Yashin.[23] Skipper Mikhail

Semichastny was a rarity, a defender who used to play on the wing. Vastly experienced and a fine on-field leader, he had, in 1936, been the Soviet Union's first ever footballer of the year. Forward Konstantin Beskov, who had put four past Cardiff City, was an industrious poacher and skilful passer who would go on to score over 120 goals for Dynamo, before becoming manager of club and country. Vsevolod Bobrov, the team's real star so far on the tour (also with four goals), was a born athlete. A feared attacker on the football pitch and ice hockey rink, Bobrov would go on to become what many people regarded as the greatest Soviet athlete of all time. Before arriving in London, he had topped the Soviet goalscoring charts in his first season in football. Unbeknown to the British, Dynamo had borrowed Bobrov from the Red Army club, CSKA Moscow. This made him just as much a ringer as Matthews and Mortensen.[24]

Arsenal would have dearly loved to take on Dynamo Moscow at their splendid Art Deco fortress, Highbury, but serious damage caused by Luftwaffe raids ruled it out. Instead, the match took place down the road at Tottenham's White Hart Lane, the same ground over which a swastika had fluttered ten years earlier. In truth, the match shouldn't have taken place at all. On the morning of the game, Wednesday 21 November, White Hart Lane was blanketed by a fog so dense no one could see more than thirty yards ahead of them. Despite this, spectators kept on arriving – in their droves (see Figure 1.3) – hoping the fog would lift in time for the afternoon kick-off. By 10.30 a.m., the police, afraid for people's safety outside the ground, ordered the gates to be opened. By the time Nikolai Latyshev arrived around noon, a crowd of 40,000 were in White Hart Lane, desperate for the match to go ahead. On being told by local 'experts' that conditions were likely to improve, the referee announced the game was on.[25]

    Up till now on the tour, British referees had officiated Dynamo's matches, according to how the British interpreted the rules of the game. So the barging of goalkeepers and tackling from behind had been allowed, whereas the obstruction of players and pulling of their shirts, which the Soviet league permitted, had not. Substitutions, prohibited in Britain, had been allowed during the Chelsea and Cardiff games, but only when players were clearly seriously injured. With Latyshev in charge of the Arsenal game in front of 54,000 baying British spectators, the tour entered new, potentially fractious territory. Latyshev's decision

Figure 1.3 Part of the queue outside White Hart Lane, London for the match between Arsenal and Dynamo Moscow, 21 November 1945. © William Vanderson/ Fox Photos/Getty Images.

to referee the match in the 'continental' fashion, with both linesmen on one side of the pitch, instead of the more conventional 'diagonal' system, was justifiable but, given the conditions, ill-advised. It made it more difficult for officials to follow the play amid the gloom and undermined the Arsenal players' confidence in the Russian's decisions.

Despite the local experts' optimism, weather conditions never really improved at White Hart Lane that Wednesday afternoon. The fog thinned on occasions over the game's ninety minutes but never enough for spectators and journalists to see the whole pitch. Players, managers and officials did at times get a good look at the action but, as British Movietone's brief report on the game put it, 'the English climate did its very utmost to wreck the whole show'.[26] Painting a complete picture of the match is difficult in these circumstances and relies on juggling partial and conflicting accounts. What is abundantly clear is how much the bizarre conditions provided a breeding ground for argument and acrimony.

The match started with a bang. Dynamo scored in the very first minute through their 'ice-man', Bobrov. Arsenal apparently hadn't even touched the ball. Cliff Bastin, the Gunners' captain, would later claim the goal had come from a disputed free kick – an early foretaste of the quarrels ahead. But other, more persuasive, newspaper accounts tell us it came from a slick move involving Semichastny and left-winger Sergei Soloviev. The Kremlin was taking a political risk in broadcasting the match live to millions on Radio Moscow, with the Soviet Union's favourite sports commentator, Vadim Sinyavsky, telling everyone Dynamo were playing an all-England side. The listeners' reaction to Dynamo's opener must have been quite something.[27]

After fifteen minutes or so, following some trademark mazy dribbles from Stanley Matthews, Arsenal equalised. Rooke scored with a simple shot from a few yards out. The bustling, thirty-three-year-old journeyman had never played top-flight football but would put in an impressive shift against Dynamo, one which probably transformed his career. Months later, Arsenal signed Rooke, and his record-breaking goalscoring helped the Gunners win their sixth league title in 1948.

Halfway through the first half, Dynamo's left-half, Leonid Soloviev, was badly injured and substituted. His replacement, Boris Oreshkin, entered the field of play before Soloviev had hobbled off. Dynamo went on to make a number of other substitutions during the game, apparently in a similar fashion. Rumours quickly spread that Mikhail Yakushin was mischievously using the Soviet substitute rule and foggy conditions to play parts of the match with an extra man. Some said that Latyshev was turning a blind eye to the cheating. There is no concrete evidence to support either of these allegations, but they were strongly believed.[28]

The serious injury to Leonid Soloviev suggests the match was turning into a physical encounter. Shortly after his departure, Arsenal's goalkeeper Griffiths took a blow to the head from not one but two Dynamo players. Concussed, he would be replaced at half time by QPR's Harry Brown, who, as luck would have it, was among the crowd. Dynamo's keeper Khomich (see Figure 1.4) also came in for some 'rough' treatment, at least according to Vadim Sinyavsky, though this might have been a case of simple British barging. The Arsenal players took particular umbrage at the Dynamos' 'unsporting' behaviour towards Matthews, 'offences' which included shirt-pulling, pushing and blatant obstruction. Latyshev had to tread a fine line, balancing

Figure 1.4 Dynamo Moscow goalkeeper Aleksei Khomich peers into the pitch gloom, White Hart Lane, 21 November 1945. © Daily Herald Archive/National Science & Media Museum/SSPL via Getty Images.

one set of acceptable practices against another. This was near impossible and tensions inevitably increased.[29]

Before the interval, the match suddenly seemed to turn in Arsenal's favour. Latching onto a clever through-ball by Rooke, Stanley Mortensen shot pass Khomich. The two Stanleys then combined, Matthews jinking past Dynamo's defence on the left to cross to Mortensen, who scored with his head. Arsenal now led 3–1, with all their goals coming from guest players. Had Arsenal reached half-time two up, the game might have been theirs. As it was, Dynamo got a quick goal back through poacher Beskov, who shot across Griffiths from the inside-left channel. The poor Arsenal keeper probably didn't see much of the shot. Griffiths was in such a befuddled state thanks to his earlier head injury, he had no idea what the score was when Latyshev blew for half time. It was 3–2 to Arsenal.[30]

Half-time breaks in the 1940s were typically reserved for tea, toilets and tactics. On this occasion, the break, which far exceeded the usual five minutes, prompted another ugly rumour: that the Dynamos were fixing to stop the game when it best suited them. According to George Allison, a Russian-speaking friend told him that he'd overheard Yakushin tell Latyshev in his dressing room that if Arsenal held onto the lead he should abandon the game, but if Dynamo came from behind it should be played to the finish. As with the substitutions charge against Yakushin, little evidence was produced to support this allegation, but it would be repeated many times after the game, indeed for years to come.[31]

The second half of the match began in almost exactly the same fashion as the first, with Arsenal half-asleep. Three minutes in, Dynamo scored. Arsenal's new goalkeeper, Harry Brown, must have wished he'd stayed on the terraces, as he fumbled a weak header by the striker Vasili Kartsev into his net. As with the game's first goal by Bobrov, captain Bastin disputed it. Sergei Soloviev, the crosser of the ball, had been blatantly offside, the Arsenal man claimed, and the linesman agreed. However, the referee unaccountably ignored his raised flag. The score was now 3–3.[32]

Presumably angered by this incident, and a penalty appeal turned down by Latyshev a few minutes later, the Arsenal players sought some sort of recompense. Rooke, a part-time RAF physical training instructor during the war, liked to put himself about and he turned his attentions to Khomich. The muscular striker charged the goalkeeper aggressively just after he'd caught a cross. This led to a scuffle between Rooke and one of the Dynamo defenders. At this point, so the story goes, forward George Drury leapt in and started throwing punches. Latyshev saw this and sent Drury off. The Arsenal man trudged over towards the tunnel but, instead of availing himself of an early bath, continued playing on the side of the pitch that was largely out of the referee's sight.[33]

With half an hour to go, and with play temporarily halted, a soon-to-be hotly disputed conversation took place between Yakushin, Allison and Latyshev on the side of the pitch. It revolved around whether the game should be abandoned due to the ever-thickening fog. Allison was all for this apparently, as was the Soviet ambassador relaying a message from the main stand, but the Dynamo staff insisted on playing on. The Soviets would later claim that Allison wanted the match stopped in order to save face. Vadim Sinyavsky also alleged that the Arsenal manager, like all greedy capitalists, had bet a lot of money on the match and didn't want to lose it all if Dynamo won.

Allison described this as risible, which, at least the second part, almost certainly was. Years later, Allison denied he'd ever been part of this three-way conversation with Yakushin and Latyshev, and claimed he'd actually appealed to Soviet diplomats for the match to be stopped on safety grounds a little later on, when Arsenal were losing.[34]

Around the sixty-fifth minute, Dynamo, having been 3–1 down before half-time, took the lead again. Bobrov scored his second goal of the game, this time with a shot from outside the penalty area. Once again Arsenal appealed for offside and once again Latyshev disappointed them. The score was now 4–3 to the tourists and Arsenal were up against it. Their opponents had scored three goals in a row and the Gunners were staring into the jaws of a memorable defeat.

Five or so minutes later, Arsenal drew level – or so it seemed. Rooke scored a beauty from a shot from twenty-five yards out, the ball thundering past Khomich as if he'd not seen it (which might have been the case). As his teammates ran to congratulate Rooke, however, they saw Latyshev had pulled play back for an infringement. Just before he'd shot, so one of the Arsenal players attested, Semichastny had jumped on Rooke's back. The Arsenal man had had to shake off the Dynamos' captain and in the process had accidentally elbowed him in the face. In Arsenal's view, given that it was Semichastny who'd committed the foul, the referee should have played the advantage and allowed Rooke's goal to stand. But now it seemed he'd blamed the striker for the infringement and disallowed Arsenal's perfectly legitimate equaliser. As it turned out, the referee had disallowed the goal but for a third infringement, handball by Rooke. The striker was flabbergasted: 'Handle it – I never had the chance to use my hands', he said later, 'they were both tied behind my back!'[35]

This fracas seems to have knocked the stuffing out of Arsenal. Perhaps many of their players figured that they were in fact playing against thirteen not twelve men, given Latyshev's clear bias in favour of the Dynamos. In the last period of the game, it was the Dynamos who looked more like scoring than the Gunners. Arsenal appeared tired, Dynamo had more of the possession, and the match drew to a close. The result was 4–3 to the Soviets.

Dynamo Moscow's players and staff were understandably euphoric after their besting of the famous Arsenal. That evening, many of them danced the night away with a bevy of local lasses at a Lyceum Hotel dinner hosted by the Gunners (whose contingent left early). Running riot against Cardiff City was one thing but triumphing over one of the most highly regarded club sides in the world was quite another. Following Sinyavsky's lead, Soviet propagandists back home went a step further, boasting that the Dynamos had effectively defeated the English national side. Celebrities like the composer Dmitry Shostakovich soon joined in, crowing about the 'higher class' of football that Dynamo's players had demonstrated and attributing the team's success directly to Soviet communism. Putting the match in a wider diplomatic perspective, it was left to the *Daily Worker* to pour some cold water on proceedings. The game had done 'little or nothing to cement Anglo-Soviet friendship in the world of sport', it lamented the day after the game. 'There appeared to be too much pushing, shoving and tripping.'[36]

Many in Britain, judging by the reaction of press and politicians, resented the Soviets' conflation of the Arsenal and England teams. They also disliked Yakushin's widely publicised complaint that during the Arsenal game 'the English' had resorted to 'methods which are considered unsporting by us'. Having grown to admire, even like the Dynamos over the past few weeks, many in Fleet Street now laid into them. It was the Soviets who had spoilt the game with their violent tactics, body checks, elbow work and so on, reporters claimed. It was the Soviets who had cheated by feigning injuries in order to abuse substitutions. And, above all, it was the Soviets who had chosen the referee for this prestigious fixture, a partisan official using a ludicrous, foreign system. In Parliament, MP Michael Foot, future Labour Party leader and life-long Plymouth Argyle fan, called on the government to pressure the armed forces into releasing players capable of standing up to the Dynamos. Ministers did nothing, but the feeling that someone in Britain needed to teach the uppity Soviets how to really play football was tangible.[37]

Making a bad situation worse, the Soviets fought back. Semichastny had plainly emerged from the Arsenal game with an enormous black eye, probably the result of his run-in with Rooke. This was categorical proof, the Dynamos argued, of English violence. The Dynamo captain alleged, in a cable to Soviet sports officials back home, that he'd been hit in the face twice by one of the opposing players and that Khomich had also been struck. The cable was leaked to Fleet

Street, where it was largely denounced as trouble-making nonsense. Arsenal officials were said to be 'amazed' by the allegations.[38]

The bad blood caused by the Arsenal match seeped into the Dynamos' last tour game, against Glasgow Rangers, at Ibrox Park at the end of November. The match was a hot-tempered affair almost from start to finish. Despite 90,000 tickets having been sold for the match, Dynamo categorically refused to turn up unless Rangers deselected their newly signed star left-winger, Jimmy Caskie. Dynamo took an early 2–0 lead during the game and in the second half were found to be playing with twelve men, having brought on a substitute without taking anyone off. Annoyed particularly by the Dynamos' penchant for obstruction, the Rangers players cut up rough. Unpleasant incidents accumulated and the game ended 2–2. Afterwards, the Soviet press listed the Dynamos' walking wounded, among them Semichastny with his bandaged head and Kartsev hardly able to walk. Even allowing for exaggeration, there's no doubt the match was a bruising encounter.[39]

As prolific an essayist as he was, George Orwell rarely wrote about football. His condemnation in December 1945 of Dynamo Moscow's tour, which appeared in the socialist weekly *Tribune* soon after the Soviets' departure, testifies to the special force the Dynamos' matches exerted on Britain. Orwell had no truck with those, like Philip Noel-Baker, who felt the tour had brought the British and the Soviet people closer together. To him, the last two fixtures, especially the foggy farce at White Hart Lane, had proven how football could provoke 'the most savage combative instincts' and 'vicious' nationalist passions. Though his language was extravagant, it's difficult to challenge Orwell's argument that the Dynamos' tour had aggravated relations between the supposed allies at, what we can now see, was a critical stage between peace and war. The Arsenal game, with all its hazy fouls, rumours and allegations, was in many ways a Cold War preview in miniature.[40]

Political point-scoring continued after the Dynamos had returned home, with the Soviets being the chief culprits. Vadim Sinyavsky took a series of pot-shots at British football and society. The British players had behaved in a shockingly rugged manner towards their fair-minded opponents, he told the readers of *Soviet Weekly*. What's more, the players had demonstrated a profound ignorance of the most elementary aspects of the game, like positioning and passing. Embarrassing too, Sinyavsky wrote, was the pitiful state of Britain's football grounds. Unlike in Soviet stadia, where, he dubiously claimed, spectators sat in modern comfort, British football fans were squeezed in like sardines to boost capitalists' profits. Meanwhile, the British press, Sinyavsky asserted, had harassed the Dynamo players and staff from start to finish. Fleet Street's focus on the Dynamos' alleged predilection for luxurious caviar during the tour was, the broadcaster said, xenophobic claptrap.[41]

Allegations of this sort made by others in the Soviet Union were still irking British diplomats two years later. In 1947, year zero of the Cold War proper thanks primarily to the announcement of the Truman Doctrine, a musical comedy about the Dynamos' tour appeared on the Moscow stage. The play portrayed the Dynamos as incorruptible socialist heroes bravely battling against corrupt capitalists and even found space for an English femme fatale endeavouring to beguile the team's best player the night before the crucial match. Seventy-five years later, with Vladimir Putin in the Kremlin, a Russian-made film about the Dynamo Moscow tour, *Eleven Silent Men*, rehearsed the same plot line.[42]

Propaganda of this sort was probably inevitable on the Soviets' part, especially as relations between Moscow and London deteriorated and many British journalists, briefed by the Foreign Office, effectively declared war on Soviet communism.[43] Yet it was also, in one important respect, unnecessary. The Dynamos had scored an overwhelming football victory in Britain in November 1945, one which successfully announced the Soviet Union's arrival on sport's international stage. The Dynamos could boast an unbeaten record; they had pulled off a major coup in defeating Arsenal; and they had demonstrated the qualities of Soviet football in front of over a quarter of a million spectators. Some British people might have thought more positively about Soviet communism because of this, but we will never know how many. Soviet politicians, eager to feed their citizens' appetite for good news, claimed that Soviet football was now the world's best. Unrealistic expectations would later lead to severe disappointment.[44]

Hopes that the Arsenal–Dynamo Moscow game, or the whole tour, would help improve British–Soviet relations in the wake of World War Two were indisputably dashed. Some goodwill was engendered on and off the pitch by a mutual love of football, but the allegations of cheating and violence, fuelled by the media on both sides, left an extremely sour legacy. Both governments were irritated by this, though both, as we've seen, also had other, less altruistic reasons for supporting the tour anyway.

Critically, allied to British football's long-standing insularity and complacency, the hostility that many in Britain felt towards the Dynamos may help explain something that has rankled football writers for decades – why Britain's football experts failed to use at least some of the lessons learned from watching Dynamo to set the nation's football on a new, modern course. George Allison, for one, felt the Dynamos had been deeply disrespectful towards the nation that had 'given' them the game. Extraordinarily, he also believed that their style was essentially British, with a minor continental twist. Others, who had fewer axes to grind, said much the same thing. British football remained blinkered.[45]

The Cold War went into deep freeze in the very late 1940s and early 1950s. The crisis over Berlin, the birth of NATO and communist China, Moscow's first atomic bomb test, then the outbreak of war in Korea all had a shivering effect. Football friendlies between Britain and the Soviet Union became unthinkable in these circumstances. However, in October 1954, the football Iron Curtain between the two countries lifted, beginning, fittingly, with an 'exhibition' match between Dynamo Moscow and Arsenal, this time in the Soviet capital. Once again, the British embassy provided the FA with the latest inside dope on Dynamo's tactics. It also warned the Arsenal players against going native by drinking too much vodka. There were no controversies on this occasion – nor any arguments over the result. On a clear, floodlit night in front of diplomats, politicians and 80,000 fans, Dynamo crushed the Gunners 5–0. Mocking the visitors' pedestrian style with ironic applause, the home crowd left the stadium chuckling at Arsenal's 'tired old men'.[46]

2 A MIRACLE AND A REVOLUTION
West Germany vs. Hungary, Bern, July 1954

It's enough to make any Chancellor cry. The closing moments of Sönke Wortmann's 2003 film *The Miracle of Bern*. Essen schoolboy Matthias Lubianski has arrived at Bern's Wankdorf Stadium in the nick of time. It's 2–2 late in the World Cup final between Cold War rivals West Germany, a parliamentary democracy on the brink of joining NATO, and Hungary, a People's Republic in the grip of communist dictatorship. Somehow (let's call it the magic of cinema), Matthias finds himself in the players' tunnel, staring at the rain-soaked pitch. His hero, Helmut Rahn, is fouled in front of him. Their eyes lock. Time slows down. Matthias throws Rahn the ball. Play continues. Moments later, a clearance falls to Rahn on the edge of the box. He cuts inside a defender and rifles a shot past goalkeeper Gyula Grosics. Six minutes later, the final whistle blows. West Germany have won the World Cup for the first time. Cue mass celebrations across the divided nation, led by ecstatic radio commentator Herbert Zimmermann. A day, and a victory, that came to be seen as the beginning of post-war West Germany. Almost fifty years later, Wortmann's blockbuster provoked a wave of nostalgia. Chancellor Gerhard Schröder wasn't the only one in tears. There was barely a dry eye in cinemas, as six million Germans flocked to watch *The Miracle of Bern*. After all, as the film's tagline said, 'every nation needs a legend'.

Cinematic portrayals of Germany's finest football hour weren't always so saccharine. The same game, featuring the same iconic commentary from Zimmermann, framed the closing scenes of Rainer Werner Fassbinder's 1979 film, *The Marriage of Maria Braun*. Where

Wortmann's film is sunshine in the rain – an uplifting ending for an uplifted nation – Fassbinder's heads down bleaker paths. The final seven minutes of the match are the final seven minutes in the life of the film's eponymous heroine, who's built her post-war success on personal ambition and political amnesia. As Zimmermann screams with joy at the final whistle, Maria's villa explodes, killing her and, Fassbinder suggests, any hope for a new Germany.

While Fassbinder's response to the 1954 final was political, Hungarian filmmakers looked the other way. Márton Keleti's comedy *A csodacsatár* ('The Football Star') was shot in 1956, with a cameo from Ferenc Puskás, Hungary's greatest footballer. When it was released in September 1957, all traces of Puskás had disappeared. The Honvéd star was abroad when the Hungarian Revolution began in October 1956. After Soviet tanks crushed the uprising, Puskás decided, like many footballers, not to come home. Teammate Nándor Hidegkuti replaced him in Keleti's film. Hungary's football defectors – not only Puskás, but also Zoltán Czibor and Sándor Kocsis – were airbrushed from history.

A miracle and a revolution. The 1954 World Cup final was a turning point for the nations that contested it. The plucky underdog became the overdog, as West Germany, and later unified Germany, went on to dominate European football, winning three more World Cups and three European Championships. The Bonn Republic, meanwhile, became Europe's wealthiest country, an 'economic miracle' to accompany the football one in Bern.

Hungarian football, in contrast, never recovered from 4 July 1954. The cover of Antal Végh's 1974 book *Why Is Hungarian Football Sick?* showed two old men leaning on a headstone to watch a game, 'as though', wrote Jonathan Wilson, 'to queue for death'.[1] Defeat to West Germany splintered the 'golden squad' (*Aranycsapat*) and fast-tracked Hungary to revolution. After 1956, optimism that football could recapture its former glories went the same way as hopes for an independent, democratic country. 'The golden flag of reparation', wrote poet Lőrinc Szabó in 'After a Defeat', turned out to be a 'delusion of miracles'.[2]

Football matches produce winners and losers, but football history is often more complicated. West Germany weren't quite the unassuming heroes of Sönke Wortmann's tearjerker. To call victory over Hungary in 1954 'a great miracle', remarks historian Nils Havemann, is 'an irrational exaggeration'.[3] What happened in Bern wasn't *that* great a surprise and didn't necessarily have the impact later ascribed to it.

On the Hungarian side, too, established narratives don't always hold up. There was no straight line from the disappointment of '54 to the uprising of '56. And football decline didn't happen overnight. Back-to-back Olympic gold medals in 1964 and 1968 (albeit in an era when the IOC's ban on professional players gave free rein to the 'state amateurs' of the Eastern bloc), plus five appearances by Hungarian clubs in European finals between 1964 and 1975, offer proof of that.

Chapter 2 tells the spellbinding story of the 1954 World Cup final, the first major showdown in football's Cold War. East against West in the hottest phase of the global conflict between communism and capitalism, just a year after the death of Stalin, a popular uprising in East Germany and the end of the Korean War. A team representing the Stalinist dictatorship of Mátyás Rákosi versus a team representing the American-backed government of Konrad Adenauer, in a country where Christian Democracy and economic resurgence jostled with the ghosts of the Nazi past. West Germany versus Hungary was full of Cold War drama, a match that stabilised the West's great anchor in post-war Europe and destabilised a key Soviet ally. But football has always been hard to pin to fixed political narratives. The 1954 final inspired conflicting loyalties, which often cut across Cold War lines. Nowhere was this more apparent than in communist East Germany, where fraternity with Hungary, and admiration for Puskás and co., clashed with pride in the achievements of the 'other' Germany.

On 14 May 1950, Hungary lost 5–3 to Austria in Vienna. Gusztáv Sebes' side wouldn't lose again until the 1954 World Cup final. Between the 5–2 win over Poland in Warsaw on 4 June 1950, and the semi-final win over Uruguay in Lausanne on 30 June 1954, the 'Magical Magyars' amassed 24 wins and 4 draws from 28 games, scoring 119 goals. Hungary won the 1952 Olympics, produced one – probably two – of the signature performances in the history of international football, and contributed to one – probably two – of the greatest World Cup matches.

Reporting on Hungary's 6–3 win over England at Wembley in November 1953, Geoffrey Green described the bewildered hosts as 'strangers in a strange world, a world of flitting red spirits'. To footballers like Bobby Robson, the later England manager, the Hungarians seemed like 'men from Mars', purveyors (Green again) of 'a new conception of football'.[4] These other-worldly qualities weren't just a reflection of English ignorance. Dynamo Moscow's *passovotchka* on their 1945 tour had offered a tantalising glimpse of communism in action: the quick movement of the ball across the turf, the fluid inter-changing of positions, and the belief in the team over the individual. 'We put collective football first', emphasised Dynamo manager Mikhail Yakushin.[5] But nobody had seen the game played with quite the collective (and individual) brilliance that Hungary displayed at Wembley in 1953. Where had it come from?

One answer, ironically, was England. After Hungary's Wembley win, Sebes remarked, 'We played football as Jimmy Hogan taught us. When our football history is told, his name should be written in gold letters'.[6] Lancashire-born Hogan coached across Europe, including two spells at MTK Budapest (1914–21 and 1925–27). Drawing on Scotland's short-passing game, and his work with Austrian coach Hugo Meisl, Hogan advocated a playing style based on movement, technique and swift combinations.

Hogan's ideas were too advanced for his native land, where – as we saw in Chapter 1 – dribbling, the long ball and the shoulder charge held sway. But they found fertile ground in Hungary. There Hogan joined an innovative football culture, associated with the coffee-houses and Jews of the capital city. A string of top players and coaches made Hungary a byword for football excellence. MTK Budapest, Hungarian champions twelve times between 1904 and 1925, featured players, Dori Kürschner and Béla Guttmann, who went on to brilliant coaching careers abroad. The diaspora also included Árpád Weisz and Ernő Erbstein, totemic figures in Italian football. It was against Italy that Hungary contested the 1938 World Cup final, losing 4–2. The national team had by this point become, in *Nemzeti Sport*'s words, 'a very serious opponent'.[7]

Hungary emerged as a football powerhouse against a backdrop of political instability. The collapse of the Habsburg Empire in 1918 and the reduction of Hungarian lands in the Treaty of Trianon. Béla Kun's communist dictatorship in 1919. The 'White Terror' under Miklós Horthy, Hungary's regent from 1920 to 1944, a period in which anti-Semitism drove many players and coaches abroad – and some, eventually, into the death camps of Nazi Germany, Hungary's ally in World War Two. Árpád Weisz was murdered at Auschwitz. Béla Guttmann and Ernő Erbstein narrowly escaped deportation east in 1944. Hungary's football brilliance was achieved despite politics, not because of it.

This changed after World War Two. Allied victory over the Axis powers gave Stalin's Soviet Union control over Eastern and Central Europe, including Hungary. Democratic hopes quickly faded. Local communists, backed by the Red Army, captured vital institutions of state power. Mátyás Rákosi, First Secretary of the Hungarian Working People's Party from 1948 to 1956, labelled the approach 'salami tactics': slicing away the opposition, until there was none left. Hungary became a People's Republic in 1949. In the same year, the show trial and execution of László Rajk, a prominent communist and founder of the secret police (AVH), began a period of repression that lasted until Stalin's death in 1953.

Communism's grip on Hungary extended to sport. Industry and agriculture were nationalised; so was football. Gusztáv Sebes became national team coach in 1949. A shrewd politician, he's easily typecast as a bureaucrat who got lucky with great players. Unlike Rákosi, however, Sebes knew when to loosen the reins. And he understood global trends. Sebes saw how Italy's all-conquering team of the 1930s came from a small number of clubs. A similar concentration would benefit Hungary, he reasoned. The country's biggest clubs, MTK and Ferencváros, were out of the question: the former because it was now under AVH patronage, the latter because of its reputation for right-wing nationalism. So Sebes chose a smaller club from the outskirts of Budapest. Kispest lacked political baggage, but it didn't lack players. Ferenc Puskás had made his Kispest debut in 1943. So had midfielder József Bozsik, another mainstay of the national team. The Ministry of Defence became the club's sponsor. Kispest became Honvéd, 'defenders of the motherland'. The team were league champions five times in six seasons between 1950 and 1955.

Six of Hungary's starting lineup in the 1954 World Cup final played for Honvéd. Leading up to the tournament, Sebes used the club as a lab experiment for the national team, testing different players and styles. Here was a paradox. Under oppressive political conditions, coached by a supposed yes-man and ardent socialist, Hungary played with a freedom absent from almost any other activity in the country. And from almost any other team in football. Under Sebes and his assistant Gyula Mándi, Hungary honed a 4–2–4 system – first trialled at MTK under Márton Bukovi – as flexible and joyful as the Rákosi dictatorship was rigid and joyless. A 'whirlpool' of movement, with Gyula Grosics as sweeper-keeper and MTK's Nándor Hidegkuti as the vital tactical shift: a deep-lying forward, who dropped into midfield to link the play and flummoxed central defenders. 'Stan, do I stay or do I go?', an exhausted Harry Johnston asked Stanley Matthews at half-time of England's friendly against Hungary in 1953.[8] England were 4–2 down, and it wasn't about to get better.

Hungary's 6–3 win at Wembley on 25 November 1953 – England's first home defeat to a continental team – marked the end of a football empire. 'The twilight of the gods', as Geoffrey Green called it in *The Times*.[9] From a less Anglocentric perspective, Hungary's triumph wasn't surprising, just one part of a body of work, compiled over four years against the world's top teams. At the 1952 Olympics in Helsinki, Hungary tore through the field. Of the 6–0 semi-final win over Sweden, Puskás said 'we were virtually irresistible'. The 2–0 win over Yugoslavia in the gold medal match was less dramatic, but of greater political importance. Rákosi called Sebes before the final, demanding victory over Tito's renegade socialist republic, which Stalin – as we'll see in Chapter 3 – had expelled from the Soviet bloc in 1948. The team obliged, though right-back Jenő Buzánsky wasn't thinking about best-ing imperialist lackeys afterwards. The gold medal was 'wonderful', he recalled, but it came with a kiss from Miss Universe, Finland's Armi Kuusela. Even better.[10]

The team improved in 1953, as Nándor Hidegkuti made the false nine role his own. More than 300,000 people sought tickets for the 1–1 draw against Austria in Budapest on 26 April, a match in which Hungary, 'modern and skillful', according to East German football weekly *Die Neue Fußballwoche*, attacked relentlessly.[11] Perhaps liber-ation was in the air. It was the golden squad's first match since Stalin's death six weeks earlier, an event that exposed cracks in the Rákosi dictatorship. A few weeks later, Hungary beat Italy 3–0 in Rome, a performance of such 'innovative passing and tactical sophistication' that they already seemed like 'the best team in the world'.[12]

That (unofficial) title was confirmed at Wembley six months later (see Figure 2.1). The 6–3 scoreline flattered the hosts. Hungary outshot England thirty-five to five and eased off in the last half hour. Prolific forward Sándor Kocsis 'was nowhere near his best', remem-bered Buzánsky. 'If he had shown his real form, the result would have been even more cruel'. 'Even halfway through the first half', wrote Leslie Edwards in the *Liverpool Echo*, 'one felt physically sick with anticipa-tion at the ultimate margin of victory'.[13] Modernity can come in

Figure 2.1 England vs. Hungary, Wembley Stadium, 25 November 1953.
© Central Press/Getty Images.

different guises. Hungary in 1953 was in political turmoil, with a struggling economy. On the football field, though, socialist progress – from the lightweight boots and warm-up routine to the lightning passing, tactical fluidity and superior fitness of the team in red – seemed beyond doubt. A coaching manual, written by Márton Bukovi and Jenő Csaknády, with an introduction by Jimmy Hogan, was soon on sale in England. Its title? *Learn to Play the Hungarian Way*.

Much has been written about 'the 6–3', much less about the return match in Budapest the following May (see Figure 2.2). Yet, as Gyula Grosics argued, the second game was more significant, 'because it proved what happened at Wembley was not just chance'.[14] Over a million Hungarians applied for tickets for the game at the recently opened Népstadion ('People's Stadium'), the showpiece construction of the Rákosi era. Official attendance was 92,000, but many more were probably there. People who'd entered the vast bowl apparently sent their tickets via carrier pigeon to family and friends waiting outside. In front of the communist top brass, it didn't look like many Englishmen had yet studied 'the Hungarian way'. The visitors were 3–0 down in thirty minutes, en route to a record 7–1 defeat. Hungary's 'remarkable

Figure 2.2 Mátyás Rákosi (left) and Imre Nagy (moustache) watch Hungary vs. England, Népstadion, Budapest, 23 May 1954. © SIMON Michou/Paris Match via Getty Images.

exposition', reckoned *The Times*, was 'as great as, if not greater than, [what] we saw at Wembley'. 'We were completely outclassed', said England manager Walter Winterbottom.[15] Hungary were red-hot favourites for the World Cup in Switzerland, now barely three weeks away.

While Hungary set the standards, West Germany's ambitions were modest. Tainted by its associations with Nazism, German sport was barred from the international stage after World War Two. The German FA (the DFB), refounded in 1949, only rejoined FIFA in September 1950. Two months later, at the Neckarstadion in Stuttgart, 98,000 spectators watched West Germany's return to international competition against Switzerland. The country's last official match, eight years earlier, was a 5–2 win over Slovakia. The coach on both occasions was a man as adept at political survival as he was at folksy football homilies: Sepp Herberger.

Ambitious and obsessive, Sepp Herberger kept 361 notebooks during the Third Reich that referenced nothing but football: 'I never had time to bother about politics'.[16] Like many DFB functionaries, though, Herberger conformed with Hitler's dictatorship to advance his career. He joined the Nazi Party in 1933. Three years later, he replaced Otto

Nerz as national team coach. Herberger kept the position for much of the next thirty years, amid war, genocide, occupation, division and (West) Germany's reinvention as a capitalist democracy.

Herberger claimed in 1946 that it was his 'modest duty' to keep the national team 'free from Nazi influences'.[17] But, like many football men of his generation, Herberger was part of the Nazi past from which he now distanced himself. Fritz Walter, Herberger's captain in 1954, played twenty-three times for Germany before the Nazi regime suspended international sport in 1942. Like many of the 1954 squad, Walter saw action in World War Two, fighting in France, Italy and Romania. Though nobody liked to dwell on it – least of all Herberger and Walter ('Let's not talk about war, let's talk about football!') – the past was very much present in post-war German football.[18]

A knee injury kept Sepp Herberger's favourite player out of West Germany's comeback against Switzerland in Stuttgart in November 1950. The hosts won 1–0, thanks to Herbert Burdenski's forty-second-minute penalty. Alfred Kunze, a top East German coach, liked what he saw, from Herberger's tactical acumen to the speed and heading ability of his team.[19]

But the Swiss game was a false dawn. Results in 1951 included defeats to Turkey and Ireland. Ten thousand Germans watched a 3–1 loss to France in Paris in October 1952, a performance so poor that Fritz Walter offered to step down. Herberger was hanging on by a thread. There were loud calls in the press for him to go. Home wins over Yugoslavia and Switzerland, followed by a 2–2 draw against Spain in Madrid, meant a brighter end to 1952. The qualification campaign for the 1954 World Cup – against Norway and the minnows of Saarland – wasn't convincing. But West Germany made it. Herberger, for now, kept his job.

Previewing the 1954 World Cup, *Die Neue Fußballwoche* reckoned 'Herberger had problems'. Injuries. Poor conditioning. The fact that half his starting lineup, including the Walter brothers, Fritz and Ottmar, played for the Kaiserslautern team just hammered 5–1 by Hannover 96 in the final of the German championship. West Germany didn't arrive in Switzerland in good shape. *Kicker* called the 3–1 win over Saarland in the final World Cup qualifier 'a shrill SOS'. Herberger said simply, 'We should be glad that this is over'.[20] Was something better about to begin? Many had their doubts, as Herberger's squad headed to its base at the Hotel Belvedere in Spiez, a picturesque town thirty minutes south of Bern.

Was 1954 the greatest World Cup? It was certainly the most entertaining. In the tournament's almost 100-year history, there have never been more goals per game than the 5.38 average in Switzerland. That's 140 goals in 26 matches. The tournament's most attacking team, Hungary, were drawn in Group 1 alongside Turkey, South Korea and West Germany. The format was bizarre. There was no round-robin. Instead, the two seeded teams – in Group 1's case, Hungary and Turkey – played the two unseeded teams only.

West Germany's preparations were low-key. In Hungary, conversely, the build-up felt like 'preparations for a coronation'.[21] Group 1 action did little to shake the consensus that Hungary were champions elect. The golden squad opened with a record 9–0 win over South Korea in Zürich on 17 June. Spared the rested Hidegkuti, the debutants had no answer to a team 'without a single weakness'. In the second half, continued the *Birmingham Gazette*, 'there appeared to be twice as many red-shirted players on the field as blue-shirted Koreans'.[22] In Bern, meanwhile, West Germany started well, beating Turkey 4–1. That set the scene for West Germany versus Hungary at Basel's St. Jakob Stadium three days later. The winner would reach the quarter finals.

After the miracle of Bern, Hungary's 8–3 win in Basel was subject to fanciful reinvention. A catastrophic defeat became Herberger's stroke of genius. Aware that West Germany were unlikely to win and would need to beat Turkey in a play-off to make the last eight, the West German boss, so the theory goes, rested eight first-teamers against the Hungarians. This saved legs for the Turkey game, while hiding West Germany's strengths from Sebes and his players, in the event of a rematch.

It's a nice idea, and one that Herberger, mindful of his reputation as a tactical genius, never dispelled. But it's mostly hindsight. Even the most far-sighted coach doesn't plan an 8–3 shellacking. 'That is the best team in the world!' crowed *Die Neue Fußballwoche*, after West Germany were 'played into the ground'. Nobody disagreed. 'It was quite obvious that only one team could win the world championship', said West German wing-half Horst Eckel, 'and that was Hungary'.[23] Defeat went down badly back home. *Der Spiegel* wondered if 'the time had come to hang the treacherous coach Herberger from an apple tree'. *Die Welt* criticised West Germany's dirty play, notably ('the meanest deed') Werner Liebrich's second-half tackle on Puskás, which left Hungary's talisman with a fractured left ankle. Brian Glanville called it 'the foul that won the World Cup', Jonathan Wilson the moment 'Hungarian football began its decline'.[24] Both are exaggerations. But Liebrich's foul, whether clumsy or malicious, was West Germany's most significant contribution to the tournament so far. The loveable amateurs, it seems, weren't averse to football's dark arts.

After the beating in Basel, West Germany and Hungary took different routes to the final. West Germany made unheralded progress. A 7–2 win over Turkey in Zürich set up a quarter-final with Yugoslavia in Geneva. Herberger's side won, somewhat luckily, 2–0. Hundreds of Germans invaded the pitch at the Charmilles Stadium at full time, 'waving national flags' and 'wildly cheer[ing] their players'. Praising the West German team's 'nerve and self-confidence' – the 8–3 now 'almost forgotten' – *Die Neue Fußballwoche* also highlighted its weaknesses, especially when under the cosh in the first half.[25]

Sepp Herberger agreed. Despite his team's success, the coach wasn't happy. For the semi-final against Austria, Herberger brought in Hamburg's Jupp Posipal at right back. He settled on Helmut Rahn, who'd started the tournament on the bench, in front of Posipal. In Basel on 30 June, everything clicked. Herberger's team thrashed their neighbours 6–1, with each Walter brother scoring twice. While Austrian football lovers despaired – writer Friedrich Torberg called it 'the most devastating defeat since Königgratz' – the world took notice of the outsiders.[26] *Die Neue Fußballwoche* praised 'the greatest success of the post-war era', built around Fritz Walter's 'masterly' second-half performance. The *Liverpool Echo* noted the tighter defence and 'a tremendously fast attack, in which every forward interchanges position brilliantly'.[27] Closer to home, *Kicker* was pleasantly surprised that West Germany won not through physicality but by outplaying a superior opponent. They couldn't repeat the trick in the final, could they?

Hungary's path was more spectacular, more controversial and, crucially, more punishing. Take the quarter-final against Brazil on 27 June, better known as 'the battle of Bern'. On a heavy pitch in driving rain, a violent match featured forty-two fouls, two penalties, four cautions and three dismissals. The bad blood sparked a post-match brawl involving players, fans and coaches. Gusztáv Sebes required four stitches for a cut above his eye. After such thuggery, Norway's *Dagbladet* righteously advocated cancelling the World Cup. British dailies likewise claimed the high ground. If this is what football domination looks like, sniffed *The Times*, 'then the British Isles are well out of it'.[28] England, of course, *were* already out of it. Walter Winterbottom's side lost 4–2 to Uruguay in the quarter-finals a day before 'the battle of Bern'. Honourable defeat, it seemed, was worthier than disreputable victory.

Lost in the moralising, police reports and FIFA investigations was the fact that Hungary versus Brazil was a brilliant spectacle. Missing the injured Puskás, Hungary raced into a two-goal lead through Hidegkuti and Kocsis, before Djalma Santos converted an eighteenth-minute penalty. Things got heated in the second half. A Brazilian pitch invasion after Mihály Lantos's penalty made it 3–1; a second Brazil goal from Julinho; and then red cards for fighting for Nílton Santos and József Bozsik. Effectively playing with nine men, with Puskás' replacement József Tóth hobbled by a thigh injury, Hungary dug deep. Kocsis' header iced the game in the eighty-eighth minute – then all hell broke loose at the final whistle.

Three days after beating one of the 1950 World Cup finalists, Hungary faced the other, Uruguay. Hungary's 4–2 win over the defending champions in Lausanne's Olympic Stadium is still regarded as one of the great World Cup matches, perhaps the greatest, given the quality of the teams, the standard of play and what was on the line. The patchy, somewhat bizarre YouTube highlights make it hard to compare the 1954 semi-final to more recent World Cup classics. But contemporaries knew they'd seen something special. 'That was football art in its purest form', purred Wolfgang Hempel in *Die Neue Fußballwoche*. 'One of the finest exhibitions of class football it has been my privilege to see anywhere', reckoned the *Liverpool Echo*'s 'Ranger'.[29]

It was pouring rain (again) in the Olympic Stadium, and Hungary went 2–0 up through Czibor and Hidegkuti, before Uruguay pulled level through two late Juan Hohberg goals. Footage shows an exhausted Uruguayan getting a vigorous chest rub before referee Mervyn Griffiths blows to begin extra time. It wasn't enough. Hungary finished like they started. Strongly. Two Kocsis goals, in the 111th and 116th minutes, sent the favourites into the final. Puskás, still missing through injury, praised his teammates' 'tremendous heart'. But it came at a cost. One hundred and twenty minutes in sapping conditions. Was there enough in the tank for the final? Would Puskás be fit?

Retrospectively, we can find reasons. Two exhausting matches. Puskás' ankle. Over-confidence. Disrupted sleep after the late return from Lausanne to the team hotel in Solothurn. The endless summer rain. But nobody previewing the 1954 World Cup final anticipated anything but a comfortable Hungary win. With or without Puskás, wrote Clifford Webb in the *Daily Herald*, Hungary were 'the hottest-ever favourites' for a World Cup final. Puskás' presence would merely pad the margin of victory. West Germany, Webb concluded, didn't have 'sufficient skill to counteract the Magyar magic'.[30]

Sepp Herberger knew this as well as anyone. But he also knew that success was 'one third skill, one third togetherness, one third luck'.[31] Herberger's squad watched Hungary's 6–3 win over England twice before the tournament. They then got a close up in Basel on 20 June. So far, so intimidating. But Herberger saw enough to know that even this great side had flaws. Rahn was a secret weapon. And the coach had Horst Eckel in mind to man-mark Hidegkuti. Eckel, despondent after the 8–3 loss, went into the final feeling quietly confident: 'we knew that if we played to 100 percent of our strengths we could beat Hungary'.[32]

Then there was the weather. In *The Miracle of Bern*, Peter Franke's Sepp Herberger tells a journalist: 'If it's sunny on Sunday, Hungary will be world champions'. But if it rains? And the pitch gets soggy? 'Then we have a chance'.[33] Fritz Walter caught malaria during the war and afterwards struggled in dry, hot conditions. But he loved it when the heavens opened. Sunday 4 July 1954 started out bright and sunny, a shimmering glaze on Lake Thun. All morning, Fritz Walter returned to the balcony at the Hotel Belvedere, hoping for something different. A few clouds dotted the sky around 11.30 a.m. Then he felt drops of rain. At lunchtime, a few hours before the 4.45 p.m. kick-off, it came down properly, 'ugly fat raindrops' across the 'grey mass' of Lake Thun.[34] Fritz Walter weather. Just in time.

For a pitch 'where every foothold was difficult', you'd need the right footwear.[35] Here, West Germany were ahead of the competition. Adi Dassler, founder and head of Adidas, was a friend of Herberger's, another Nazi fellow-traveller whose sporting enthusiasms overrode distaste for the Third Reich. Adidas had developed a new football boot: lightweight with screw-in studs. Only one team had it in Bern in July 1954. Dassler's revolutionary footwear gave West Germany an advantage in heavy conditions. Herberger's side had technological expertise on its side, an example of the high-quality manufacturing goods driving West Germany's economic recovery. So much for scrappy underdogs.

Neither the rain nor the screw-in studs seemed to matter in the early going. Hungary started, as usual, like a train (see Figure 2.3). Six minutes: a Czibor shot deflects off Eckel to the returning Puskás, who beats Toni Turek with a low shot into the corner. Eight minutes: a mix-up between Werner Kohlmeyer and Turek gives Czibor the softest of goals. Cut in the YouTube highlights to a shocked looking German in the crowd of 62,000. The Longines match clock reads Ungarn 2 Deutschland 0.

But West Germany hadn't started badly. They'd had promising attacks before Puskás' opener and, vitally, pulled a goal back immediately after Czibor's strike. Again, it's poor defending. Bozsik's attempt to clear Rahn's cross diverts the ball to Max Morlock, who pokes it past Grosics. We've played ten minutes, and it's already 2–1. Eight minutes later, West Germany equalise. Grosics flaps at Fritz Walter's corner and Rahn scores at the back post. The dark horses have discovered that 'all

Figure 2.3 The World Cup final, Wankdorf Stadium, Bern, 4 July 1954. © Bob Thomas/Popperfoto via Getty Images/Getty Images.

the Hungarian magic is in their forward line: the defenders are merely humans'.[36]

Being pegged back wasn't in the script, but it had happened before, most recently against Uruguay, and Hungary usually regrouped to win. This could have happened in the Wankdorf Stadium. The balding Hidegkuti, hands half raised in celebration, hits the post. During a dominant spell early in the second half, a third Hungary goal seems inevitable. 'Only the Teuton gods in Valhalla', reported *The Guardian*, 'can explain how [West Germany] survived the dodgings and the feintings, the twists and turns, the hurricane shots'. Turek makes some great saves and, when the ball gets past him, Kohlmeyer is there to clear it off the line. It's not one-way traffic. West Germany threaten on the break and, as the *Daily Herald* noted, 'lasted the pace better'.[37]

Only six minutes remain when Helmut Rahn sends Herbert Zimmermann into ecstasy: 'Schäfer sends a cross into the box ... Header cleared ... Goal, goal, goal, goal!' Then comes the moment of controversy. Puskás runs on to Mihály Tóth's pass and slots the ball past Turek. A crestfallen Rahn hasn't heard the whistle. But Fritz Walter has: 'That was offside, Helmut'.[38] Surviving footage makes it hard to know whether Welshman Mervyn Griffiths was right to raise his flag. In his history of German football, Ulrich Hesse-Lichtenberger calls the decision 'dubious'. The *Daily Telegraph* closed ranks around Griffiths and English referee William Ling: the goal had been 'rightly disallowed'. Puskás was furious. 'I couldn't believe it ... To lose a World Cup on such a decision just isn't right'. What would have happened to West Germany, wonders Günter Grass' narrator in *My Century*, 'if we'd left the field defeated again?'[39] What would have happened to Hungary if Puskás' goal had stood, and the favourites had gone on to win in extra time?

Instead, West Germany held on, surviving a last-minute shot from Czibor, superbly saved by Turek. As Maria Braun's villa explodes, and Zimmermann explodes with happiness, the wives of the Hungarian players don't know what to do with the flowers they've brought for their husbands. West Germany, not the Magical Magyars, are world champions (see Figure 2.4). As Fritz Walter lifts the Jules Rimet trophy, twenty thousand Germans in the Wankdorf Stadium burst into song. The national anthem, 'Deutschland über alles'. But not the post-war version, with its emphasis on unity, justice and freedom. Instead, the crowd sing the discredited pre-war first verse, with its nationalistic striving for a Germany 'from the Maas to the Memel/from the Etsch to the Belt'. East German and Swiss broadcasters cut transmission. The awkward moment doesn't feature in Sönke Wortmann's 2003 film. The sun has broken through the clouds. The shadows of history are forgotten in a moment of pure joy.

'Over, over, over – over!! The game is over! Germany are world champions!' Most Germans of a certain age know these lines from Herbert Zimmermann. They're seared in collective memory like Kenneth Wolstenholme's commentary on England's fourth goal in the 1966 World Cup final: 'some people are on the pitch, they think it's all over, it is now!' As Zimmermann scaled the peaks of euphoria – caution long since abandoned ('call me mad, call me crazy!', he screamed after Rahn's second goal) – his Hungarian counterpart György Szepesi stared into the abyss. Holding back the tears, he too says at the final whistle, 'It's over, it's over'.[40] But the shared phrase had opposite meanings. These were two very different endings.

In West Germany, joy was all the greater for being unexpected. Strangers hugged in the streets. National flags hung from windows.

Figure 2.4 Sepp Herberger (left) and Fritz Walter (with the Jules Rimet trophy) are held aloft by celebrating West German players after the 1954 World Cup final. © Schirner/ullstein bild via Getty Images.

Schools and shops closed to celebrate. In towns across the country, a 'joyous inferno' (Essen) swept across public spaces. An 'ecstatically excited, raging, screaming, laughing and weeping crowd' (Fürth) hailed the world champions.[41]

The team returned from Switzerland by train, stopping, like the emperors of old, for acclaim at every station. From Spiez to Interlaken, through Baden-Württemberg and Bavaria, the passengers in the 'Red Flash' were mobbed. At Singen, more people welcomed the team than there were people in the town (25,000). The players were buried beneath a mountain of gifts: porcelain sculptures, wines, books, hair lotion, candles, underwear, cow bells (Kempten), silver ashtrays (Kaufbeuren), pungent cheeses, a football made from Allgäu alpine flowers. Fritz Walter called the journey home 'an unprecedented reception'.[42] It culminated on Marienplatz in Munich on 6 July, where 500,000 people acclaimed the heroes of Bern.

In Hungary, the mood quickly turned ugly. By 9 p.m. on 4 July, a few hours after the final whistle, 400 people had gathered at Oktogon, close to AVH headquarters in central Budapest, to abuse Puskás and Sebes, whose apartment windows were smashed that night. Numbers swelled, as the crowd moved to the buildings of the National Committee for Physical Education and Sports and Magyar Rádió, where the captain and coach were warned 'not to come home, because they would be executed'. There were bigger demonstrations the following night, when 10,000 people were on the streets, and further protests on 6 July, when 4,000 people gathered outside the National Theatre. Police broke up the crowds, whose inchoate rage – overturning trams, making anti-Semitic remarks about Sebes, vandalising the offices of the state-run sports lottery – only slowly abated. Two weeks after the final, a mob burned pictures of Puskás and smashed windows at *Nepsport* before heading again to Magyar Rádió. An AVH officer threatened to open fire if the crowd didn't disperse.[43]

Two different manifestations, then, of football's mass power. But what did they mean, and where did they lead? Historian Joachim Fest wasn't the only observer to describe 4 July 1954 as 'the moment the Federal Republic of Germany was truly born'. The miracle of Bern, in the now standard reading, brought unity, confidence and identity to a country lacking all three. West Germany's post-war history – the history of an economic and football juggernaut – begins not in 1949, when the Basic Law created the Federal Republic, but five years later, when eleven humble footballers defeated the world's greatest team. A myth's power can be measured by how many people buy into it. And Germans of all stripes – footballers, journalists, historians, politicians – bought into the idea that 4 July 1954 made (West) Germany, in Franz Beckenbauer's words, 'somebody again'.[44]

In fact, reaction to West Germany's win over Hungary was more mixed and uncertain than legend would (often much later) have it. Writing in 2005, Rudolf Oswald identified three strands of public opinion in July 1954: a euphoric, almost 'anti-national' public response; a glorification of football as *Volksgemeinschaft* (national community) among the DFB leadership; and a cautious distance from the triumph in government circles. The latter left the field open to the nationalistic messaging of DFB boss Peco Bauwens. His speech to the team in Munich on 6 July invoked the German god of war Wotan and Hitler's *Führerprinzip* (leadership principle).[45]

Bauwens' speech, like fans singing the first verse of 'Deutschland über alles', provoked uncomfortable echoes of a past most Germans wanted left behind. Munich's biggest paper, the *Süddeutsche Zeitung*, called Bauwens' 'Sieg Heil' effort an 'embarrassment'; *Die Zeit* feared such 'hysterical expressions' would provoke 'suspicion' of Germany abroad. West German president Theodor Heuss eschewed political interpretations of victory in Bern. Sport, he said, should be 'kept out of politics'.[46]

This reflected the public mood on both sides of the Iron Curtain. Readers' letters to publications in East and West Germany emphasised the sporting achievement – what communist youth newspaper *Junge Welt* called 'altogether the greatest German triumph in the history of football' – and rejected the intrusion of politics: 'I don't see what such a beautiful football win has to do with our national situation', one man told the *Süddeutsche Zeitung*.[47]

Of course, the win had plenty to do with politics. In West Germany, where gathering Cold War confidence found further expression in NATO membership (1955) and the founding of the European Economic Community two years later. And in East Germany, where sport and politics ran into unavoidable Cold War contradictions. The East German media balanced praise (often extravagant) for its socialist ally, Hungary, with praise (often grudging) for its 'brother state', West Germany. But 'strict neutrality' got harder as the 1954 tournament progressed. In commentary on the final, Wolfgang Hempel broke protocol, describing 'the West German team' as 'the German team' and 'the Germans', a slippage that inadvertently endorsed the Federal Republic's claims to represent the German nation. As Hempel later stated, the result in Bern sparked 'just as much jubilation' in East as in West Germany: 'everyone still felt German'.[48]

Der Spiegel wondered if beating Hungary offered Germany, or its Western half, a better basis for 'national existence', 'after two thousand years of historical aberration': 'Never before have the collective feelings of Germans bubbled over so exclusively for nothing but their football team'.[49] This was itself a political discovery. But it didn't last long. As Franz-Josef Brüggemeier has shown, after the initial outpouring of joy, 'the miracle of Bern' was often forgotten – at least in the public record. The final left few traces in archives, newspapers or memoirs. The post-war elites 'were just not interested'.[50]

It wasn't, arguably, until fifty years later that 'the miracle of Bern' lodged itself in collective memory, as 'an unforgettable day in Germany's postwar history ... the real birthday of the Federal Republic'.[51] Sönke Wortmann's film came out shortly before the fiftieth anniversary of the 1954 final, as Germany prepared to host the World Cup for the first time as a unified nation. With football now a lucrative arm of the culture industry, the need for a comforting national story was paramount. An against-the-odds triumph fit the bill better than the more complicated truth about a 'miracle' that was also a triumph of sporting continuity, economic strength and technological innovation.

Innovation that may have included performance-enhancing drugs. Doping suspicions have long swirled around the winning team. Wankdorf groundsman Walter Brönnimann claimed he found used syringes in the West German changing rooms after the final, allegations repeated, without much evidence, by Puskás (still sore about that offside goal) and the magazine *World Soccer*. A 2010 University of Leipzig study suggested West German players didn't take glucose supplements, as they'd claimed, but Pervitin, the German brand name for methamphetamine, a drug handed out like candy to Wehrmacht soldiers during World War Two. The Pervitin theory remains unproven, or unprovable. But it's a reminder that doping controversies in Cold War sport didn't begin and end with the Olympics. And that the 'spirit of Spiez' might have been fuelled by something stronger than camaraderie.

If the 1954 final's impact on West Germany was a slow-burner, its impact on Hungary was immediate – and explosive. In Márton

Keleti's *A csodacsatár*, people take to the streets after the fictional country of Footballia's defeat in a vital match. The country's dictator, Admiral Duca, frets that 'This is a rebellion, this is chaos, this is a revolution!'[52] The scene would have resonated with Hungarian audiences when the film came out in 1957. Gyula Grosics felt post-match protests in July 1954 created 'a bitter atmosphere [that] could be felt months later'. In these protests, he claimed, 'lay the seeds of the 1956 Uprising'.[53]

Anger was so fierce in July 1954 because it targeted the one part of the communist regime, the golden squad, that everyone loved. Perhaps, with football's role as the shining light in a grim dictatorship suddenly and unexpectedly dimmed, the scales fell from people's eyes. The 1956 uprising had more to do with Stalin's death, miserable living standards, AVH repression, hatred of Rákosi and Nikita Khrushchev's secret speech than a 3–2 defeat. But, as Tamás Aczél and Tibor Méray wrote in 1982, 'there was something that [the people] did not forget'.[54] That 'something' was the first illustration of people's power, displayed on the streets of Budapest after Helmut Rahn broke the nation's heart.

Hungarian football didn't die in the Wankdorf Stadium on 4 July 1954. Or when Soviet forces invaded Hungary on 4 November 1956. Ferencváros' Flórián Albert won the Ballon d'Or in 1967. His club won the 1965 Fairs Cup, beating Juventus in the final. Hungary's national team, led by Albert, reached the quarter-finals of the 1962 and 1966 World Cups, the latter after beating defending champs Brazil 3–1, a performance, eulogised the *Daily Mirror*, 'to match the magnificent heights of Magyar memory'.[55] In the 70s and 80s, Hungarian clubs reached European finals: Ferencváros versus Dynamo Kyiv in the European Cup Winners' Cup (1975); Videoton versus Real Madrid in the UEFA Cup (1985).

Nonetheless, the combined blows of 1954 and 1956 devastated Hungarian football. Defeat in Bern was a wound that didn't heal. Decades later, it provoked furious debate, 'as though', said striker Tibor Nyilasi, 'Hungarian football is frozen at that moment, as though we have never quite moved on'.[56] In the short term, the golden squad recovered, putting together another long, unbeaten run (eighteen games) between September 1954 and February 1956. These were still the Magical Magyars. Before Scotland's 3–1 defeat to Hungary in Budapest in May 1955, winger Billy Liddell admired his opponents' 'sartorial elegance', a contrast to the drab clothing of ordinary Hungarians: 'they were looked upon by almost everybody as national heroes'.[57]

Behind the scenes, though, all was not well. The coaching structure around Gusztáv Sebes was dismantled, as the communist leadership fractured. Eventually, the team started losing: a 3–1 defeat in Turkey in February 1956, just before Khrushchev's secret speech in Moscow lit a fuse beneath the communist bloc; a 4–2 loss to Czechoslovakia at a rainy Népstadion in May; and a 5–4 loss to Belgium in Brussels on 3 June, a game the visitors led 3–1. After the match, Sebes was sacked, a month before Matyas Rákosi got his marching orders. The golden squad would now be managed by committee, headed by Márton Bukovi. The swansong came at Moscow's Lenin Stadium on 23 September. In front of 105,000 people, the recalled Gyula Grosics outplayed the young Lev Yashin; Zoltan Czibor scored early on; and Hungary, after a long (and, to some, suspicious) series of draws, secured a first win over the Soviet Union. A month later, Soviet troops would be in Budapest, ensuring a much bloodier victory.

In the confusion of the Hungarian Revolution, reports surfaced that Ferenc Puskás had been killed. A heroic death, waxed *The Guardian*, 'manning the barricades in the fight for freedom against tyranny'.[58] In fact, Puskás and his Honvéd team, like their MTK counterparts, were out of the country, whisked away from trouble on European tours. Many of those players never played in Hungary again. A FIFA document from 1957 reveals the scale of the exodus. Twenty national team players, including Puskás, Grosics, Czibor and Kocsis, were listed as suspended 'refugee footballers'. A further 171 first and second division players – including almost the entire squads of Soproni Vasutas, Nagykánizsai Bányász and ETO FC Győr – were granted transfers abroad from 21 October.[59] The player drain was the blow from which it proved hardest to recover. Puskás' denuded army team went from powerhouse to relegation fodder in the blink of an eye. Hungary, in Jonathan Wilson's words, 'were never so good again'.[60]

Sebes, that committed communist, had no doubts. 'If Hungary had won the football World Cup, there would have been no counter revolution but a powerful thrust in the building of socialism in the country'.[61] Perhaps. Perhaps not. It's often tricky to measure football's political impact, especially for a game as significant as the 1954 World Cup final.

Less debatable, in sporting terms, is the sense of a wrong ending on 4 July 1954. Not for West Germany, of course, but for the team destined to win. Overwhelming favourites, Brazil lost the 1950 World Cup final on home soil to Uruguay. But Brazil recovered, winning three World Cups between 1958 and 1970. There was no redemption for the Magical Magyars after Bern. This remains a source of regret, not only in Hungary but among football lovers everywhere. Gyula Grosics once said, 'For me the world opened thanks to the Aranycsapat'.[62] It's equally true that the 'golden squad' opened the eyes of the world. In December 1954, Bill Shankly, manager of lowly Workington Town, was on a train to London with his team, when he got wind that Puskás, Hidegkuti and co. – travelling south after Hungary's 4–2 victory over Scotland – were on board. Shankly hurried his lads to the first-class carriages to get autographs, hear stories and pick brains. 'Some of their magic rubbed off on us', he said, after Workington beat Leyton Orient 1–0 in the FA Cup.[63] The magic is still there. Few teams have been as beloved as Hungary's greatest team. But the golden squad couldn't take its shot at the ultimate golden moment. Hungary's players were football gods, whatever your politics. It hurt to find out, on the quagmire at the Wankdorf Stadium, that they had feet of clay.

3 FOOTBALL BEATS GOD
Ireland vs. Yugoslavia, Dublin, October 1955

May 2002. Ireland is at war with itself, not over territorial or sectarian issues, but over football. In the run-up to the World Cup finals in South Korea and Japan, Ireland's choleric captain, the Manchester United midfielder Roy Keane, lets fly at the 'amateurish' Irish Football Association. Keane accuses the FAI of shoddy preparations for the tournament, including hazardous training facilities at the squad's base on the volcanic island of Saipan. A blazing, expletive-laden row ensues between Keane and team manager Mick McCarthy. 'You can stick your World Cup up your arse,' the future Sky Sports pundit allegedly shouts. Keane is sent home in disgrace.

In Ireland, the 'Saipan incident' spectacularly catches fire. Journalists, the public and politicians are deeply divided over Keane's behaviour. Prime Minister Bertie Ahern, a Manchester United fan, offers his services as a mediator but to no avail. Ireland's star player misses the World Cup, and his team goes out in the second round on penalties to Spain. For many, the whole row encapsulates the battle between the 'new' Ireland, a Celtic Tiger emboldened by recent footballing success under manager Jack Charlton and unwilling to accept second best, and the 'old' Ireland, happy merely to be invited to the party.[1]

Reach back fifty years before the Saipan incident to October 1955 and we find Ireland mired in another football controversy. This, too, has shades of the 'old' versus 'new' but it's more serious, for it pits football against faith. Ireland are due to play a friendly at the home of Irish football,

Dalymount Park in Dublin, against a team from the Federal People's Republic of Yugoslavia. Football fans are excited; Ireland doesn't host that many international matches and Yugoslavia are one of the finest teams in Europe. However, the Archbishop of Dublin, John Charles McQuaid, guardian of the country's rectitude, is outraged. Yugoslavia is run by the atheist dictator Tito, McQuaid insists, who imprisons and tortures Catholic priests. Ireland is a God-fearing Catholic country and must take a stand against evil in the Cold War. The match, McQuaid decrees, must not go ahead.

It's often said that football and faith are comparable. 'Football is like a religion to me', Pelé once confessed, 'I worship the ball and treat it like a god'.[2] This is the story of an episode during the Cold War when football and faith clashed head-on – and God lost. In what became a test of the power of the Catholic Church in Ireland, Archbishop McQuaid suffered a rare defeat. Despite intense pressure to call off the Ireland–Yugoslavia game, the men in blazers at the Irish FA – characters much like those so derided by Roy Keane five decades later – stood firm and the match took place. Tito's team showed the Irish no mercy, winning easily and confirming their reputation as the emerging powerhouse of Eastern European football. Yet a victory for communism was well worth it, some in Ireland claimed. The Irish team might have lost on the pitch. But by putting a dent in the Catholic Church's overbearing authority, football helped the country in the long term win off it.

What, we might ask in the first place, was the Yugoslav national team doing playing a friendly in 1955 in Ireland? Ireland was a footballing backwater and a long way, geographically and ideologically, from Yugoslavia's natural base in the Balkans and Eastern Europe. Can it be attributed to the East–West thaw following the recent death of Joseph Stalin? Was the Yugoslav team trying to mimic Gusztáv Sebes' Hungary, who journeyed across Europe advertising the wonders of communist football? Was Tito, a big fan of the Croatian team Hajduk Split, maybe even using his country's favourite sport to convert Catholics into Marxists? The answer is rooted in the peculiar position in which Yugoslavia found itself during the Cold War.

Communist Yugoslavia was synonymous with Josip Broz Tito. Having risen to power as the heroic leader of Partisan resistance to fascist occupation during World War Two, Tito dominated the country for almost four decades. Unusually for an Eastern European state, his regime was both politically repressive and economically liberal. It also reached out to the West far more than any of its neighbours, embracing visiting holidaymakers, pop stars and football clubs.[3] Yugoslavs regarded Tito as a living god. On being told of his death on 4 May 1980, the referee of a match between Hajduk Split and Red Star Belgrade immediately halted play. Players and officials burst into tears, and the 50,000-strong crowd sang 'Comrade Tito, we swear an oath to you, that we will not deviate from your path!'[4]

At the outset of the Cold War, Yugoslavia was Moscow's most trusted ally. Belgrade housed the headquarters of Cominform, the central organisation of the international communist movement. However, in 1948 Stalin split from Tito over political differences. The Soviet Union effectively declared war on Yugoslavia, which was expelled from the Eastern bloc. Tito, already authoritarian and now fearful of Soviet subversion, bore down more heavily on dissidents, including prominent Catholic priests. Thereafter, Yugoslavia pursued a Third Way in the Cold War, ploughing an independent furrow in the communist world and cultivating relations with the West for economic and military assistance. Tito co-founded the Non-Aligned Movement, through which Yugoslavia built up valuable diplomatic and financial connections with Africa and Asia.

Football acted as both a unifier and a tool of cultural diplomacy under Tito. Yugoslavia was a young, fragile country with deep ethnic divisions that would eventually lead to bloody civil war in the 1990s. Tito's government used football as a powerful force for integration. The game was structured to mirror the state, with associations for each republic (Serbia, Croatia, Slovenia, Macedonia, Montenegro, Bosnia and Herzegovina) brought together in an overarching federal body. Unifying competitions incorporated teams from every part of Yugoslavia, while multi-ethnic clubs were nurtured and others with violently nationalist paths disbanded. Football stadiums could still be hotbeds of nationalism and matches marred by politically inspired violence on and off the pitch. But the football landscape in Yugoslavia played an important role in underpinning the Communist Party's doctrine of 'brotherhood and unity'.

Yugoslavia's national team, or *reprezentacija*, was also organised along multi-ethnic lines, which had the added advantage of pooling talent from across the country. This, as well as the weighty financial and technical support the government gave it, helps explain why the team was so formidable. For Tito, a successful national team would not only unite his people. It would also promote the country and its brand of 'self-managed socialism' overseas. This, in turn, would help to overcome Yugoslavia's isolation within the communist world and grease the wheels of diplomacy and international trade. Financial rewards and other perks naturally came the elite players' way. Ostensibly 'state amateurs' who worked in factories and foundries, in reality many of them were, like Dynamo Moscow's British tourists in 1945, full-time, privileged ambassadors.[5]

Tito's football-as-marketing strategy was given an enormous boost at the Helsinki Olympics in 1952. With the world watching, Yugoslavia played the Soviet Union in a communist showdown. Their game was only in the first round of the football tournament, but both sides treated it as a do or die affair. A rampant Yugoslavia were 5–1 up with fifteen minutes remaining, only for the Soviets to draw level by scoring four goals, all, bizarrely, from corners. Yugoslavia won the replay 3–1, silencing the Soviet journalists who had celebrated their team's comeback against Tito's 'fascist clique'. The Yugoslavs' victory represented a major propaganda coup. The team's members – many of whom played against Ireland in October 1955 – would be national heroes for decades.[6]

Yugoslavia's triumph over the Soviet Union, and their silver medal at the 1952 Olympics, was, as historian Richard Mills tells us, no flash in the pan. Yugoslav football entered a golden age soon after World War Two. The *reprezentacija* qualified for every World Cup finals between 1950 and 1962. It reached the quarter-finals in 1954 and 1958, and finished fourth in Chile four years later. In the European Championship, the team did even better, reaching the final in both 1960 and 1968. The Olympic side, largely a youth team after Helsinki, won its third silver medal in a row at Melbourne in 1956 and took gold in Rome in 1960. Yugoslav players were highly rated across Europe. Four of the Rest of the World XI that drew 4–4 with England at Wembley in October 1953, for instance, hailed from Yugoslavia. The older the Cold War grew, and the more open Yugoslavia became, the more the country's players found clubs overseas.[7]

Capitalising on and underpinning this success, Yugoslavia's footballers were devoted travellers. The country's national team and leading clubs like Hajduk Split and Dinamo Zagreb clocked up a remarkable number of air miles. The Middle East, South America,

East Asia, Africa, Australia – the list of locations almost appears endless. When touring, often for weeks on end, footballers played a vital role as foreign currency earners and sporting emissaries. Their job was to boost Yugoslavia's image and coffers and to spread the gospel of socialism. The team's focus changed according to Yugoslavia's needs and the Cold War's changing climate. In the mid-1950s, when the country largely stood alone in the East and sought friends elsewhere, it turned its attention to the West, including Ireland.[8]

Like Yugoslavia, the Republic of Ireland occupied an unusual position during the Cold War. On the one hand, the young country was officially neutral. This relieved it of costly commitments but, in theory at least, laid it open to communist influence. On the other hand, Ireland faced strongly towards the West. It received Marshall Aid from the United States after World War Two and in the mid-1950s secretly began feeding information to the spies of the Central Intelligence Agency. More importantly, Ireland was among the most stridently Catholic countries in the world. The immense power of the Catholic Church in Ireland left little to no space for atheistic communism or support for the Eastern bloc. An Irish communist party existed but was tiny compared with the country's two major political parties, Fianna Fáil and Fianna Gael.[9]

During the Cold War, football in Ireland received nowhere near as much political support as it did in Yugoslavia. The parlous state of the Irish economy didn't allow for this but, more significantly, football was frowned upon by many nationalists, who labelled it a 'foreign' sport foisted on Ireland by English colonialists. Sport was an ideological battlefield in Ireland. From the 1880s to the 1970s, the powerful Gaelic Athletic Association banned its members from playing or even watching football (as well as rugby, cricket and hockey) in favour of more authentically 'Irish' sports like hurling and camogie. Youngsters in the 1950s who played football, like the great Johnny Giles of Leeds United fame, were made to feel un-Irish.[10]

Despite these obstacles, football was hugely popular. When Yugoslavia came to town in 1955, the Irish football league was in rude health. Attendances were at an all-time high, with the biggest games attracting 20,000 spectators. Thousands more people listened to matches on Radio Éireann and press coverage of the game boomed. The fifties were a bleak decade in Ireland. Unemployment was high and welfare benefits measly. Industry slumped and a fifth of the population emigrated.

Live football offered a brief, relatively cheap escape from this desolate environment. The Dublin derbies, between Shamrock Rovers and Drumcondra, gripped the capital city. 'Long queues stretched back down Pearse Street, full of fans anxious to make kick-off', recalls Eamon Dunphy, who grew up close to Drumcondra's ground and played for Ireland in the 1960s. 'All week I'd worry about the outcome of the game.'[11]

The Irish national team, meanwhile, was on the up. It wouldn't qualify for a World Cup finals until 1990, but the team boasted some outstanding players. Manchester United's legendary captain Johnny Carey was among many who played in the English top-flight. Ireland took some notable scalps in the decade after World War Two. Most notoriously, they beat West Germany 3–2 in Dublin in 1951. The Germans thought they'd scored a last-minute equaliser from a corner only to learn that English referee William Ling – who'd take charge of the 1954 World Cup final – had blown for full time when the ball was in mid-flight. Most famously, in a friendly at Goodison Park in September 1949, Ireland (see Figure 3.1) beat England 2–0 thanks to

Figure 3.1 Ireland about to defeat England 2–0 at Goodison Park, Liverpool, 21 September 1949. Con Martin is rear, second from left, and Peter Farrell is front, second from right. © Daily Mirror/Mirrorpix via Getty Images.

goals by Con Martin and Peter Farrell, both of whom would play against Yugoslavia. 'Anybody who thinks the Irish have any chance', Henry Rose of the *Daily Express* had written before the match, oozing English hubris, 'should make an appointment with a Harley Street psychiatrist'. The result made history: this was the first time the mighty England had been defeated on home soil. The match marked Ireland's arrival as a footballing nation.[12]

One of the unsung heroes in developing Irish football during this era was Joe Wickham. Educated at a Christian Brothers school and a founder of the Dublin railwaymen's team Midland Athletic, Wickham took over as secretary of the Irish Football Association (FAI) just before World War Two. He would die in post, during a game between Ireland and Poland in Chorzów in 1968. Wickham was a gifted administrator and diplomat and usually one of the FAI five selectors who picked the international team. He was also a practising Catholic, two of whose sisters were nuns.[13]

Joe Wickham was one of two characters at the centre of the row over the Ireland–Yugoslavia match in 1955. John Charles McQuaid, possibly the most powerful man in Ireland, was the other. McQuaid was the Catholic Primate of Ireland and Archbishop of Dublin from 1940 to 1972. Educated at writer James Joyce's old college, and a long-time acquaintance of Éamon de Valera, the colossus of Irish politics, McQuaid (see Figure 3.2) embodied the Irish establishment. He believed that God, ruling through the Catholic Church, was the authority of the land and that everything had to be sacrificed for the one absolute requirement: the salvation of souls. McQuaid interfered in any matter he believed threatened the spiritual welfare of his flock. This included policing plays and films, denouncing female athletes as 'un-Irish and un-Catholic' and banning football matches on Good Friday during World War Two. Few people dared challenge the word of a man who spoke in the name of Jesus Christ.[14]

Archbishop McQuaid was, on top of this, resolutely anti-communist. Like Pope Pius XII, a highly contentious figure whose role as one of the West's great Cold Warriors is often overlooked, McQuaid preached that Marxism and Catholicism were antithetical. Communism, like all evils, had to be rooted out, he urged, especially where it threatened religious freedoms. As a Cold War crusader, in Ireland McQuaid used the Catholic Information Bureau to spy on left-wingers and to tell parish

Figure 3.2 Archbishop John Charles McQuaid with Éamon de Valera (holding hat). Location and date unknown. © Independent News and Media/Getty Images.

priests the identity of 'communists' in their midst. Looking overseas, he raised money to help the Christian Democrats defeat the Communist Party in the pivotal Italian election of 1948 and campaigned vigorously for the release of Catholic priests imprisoned behind the Iron Curtain.[15]

One of these priests was the Croatian cardinal Aloysius Stepinac. Despite the state's official atheism, Roman Catholicism remained a powerful force in communist Yugoslavia, particularly in Croatia. Tito, who was Croatian-born, trod a fine line between respecting ordinary Catholics' convictions and clamping down on outspoken clerics. Tito's government branded Aloysius Stepinac a traitor and criminal for having collaborated during World War Two with the Croatian Nazi puppet regime, the Ustaše, and been complicit in forced religious conversions. McQuaid portrayed the cardinal as a Catholic martyr standing up to radical secularism. In May 1949, more than 100,000 people gathered in the streets of Dublin to protest at the treatment of Stepinac and Cardinal József Mindszenty, who was incarcerated in Hungary. This was the largest demonstration Dublin had ever witnessed.[16]

In late 1954, Joe Wickham's FAI invited the Yugoslav national team to play a friendly in Dublin the following autumn.[17] Wickham had issued a similar invitation in 1952, only to quietly withdraw it after learning of Archbishop McQuaid's objections. Because the Cold War had thawed somewhat in the intervening years, Wickham believed the game could now go ahead and it was scheduled for Wednesday 19 October 1955.[18] When news of the match broke in Ireland that summer, the football press and fans reacted with eager anticipation. There were one or two criticisms; inviting the communist Yugoslavs broke all Christian principles, senior Waterford Football League officials protested.[19] But McQuaid's office was silent on the matter.

Once October arrived, however, things radically changed. Days before the game was due to take place, John O'Regan, McQuaid's right-hand man, phoned Wickham and asked him to call off the match as a protest against Marshal Tito's persecution of Cardinal Stepinac. McQuaid's late intervention might have been due to the distraction of other work or a desire to put the FAI on the spot. Either way, it left Wickham in an unenviable position. Wickham politely told O'Regan that Ireland and Yugoslavia belonged to UEFA, which had no interest in either politics or religion, and that it was now too late to call the match off.[20] Cue pressure from other quarters. Following discussions between McQuaid and Prime Minister John Costello, the Department of Justice rattled the FAI by demanding it guaranteed to pay the costs of repatriating any Yugoslav player who might try to defect. The Irish President, Sean O'Kelly, who was due to receive the Yugoslav team at the national stadium, Dalymount Park, then announced he would not attend the game. Government ministers followed suit.[21]

Faced with these unprecedented actions, the FAI called an emergency meeting. If McQuaid's office expected the 'soccer crowd' to cave in, they were to be sorely disappointed. Two committee members did wobble, regretting the political and ecclesiastical stink the game had caused. Another member, from the Army Athletic Association, the aptly named Lieutenant-Colonel Gunn, who'd likely been leant on by the military brass, opposed holding the match. But the rest of the committee stood behind Wickham's initial response to O'Regan. Summing up their views, FAI chairman Sam Prole announced that the match had been arranged in 'good faith' and its cancellation would jeopardise Ireland's position in international football. Worse still, the game's abandonment could ruin the terrific record football had as an ambassador for Ireland 'in bringing the National Flag to places it had never been seen'. On a show of hands, all members, except Gunn, voted for the game to go ahead.[22]

By now, a bitter public dispute raged around the Yugoslavia game in Ireland. Aware of McQuaid's opposition, the Army Band, which traditionally opened football match proceedings with the national anthems, reneged on its engagement. Most trade union leaders, who were ardently anti-communist, supported the archbishop's line, and Transport FC, a factory works team from Leinster, pulled out of the post-match banquet meant to honour the Yugoslavs. The radio commentator, Philip Greene, the voice of Irish football, first refused to work on the game, prompting the superb newspaper headline 'Reds Turn Greene Yellow'.[23] Then Radio Éireann announced they would not provide any coverage. To top it all, the Irish team's part-time trainer, Dick Hearns, a serving police officer, declared he was unavailable for the match. And rumours circulated – ultimately unfounded – that some of the Irish players were going to drop out.[24]

Protests against the Yugoslavia game, and calls to boycott it, came from a variety of Catholic organisations. The Catholic Association of International Relations wrote an open letter to the Yugoslav team branding them instruments of tyranny. The League of the Kingship of Christ encouraged the Yugoslav players to defect. The chief of the Catholic Boy Scouts accused the FAI of entertaining 'the tools of Tito', while a Limerick educational body expressed hope that in coming to 'the Island of Saints and Scholars' some of the Yugoslav players might become Catholic converts.[25] A letter read out from the pulpit of every church on the Sunday before the game ordered people not to attend on pain of mortal sin. In the north of Ireland, Protestants and Unionists were quick to score points off McQuaid's intervention. It was 'grotesque', the *Belfast Telegraph* proclaimed, and proved the existence of an 'invisible curtain' of religious division between Northern Ireland and the Republic that was as real as 'the iron one' between East and West.[26]

The Yugoslavs arrived at Dublin Airport via London two nights before the game and were driven under heavy police escort to the plush Gresham Hotel on O'Connell Street. Aware they had flown into a political storm, their spokesmen staked out the moral high ground. The team had played on all five continents, said the Yugoslav Football Association president Rato Dugonjić, and this was the first time a protest had been lodged against the team. More caustically, Vladimir Velibit, Yugoslavia's ambassador to Britain, accused Archbishop McQuaid of defying a recent ruling by Pope Pius XII that politics should not interfere with sport. Goodness knows what, if he heard about it, McQuaid thought of this gibe. The morning of the match, as if shooting into an open net, Yugoslav officials publicly accused the Archbishop of waging a 'campaign of intolerance'. Meanwhile, the Yugoslav players amused themselves by going window-shopping on Dublin's high streets.[27]

Coming into the game at Dalymount Park, both the Yugoslav and Irish teams were in fine fettle. Ireland had recently beaten the Netherlands at home and Norway away. More impressively, Yugoslavia hadn't lost in well over a year and had recently notched up victories over Italy and World Cup winners West Germany. Though the Irish players each got £30 for the match, it was the Yugoslav 'amateurs' who were the far more professional outfit. Ordinarily, before games they trained for a fortnight at Partizan Belgrade's ground. Their manager, Aleksandar Tirnanić, had experience as a player and coach and, critically, the power to pick the team. In contrast, the Irish players usually gathered on the day of matches, with many of them exhausted having travelled by boat overnight from their English clubs. The Irish team had no manager and largely relied on senior players to handle tactics and half-time talks. The team was picked by an FAI committee largely made up of aged businessmen whose knowledge of the game was limited to say the least.[28]

Four of the Yugoslav team that played against Ireland would be shoe-ins for the country's all-time XI. Nicknamed 'the ballet dancer with hands of steel', goalkeeper Vladimir Beara (see Figure 3.3) played sixty times for his country. He won three league titles with Hajduk Split before making the highly provocative move to Serbian rivals Red Star Belgrade, who reportedly sold their team bus to finance the deal. Beara was Red Star's keeper against Manchester United immediately before the 1958 Munich air crash.[29] Branko Zebec was a highly versatile left-sided midfielder who earned sixty-five caps for Yugoslavia, bagging seventeen goals. Extremely fast, he had been top scorer at the 1952 Olympics and, unusually because of their fierce rivalry, played for both Belgrade teams, Red Star and Partizan.

Known as the Blond Buzzer, centre-forward Miloš Milutinović played 213 matches for Partizan Belgrade, scoring a remarkable 231 goals. Milutinović was in red-hot form for the Ireland game; that season saw him notch six goals against Sporting Lisbon and a further two against Real Madrid in the inaugural European Champions Clubs' Cup, forerunner of the Champions League. Widely regarded as the greatest Croatian player of all time, captain Bernard Vukas played

Figure 3.3 Yugoslavia's goalkeeper Vladimir Beara in training, at an unknown location sometime in the 1950s. © Popperfoto via Getty Images/ Getty Images.

over 600 games for Hajduk Split and fifty-nine times for Yugoslavia. The slightly built Vukas was nominally a forward but had the ability to ghost into a variety of positions during games, making him the perfect playmaker. Two months before the Ireland game, Vukas had scored a hat-trick for a European XI against a UK side in Belfast.[30]

Ireland's line-up was less star-studded. Talisman Johnny Carey had recently retired, leaving a big hole, especially in the centre of the park, and several players, like left-winger Liam Tuohy, were lacking international experience. But Peter Farrell, who played for Everton, was an inspirational captain and talented right-half. Blessed with a saintly air on and off the pitch, Farrell was forced when he retired to formally announce he would not be joining the priesthood. Centre-forward Shay Gibbons was the Irish league's most prolific goal poacher of the 1950s, and inside-forward Arthur Fitzsimons, who played just behind future Nottingham Forest manager Brian Clough for Middlesbrough, was a sturdy provider. Aston Villa's versatile central defender Con Martin was the team's biggest character. Martin was a renowned Gaelic footballer in his youth and, after switching codes, played in multiple positions for Ireland throughout his career, including as goalkeeper. Martin offered a powerful physical presence and fierce determination, and was skilful with both feet.[31]

A crowd of around 22,000 turned up to watch the match at Dalymount Park. For a midweek game kicking off in the afternoon, when many people would be at work, this was exceptionally large. Clearly, Archbishop McQuaid's boycotting campaign had failed. Some people presumably stayed away on McQuaid's orders, but we know others went along explicitly to defy him. The maverick Tipperary revolutionary-turned-politician, Dan Breen, an atheist who cared little for football, was among these. So was a group of writers and artists, including the poet and novelist Paddy Kavanagh. A heavier than usual police presence bolstered the numbers in attendance, adding to the tensions surrounding the match. Some officers were in plain clothes – watching out for absconding Yugoslavs, perhaps. The authorities feared there would be vociferous pro- and anti-game demonstrations outside the ground, but on the day protests were confined to a solitary man carrying a yellow-and-white Papal flag.[32]

Inside the ground, everything went smoothly before kick-off. Standing in for the nation's president, Oscar Traynor, the FAI's president, welcomed the Yugoslav players on the pitch alongside Joe Wickham. Traynor was a highly respected former defence minister who used to keep goal for Belfast Celtic. The spectators surprised Rato Dugonjić with the warmth of their cheers, and the recorded national anthems playing over the loudspeakers hit the right notes.[33] The only hiccup was with the Yugoslavs' red, white and blue flag, which embarrassingly was run up the flagpole upside down, before being righted. It's likely this was more cock-up than conspiracy, but the visitors can't have been best pleased.[34]

Despite this, there was no hint of any bad blood between the players as they warmed up and shook hands. This is maybe because they'd more in common than many let on. A number of the Yugoslav players, particularly the Croats, were practising Catholics. For some of them, playing in Ireland against brothers-in-arms might have had a certain appeal. Liam Tuohy saw several Yugoslav players blessing themselves as they came out of the tunnel. 'There were nearly more Catholics on their side than there were on ours', he recalled years later.[35]

Distracted perhaps by the flag fiasco, the blue-clad Yugoslavs started the match poorly. The Irish, in green, had the better of the opening skirmishes. The pitch was heavier than the visitors were used to, and the 'Irish weather' (breezy, cold and drizzly) played to the hosts' advantage. A Fitzsimons' wind-assisted long shot gave the home fans cause for optimism, despite going well wide and knocking over a crouching photographer. But it was the visitors that made the first dangerous move, as Vukas – who would go on to torment the Irish – took a return pass from Zebec in the opposition box before goalkeeper Jimmy O'Neill snuffed out the threat.

In the tenth minute, the Yugoslavs took the lead. English referee Alec Murdoch adjudged that Irish wing-half Frank O'Farrell had handballed just outside his box. Milutinović took the free kick and his low drive deflected off a defender past the unsighted O'Neill into the net. Milutinović had struck the free kick with his customary force but the home team hadn't helped themselves much by building a ramshackle wall.

If this was bad fortune, the next Yugoslav goal, in the fourteenth minute, was down to a schoolboy error. Con Martin played a horrendously short back pass to O'Neill, Milutinović intercepted, side-stepped the keeper, and calmly slotted into an empty net. The Yugoslavia game should have been cause for celebration for Martin. It was his twenty-eighth international, which entitled him to share the record for the most caps for Ireland with Johnny Carey. Unfortunately, Mr Versatile came into the match with an ankle injury and had an all-round stinker.

With the Yugoslavs now in a comfortable 2–0 lead, Vukas took over. The Croat wore the number nine shirt, but this was a ruse. Instead of playing centre-forward, Vukas roamed all over the pitch, playing so deep at times he resembled a half-back. This pulled the Irish players, especially Peter Farrell, out of position, leaving space for his Yugoslav colleagues to exploit. Vukas often found these colleagues with cute lobs or crosses. At other times, coming from deep, he waltzed through the uncertain Irish defence with ease. Vukas' teammate Milutinović, wearing number eight, played centre-forward, but was rarely picked up by the Irish markers. The two of them – Vukas the architect, Milutinović the marksman – put Ireland to the sword.

Against the run of play, in the thirty-second minute Ireland pulled a goal back. The Yugoslavs had by far the better ball control than the home team but even they could make the odd slip. When Zebec, deep in his own half, dallied in possession, Fitzsimons – Ireland's man-of-the-match – pounced and on the turn hit the ball first time past goalkeeper Beara. For a brief period, the Irish looked like reviving. Martin's long punts into the Yugoslav box were designed to heap increasing pressure on Beara, who, like all continental keepers, was thought to be timorous and suspect in the air. Beara was regularly charged by the Irish forwards, which led to several scuffles and complaints to the referee. However, instead of capitulating, just before the interval the Yugoslavs went further ahead. Right-winger Zdravko Rajkov jinked past his marker, pushed the ball out to Vukas, who flicked it on to Milutinović. The Blond Buzzer's shot past O'Neill completed his hat-trick and the striker raised his arms in celebration. Half-time: 3–1.

For long periods in the second half the Irish, rallied by Farrell, had the Yugoslavs pinned in their own half but wasted chance after chance. Shay Gibbons and Luton Town's George Cummins had gilt-edged opportunities to reduce the arrears following errors by centre-half Tomislav Crnković. Each had only Beara to beat, but clean through on goal Gibbons hit the ball straight at the advancing keeper, and Cummins, with everything in his favour – Beara was on the ground – struck the keeper's foot with a ten-yard shot. When the Irish hit the target on other occasions, they found the Red Star Belgrade man on top form. His acrobatics might have been a tad flashy for Irish tastes, but no one could doubt his prowess. Beara's ability to hold on to shots – without gloves, of course – rather than parry them exuded confidence. Beara left the field injured towards the end of the game, having been 'buffeted' by the Irish forwards once too often. His replacement, Branko Kralj, was just as solid.

It's debatable whether the Yugoslavs were in trouble during this phase of the game or were merely taking it easy, sitting on their lead. In matches, the Yugoslavs usually preferred to defend by retreating in numbers and effectively building a wall around their half-backs, Vujadin Boškov and Dobrosav Krstić, outside the penalty box. More often than not, this frustrated the Irish, who were reduced to hitting wasteful shots from distance. Just as often, the Yugoslavs would dispossess the Irish players at close quarters and then methodically build their attacks from within their own half or hit the opposition quickly on the break. Either way, like fellow communist sides Dynamo Moscow and the Magical Magyars, the Yugoslavs eschewed hopeful long-distance shots in favour of a short-passing game based on greater movement that culminated with close-range efforts on goal.

The Yugoslavs had a clearly identifiable system, a 'science' as one admiring Irish journalist, Sean Piondar, put it. They had a more flexible formation, technically more proficient players, cooler finishers, and were fitter. 'Bewitched and bewildered' by all of this, as another reporter, Frank Johnstone, wrote, the Irish by comparison looked disorganised, cumbersome and unimaginative. They lacked a plan in truth. There's no evidence the team had done any homework on the Yugoslavs, let alone figured out a strategy of how to beat them. They also didn't have a manager on the touchline who could identify problems and make the necessary changes.[36]

The Yugoslavs' superiority was confirmed clearly in the seventy-sixth minute when the game was put to bed with their fourth goal. Following a period of sustained Yugoslav possession, a tiring Martin blundered again. Casually sticking out a foot to intercept an attempted pass from Milutinović, the defender only got a heel to it, leaving the inside-left, Todor Veselinović, free to sweep a fierce shot beyond the hapless O'Neill. Towards the end of the game, Martin embarrassed himself with another error but the Yugoslavs, for once, failed to capitalise.

The match ended with a 4–1 victory for Yugoslavia. The heaviest home defeat the Irish had suffered in six years. Though disappointed, their fans gave the Yugoslav players a standing ovation.

With the Ireland–Yugoslavia game now over, we might expect the controversy surrounding it to have petered out. Not so. On the next two Sundays after the match, Joe Wickham's local priest denounced him from the pulpit. The FAI secretary was a Judas who had sold Christ the King for a game of football, the priest declared, and, worse still, was 'a Protestant Catholic'. Wickham was so upset at being categorised as 'a poor class of Catholic' among his neighbours, he appealed to the Pope's diplomatic nuncio in Ireland. The nuncio passed Wickham's letter on to Archbishop McQuaid, who grudgingly admitted the priest's excessiveness and promised to have a quiet word with him about the matter. No one apologised to Wickham. It's not known whether Wickham asked his sisters' forgiveness for blackening the family name.[37]

In Northern Ireland, opinion on McQuaid's actions hardened. Government ministers added to the *Belfast Telegraph*'s earlier words about the religious cold war between Ulster Protestantism and Irish Catholicism. The Minister for Education, Harry Midgley, condemned McQuaid's role as 'one of the most monumental pieces of clerical interference' ever seen in Ireland, one that demonstrated how the Catholic priesthood believed it had the right to control every aspect of people's lives. The Belfast-based writer and broadcaster Sam McAughtry later claimed that McQuaid's actions had an enormous impact on Ulster Protestants, sparking heated debates in the city's pubs about the nature of Catholic rule in the south. McQuaid received several tart letters from ordinary Ulster Protestants describing Ireland as 'the Papal State' and praising Wickham and the FAI for defying the might of the Roman Church.[38]

News of Archbishop McQuaid's belated efforts to stop the game also triggered comment outside of Ireland, some of it positive, most of it excoriating. From Paris, the Croat section of the Confederation of French Christian Workers wrote to thank McQuaid for his boycott campaign and his ongoing efforts to free Cardinal Stepinac. In Britain, McQuaid was the butt of jokes on television and accused of being a fascist. In Italy, even the right-wing, fervently anti-communist magazine *Il Borghese* lampooned McQuaid, calling him 'a monsignor of olden days'. The Soviet news agency, TASS, attacked McQuaid as a Cold War churchman.[39]

Motivated by revenge perhaps, McQuaid reacted to all of this by trying to wrestle control of the Irish Football Association. The Archbishop set up a secret committee of four priests tasked with pushing the FAI in a more Catholic-friendly direction. This involved priests taking up senior administrative positions in Ireland's football clubs, organising leagues between altar boys from different parishes, and even the setting up of a priests' football team. This strategy doesn't appear to have had as much success as McQuaid would have liked. Months later, McQuaid was encouraged by the numbers of 'boy footballers' who were attending Catholic retreats, but his committee's efforts to persuade boys to go to Mass on Sunday mornings instead of having kickabouts in Dublin's Phoenix Park fell on deaf ears. In 1957, McQuaid's committee leant on Joe Wickham's FAI to call off a planned B international between Ireland and Romania in Dublin via an informal request to FIFA. It failed, and another football team from behind the Iron Curtain paid Ireland a visit.[40]

Today, debate continues in Ireland about the significance of Archbishop McQuaid's defeat at the hands of the FAI in 1955. Back then, the Association of Civil Liberties in Ireland claimed that the 22,000 attendance at the Yugoslavia–Ireland game proved the country was no longer a clerical state, but this assessment was well wide of the mark. Ireland remained fervently Catholic and McQuaid one of its most influential figures for years to come. The radical historian and activist Conor McCabe argues the whole row represented an important protest against Irish conservatism's attempt to interfere with football, working-class Dublin's most popular cultural activity. Looking at the row less politically, one of Ireland's leading sports historians, Paul Rouse, claims it represented a triumph of sport over religion. What everyone can agree on is how much the controversy passed into Irish folklore and that the match was an unprecedented example of resistance to McQuaid. By digging in his heels over the Yugoslavs' visit, the Archbishop scored a proverbial own goal. He was the long-term loser from the game, a man whose stern rule at least some Irish people now began to question.[41]

We can take this a step further. The controversy over Yugoslavia's visit to Ireland in October 1955 illustrated how football could serve as an important arena for ideological and religious arguments during the Cold War. It's highly unlikely the row and match converted any Catholics into leftists, let alone communists. But they did trigger opposition to the control that the Catholic Church exerted in Ireland. The controversy would have turned few if any Irish people into enemies of Western democracy, yet many did perhaps begin to think afterwards about how Irish democracy could be modernised. Football could, in other words, destabilise politics in the West and, as we shall see in later chapters, in the East.

The *reprezentacija*'s impressive display at Dalymount Park in 1955 was a public relations triumph for Josip Broz Tito's Yugoslavia. After the match, one or two Irish journalists – like their English counterparts during Dynamo Moscow's tour of Britain in 1945 – did stereotype the Yugoslav team as mere 'cogs in a machine', a machine that was unfairly bankrolled by its communist regime. Yugoslavian officials clumsily retaliated by gloating about the merits of their country's collective approach to football and life and sledging the Irish for not having 'played as a team'. But the Irish football fraternity overwhelmingly purred over the Yugoslavs' performance. Reporters Sean Piondar and

K. J. Kenealy, among others, called Yugoslavia one of the best football teams in Europe, if not the world. The Yugoslav team had, moreover, behaved like respectful ambassadors, on and off the pitch. Amid intense controversy, the players had been a credit to their nation and ideology. Through no fault of their own, by their mere presence, they had also embarrassed, if not challenged, the Irish establishment.[42]

From a footballing and diplomatic point of view, Ireland had less of a stake in the game's result than Yugoslavia. The Irish were underdogs and the defeat was not unexpected. However, the gulf in footballing ability the match highlighted not only punctured the FAI's balloon. It also prompted the FAI to immediately appoint Johnny Carey as Ireland's first recognised manager. Carey's first match in charge, at home against Spain in November 1955 (a 2–2 draw), generated so much excitement that over 40,000 people crammed into Dalymount Park. Hundreds of spectators got in free – like those at the chaotic Chelsea–Dynamo Moscow game at Stamford Bridge a decade earlier – by pulling down the stadium gates.[43]

Carey managed Ireland for forty-five games through until the late 1960s but he was not the new broom the country needed. He only did the job part-time (juggling it with managing clubs like Blackburn Rovers), was given little time to prepare before matches, and the five-man FAI committee continued to select the team. In 1969, former Ireland international Mick Meagan was appointed as manager with full executive powers for team matters, but it wasn't until Englishman Jack Charlton took over in the mid-1980s that Ireland really became a fully professional set-up. Charlton's reign between 1986 and 1995 – with its widened pool of players and a strategy based on exploiting the space behind the opposition's defence – produced Irish football's golden generation and helped transform the country's identity.[44]

Unlike Ireland, the Yugoslavs had no need to change their football management structure in the wake of the match in Dublin. Yugoslav commentators did question whether their footballers were travelling too much. This was not because some of the players visiting Ireland defected – none of them did, much to Joe Wickham's relief presumably. But the team looked jaded, and the commentators seemed to be suggesting the Belgrade political authorities ought to lighten the players' ambassadorial loads.[45]

In the event, on the back of wins like that against Ireland, Yugoslavia extended its footballing tentacles in the years ahead. In

1957, Bernard Vukas became the country's first player in the Cold War era to be allowed to sign as a professional at a club in the West, Bologna. Others followed, including Todor Veselinović at Sampdoria, Vladimir Beara and Branko Zebec at Alemannia Aachen, and Miloš Milutinović at Bayern Munich and then Racing Paris. Soon, a number of Yugoslavia's world-class coaches also found work overseas. Ljubiša Broćić probably gets top prize for globe-trotting managerial positions. The boss at Red Star Belgrade in the early 1950s, Broćić had the pick of jobs in Italy, Spain, the Netherlands, Australia and Saudi Arabia through until his retirement in the 1980s.[46]

A remarkable number of players involved in the 1955 Ireland–Yugoslavia game themselves went on to become managers. The 'handballing' Frank O'Farrell took Leicester City to the 1969 FA Cup Final before failing disastrously to step into Matt Busby's shoes at Manchester United. Debutant Liam Tuohy briefly managed Ireland in the early 1970s, while also working as an ice cream salesman. Con Martin became player-manager of Dundalk before 'apprenticing' two sons into the professional game, one of whom, Mick, played for Ireland. Winger Zdravko Rajkov coached the national teams of Iran and Algeria. Branko Zebec led Bayern Munich to their first Bundesliga title for thirty-seven years in the late 1960s. And half-back Vujadin Boškov won Serie A with Sampdoria in 1991. Boškov became a revered figure at Sampdoria. His laconic comments in tense post-match interviews – like 'The team which makes fewer mistakes, wins . . . we made more mistakes, we lost' – often resembled the equally gnomic utterances of Sepp Herberger.[47]

In September 1999, forty-four years after his last visit to Ireland, Vujadin Boškov returned. He must have felt that history was repeating itself. The Cold War was over but Boškov was now manager of the new, non-socialist Federal Republic of Yugoslavia (or FRY), whose president, the Serb Slobodan Milošević, was at war with the West over Kosovo. Boškov's team was in Dublin to play Ireland in a qualifier for the 2000 European Championship in Belgium and the Netherlands. This time around, even fewer of the locals wanted Ireland's match against Yugoslavia to go ahead, largely for fear of the propaganda coup it could bring Milošević. The Irish government, FAI and manager Mick McCarthy all expressed opposition to the game, but UEFA insisted it be played. Ireland won 2–1, thanks to an instinctive first-time shot by teenager Robbie Keane and a twenty-five-yard, left-foot screamer from Mark Kennedy.[48]

Months later, after games against other teams, Boškov had the last laugh. Ireland didn't qualify for Euro 2000, falling at the last hurdle in a bad-tempered play-off with Turkey in Bursa that saw the Irish forced to train on a cabbage patch and ended in a brawl-cum-pitch invasion. Several players blamed the FAI's poor organisation for this defeat, which might help explain captain Roy Keane's outburst in Saipan a few years later. However, FRY did go to the Euros, as group winners. They acquitted themselves well and reached the quarter-finals, before being smashed 6–1 by the Netherlands. Three years later, FRY adopted the name Serbia and Montenegro. No team calling itself Yugoslavia, a name steeped in footballing history, has existed since.[49]

4 SETTLING OLD SCORES
Spain vs. Soviet Union, Madrid, June 1964

For Nikita Sergeyevich Khrushchev and Francisco Franco Bahamonde, this is more than a football match. It's just before 6.30 p.m. on Sunday 21 June 1964. Father's Day at Madrid's Santiago Bernabéu Stadium. A crowd of 79,000 await the arrival of Spain and the Soviet Union for the final of the European Nations' Cup. The players line up for the national anthems, in shirts emblematic of the twentieth century's great ideological struggle: Bolshevik red against Falangist dark blue (see Figure 4.1). Communism versus fascism. Barcelona midfielder Chus Pereda was under no illusions that night: 'When we played in Madrid, it was pure politics – any fool realised that. It was Franco against communism. For him, it was not just a battle, it was war.'[1]

Khrushchev probably didn't watch the match. He was in Scandinavia, on the final day of a five-day visit to Denmark (see Figure 4.2). More hunter than athlete, Khrushchev wasn't known for his love of football. Like any good Marxist, he considered sport frivolous. Other topics – from agricultural reform and dismantling the cult of Stalin to peaceful coexistence with the West – occupied his mind. Franco, in contrast, listened to commentary on his beloved Real Madrid while shooting grouse, did the football pools every week (under the pseudonym Francisco Cofran) and binge-watched sport on the multiple TV sets dotted around the Royal Palace of El Pardo. Still, in the week before the final, he wasn't sure about attending. Fear of defeat weighed on his mind. It was José Solís Ruiz, Secretary General of Franco's National Movement, who convinced the dictator to go to the Bernabéu. So, Franco and his wife Carmen Polo made their way to the

Figure 4.1 Spain vs. the Soviet Union, European Nations' Cup final, Madrid, 21 June 1964. © Gianni Ferrari/Cover/Getty Images.

VIP seats before kick-off, milking the applause and basking in the orchestrated chants of 'Franco! Franco! Franco!' 'The enormous gathering', effused the dictator, 'could not have been more affectionate'.[2]

Sunday 21 June 1964 turned out better for *el Generalísimo* than the Soviet leader. Spain beat the defending champions 2–1 to win the country's first major football trophy, capping the regime's celebrations of '25 years of peace' since the end of the Civil War. Francoist newspaper *ABC* crowed that 'in this quarter of a century there has never been displayed a greater popular enthusiasm for the State born out of the victory over communism'.[3] Spain's win was a shot in the arm for the Franco regime, showcasing a popular, modernising state committed to Cold War détente. Here, gushed journalist Matías Prats Cañete, was 'the image of a happy and hospitable Spain, basking in the social peace established by our good protector and Caudillo, Francisco Franco'.[4]

For one side, a resounding propaganda triumph; for the other, a bitter defeat. Khrushchev was furious. Not only with the result, but

Figure 4.2 Nikita Khrushchev at the Zealand Cattle Show, Denmark, 20 June 1964. © Terry Fincher/Mirrorpix via Getty Images.

with Soviet television beaming pictures of a smiling Franco into living rooms from Lviv to Vladivostok. Two days after the final, Soviet coach Konstantin Beskov, who'd played for Dynamo Moscow in Britain in 1945, was sacked. Khrushchev wasn't far behind. Politburo machinations against the unpopular leader, whose scattergun liberalisation and erratic behaviour alienated key figures in the party and the KGB, led to his ouster in October 1964. Khrushchev's replacement was a safer pair of hands and a bigger football fan: Leonid Brezhnev.

Chapter 4 tells the story of 'one of the most politicised football matches ever', a genuine grudge match, in which communism played anti-communism – and lost.[5] Perhaps the most bitterly contested and distinctive of all Cold War football clashes, the 1964 final was a throwback to the political battles of the 1930s, a game that boosted and rebranded Franco's dictatorship, and helped bring down the curtain on Khrushchev's era of experiment. It's a window into two authoritarian regimes looking to reform and score propaganda victories through sport, two football cultures reluctantly coming together, and two legends of the European game – Ballon d'Or winners Luis Suárez and Lev Yashin – facing off for the continent's biggest prize.

After victory in June 1964, one word dominated the Spanish press: *furia* ('fury'). *La Furia Española* ('the Spanish fury') meant a team built on 'hard work ... spirit and physical strength'.[6] Technique and tactical sophistication, cornerstones of Spanish football in the twenty-first century, had little place here. Spain's first Euros triumph, opined *Marca* on 22 June, wasn't about skill, but about knowing how to 'win games out of courage'. The president of the Royal Spanish Football Federation (RFEF), Benito Pico, agreed: 'Spain won in a Spanish manner, with a lot of courage and guts'.[7]

Though the term meshed with Francoism's self-image of virile patriotism, the fury had deep roots in Spanish football. Spain's football mythology originated in the performances of 'the lions of Antwerp', the team that won silver at the 1920 Olympics. One moment stood out: José María Belauste's equaliser against Sweden on 1 September, a vital strike en route to the podium. Journalist Manolo de Castro described a header of such strength 'that [Belauste] and various Swedes tumbled together into the goal'. Goalkeeper Ricardo Zamora's autobiography had Belauste driving the ball over the line with 'four Swedes clinging to his shirt'.[8] Reading accounts of the goal, you're not sure if it's a header or a shot. But that's not the point. Belauste's goal, however it went in, was a force of nature. It symbolised a rugged playing style that remained the benchmark forty-four years later. After beating the Soviet Union in Madrid, Spain's coach José Villalonga evoked 'the epic story of Antwerp', as did many newspapers. *Marca* praised Spain for heading corner kicks 'like Belauste in Antwerp'.[9]

The fury was coopted, or nationalised, by the Spanish right, but its core values were more Basque than Spanish. The Basque country was the heartland of Spanish football. The team whose style most closely reflected the fury's physicality was Athletic Bilbao, a club tied to Basque nationalism. Thirteen of the 1920 Olympic squad came from the Basque country. Belauste dedicated his goal against Sweden to Sabino Arana, founder of the Basque Nationalist Party. While Basque nationalism, like its counterpart in Catalonia, would be proscribed under Franco, core Basque values – 'cojones, a lot of cojones ... to run more and throw everything at the opposition' – were transmuted into Spanish ones, on and beyond the football field.[10]

Before then, Basque nationalism would be responsible for Spanish football's first encounter with the Soviet Union. It came during the Spanish Civil War, as Republicans, including the Basque government of ex-Athletic player José Antonio Aguirre, fought a rearguard action against Franco's Nationalists, who'd launched an uprising to topple the country's democratic government in July 1936. The conflict caught the world's attention. The Soviet Union spearheaded international efforts to fight Franco and fascism. Moscow sent the Republicans men, weapons and financial aid in what it and communists across the world saw as a Manichean conflict between left and right. The beleaguered Republic, though, always needed more support. So, Aguirre sent the *Euzkadiko selekzioa* on tour. The European leg began in Paris in April 1937, two days before the Luftwaffe bombed the Basque town of Guernica. It then headed east to Czechoslovakia and Poland, before arriving in Moscow on 16 June, three days before Franco's army captured the Euskadi capital, Bilbao.

Stacked with Spanish internationals, the Basque team spent ten weeks in the Soviet Union, winning eight of nine games. The tour's value for the visitors was questionable. The Civil War was turning Franco's way, however many victories Pedro Vallana's team accrued. Athletic Bilbao midfielder Ángel Zubieta remembered no great cultural exchanges: 'Playing football, drinking vodka, and staying in the hotel was how we spent our time in that faraway and strange land and we had no contact with anyone other than the world of sport'.[11]

Conversely, the Basque tour was a turning point for Soviet football. It came as the communists began to take football seriously, introducing an All-Union competition, the Soviet Top League, in 1936. The arrival on Soviet soil of a team featuring stars like striker Isidro Lángara, captain Luis Regueiro and goalie Goyo Blasco was big news. *Izvestia* reported that the games against Lokomotiv, Dynamo and Spartak were 'the most eagerly awaited matches ever to be seen in Moscow'.[12] There were two million ticket requests. Ninety thousand people watched the 2–1 Basque victory over Dynamo Moscow on 26 June.

The sporting buzz, during Stalin's Great Terror, was palpable. 'Not before or since has there been that much excitement around football', wrote Spartak's Nikolai Starostin. Excitement peaked when Soviet football managed a win over its storied opponents. At the ninth and final attempt, Spartak Moscow, with the help of a dodgy penalty and ringers from rival clubs, beat the exhausted Basques 6–2 on 8 July at the Dynamo Stadium. If you want proof of the importance of this victory, look at the photo of the Spartak team at the 1937 Physical

Culture Day Parade in Moscow. They stand on a float shaped like a giant football boot, on which '6–2' is emblazoned in huge letters.[13]

The Basque tour was a wake-up call for Soviet players and coaches. Using a variant on the W-M system pioneered by Herbert Chapman's Arsenal, the Basque side's skill and intensity offered evidence, *Pravda* admitted, that 'our best teams are far from high quality'.[14] The lesson from the tour was simple: Soviet football needed to engage with the world, to play serious opponents, and to develop sophisticated tactics. The first proof of that pudding, as we saw in Chapter 1, was Dynamo Moscow's tour of Britain in 1945.

Football contacts between the Soviet Union and Spain broke off after the Civil War. Though Spain was neutral during World War Two, Franco's zealously anti-Bolshevik regime openly sympathised with the Axis powers. The Soviet Union, meanwhile, fought 'Hitler fascism' at the cost of around twenty-seven million lives. No sooner was the Great Patriotic War over than the Cold War began, ensuring Spain and the Soviet Union remained on opposite political sides. Initially ostracised by the West, Spain worked its way into the anti-communist fold, building relations with the United States and its allies. The UN lifted its embargo on Spain in 1950. In the same year, the national team finished fourth at the World Cup in Brazil. This was a rare high point. Spain went through sixteen coaches between 1950 and 1962. Like the Soviet Union, who entered international football at the 1952 Olympics, Spain muddled along in the second tier of European teams. Wins against Ireland and Portugal, like Soviet wins over Bulgaria and Finland, couldn't hide deficiencies against elite opponents. Spain didn't qualify for the 1954 or 1958 World Cup. The Soviet Union made it to Sweden in 1958, losing 2–0 to the hosts in the quarter-finals. But neither country had unlocked its potential.

The long sporting estrangement between Spain and the Soviet Union looked to be over in 1960. Qualification for the inaugural European Nations' Cup – the long-mooted vision of Henri Delaunay – had begun in 1958, three years after the Frenchman's death: three rounds of home-and-away fixtures, before the semi-finals and final in France. Spain and the Soviet Union came through round-of-sixteen matches against communist opposition – Hungary and Poland, respectively – to set up a quarter-final tie. The two matches were scheduled for 29 May (Moscow), where tickets quickly sold out, and 9 June 1960 (Madrid). It was an eagerly awaited clash, especially in Spain. Optimism about the team, under new coach Helenio Herrera, was growing. Goalscorers in the 7–2 aggregate thrashing of Poland included 1960's European Footballer of the Year, Luis Suárez; Real Madrid's Argentine-born Alfredo Di Stéfano, one of the greatest players of all time; and Di Stéfano's teammate, the brilliant winger Paco Gento. Eleven days before the scheduled game in Moscow, a Real Madrid team featuring Gento, Di Stéfano and Ferenc Puskás beat Eintracht Frankfurt 7–3 to win a fifth successive European Cup. A crowd of 127,000 at Hampden Park in Glasgow witnessed an otherworldly performance. 'The Spanish side's artistry was so immensely superior', purred *The Guardian*, 'that its players gave the appearance of putting on an exhibition'.[15]

For the Franco regime – a dictatorship built on nationalism, the Catholic Church and the Caudillo's authority – Real Madrid's European Cup brilliance was great propaganda. Albeit propaganda undercut by the fact that its best players weren't native Spaniards but Argentine (Di Stéfano and José Santamaría), French (Raymond Kopa) and Hungarian (Puskás). The dictator didn't have the same faith in the national team, despite its Real contingent and Herrera's burgeoning reputation. Confidence was further shaken by the Soviet Union's 7–1 win over Poland on 19 May 1960. Among the crowd of 85,000 at Moscow's Lenin Stadium were Helenio Herrera and some worried-looking Spanish selectors.

The Soviets were just as worried. The head of the Soviet Football Federation, Andrei Starostin (Nikolai's brother), compared Spain to the Brazil side that had won the 1958 World Cup. Di Stéfano, he raved, who'd become a Spanish citizen in 1956, was 'a centre forward for all the ages'. Starostin was promptly censured for 'exaggerating the qualities of the Spanish team'. *Pravda* presented Spain's 3–0 win over England in Madrid on 15 May as meaningless, since the English FA had fielded a youth team. This was a fabrication. But, in the lead up to the 1960 matches, it was a question of who blinked first. And it wasn't going to be the more media-savvy Soviet regime.[16]

Spain had ventured behind the Iron Curtain to reach the quarter-finals, defeating Poland 4–2 in Chorzów in June 1959, before finishing the job back home three months later. Real Madrid played several communist opponents in the European Cup in the late 50s. The first clash, against Partizan Belgrade on Christmas Day 1955, had already required Real officials to cajole a reluctant Franco into engaging with the enemy. But the Soviet Union, said the club's vice-president Raimundo Saporta, was 'a qualitatively different case' than Hungary, Poland or Yugoslavia.[17] Franco's distaste for the headquarters of international communism was as strong as ever in 1960, and Cold War relations were frostier than they'd been in 1955.

Weeks before the scheduled first leg in Moscow, an American Lockheed U-2 spy plane was shot down over Soviet territory, ratcheting up tensions between the superpowers, particularly in Berlin, a city divided between East and West since 1945. The Berlin crisis didn't directly concern Franco. Nor did the fate of the American spy plane pilot, Gary Powers. But his government didn't want to upset its US patron. President Eisenhower had visited the Torrejón Air Force Base near Madrid in December 1959, a landmark moment in Spain's rapprochement with the West. The dictatorship wanted NATO membership, plus the economic and diplomatic benefits that came from close relations with the United States and its allies. Anything that smacked of appeasing the Soviets looked risky. Particularly if it might end in sporting humiliation.

Behind the scenes, both sides made their case. José Solís and Foreign Minister Fernando María Castiella pushed for the matches to go ahead. So did the head of the Falangist National Sports Delegation (DND), José Antonio Elola Olaso, and his RFEF counterpart, Alfonso de la Fuente Chaos. The latter pair went to Franco's villa to persuade the dictator of 'the short-sightedness of banning these two matches'. All four men understood the importance of riding on Real Madrid's coat-tails, of playing in order to soften the Franco regime's rabidly anti-communist image. As Saporta said in 1986, the games would allow Spain 'to appear moderate and forgiving in the eyes of the international sporting community, rather than as the backward-looking isolated bastion of reactionism'.[18]

But the hardliners won the day. Led by Interior Minister Camilo Alonso Vega, a childhood friend of Franco's, and Minister for Information and Tourism Gabriel Arias-Salgado, they sensed a communist conspiracy. Veterans of the Falangist Blue Division, which fought Bolshevism in World War Two, still languished in Soviet prison camps. Police reports predicted pro-Soviet demonstrations at the Bernabéu Stadium on 9 June. The Soviets rejected Franco's request to play both legs on neutral ground. And then requested that their flag fly, and their anthem be aired, before the game in Madrid. This was too much. The DND informed the RFEF on 21 May that 'the highest organ of the state' (we know who that was) had decided to call off the two games.[19] UEFA was informed at an executive meeting in Frankfurt on 28 May. Herrera's squad never boarded the plane to Moscow. Spain forfeited the tie. The Soviet Union received a bye into the semi-finals.

After Spain's withdrawal, the Soviet Football Federation condemned a government that 'tramples over the principles of the international sports federations' and 'tries to bring into sport the elements of the Cold War'. 'From Franco's position as the right-sided defender of America's prestige', the Federation declared, 'he has scored an own goal'.[20] It was hard to disagree. The boycott was a PR disaster for the Franco regime. The Soviet Union won the first European Nations' Cup, defeating Yugoslavia 2–1 in the final in Paris on 11 July. The cancellation, reported the *Daily Telegraph*, had caused 'the greatest displeasure among the Spanish public', not least because of the media blackout surrounding it. Displeasure was even greater for the Spanish team, which had fancied its chances against the Soviets. Chus Pereda recalled the 'huge sense of sadness' in an interview in 2010, a year before he died of cancer.[21] Resentment at blatant political interference was widespread, from Herrera and the players to RFEF officials and fans. The Spanish authorities wouldn't make the same mistake in 1964.

By the time Spain hosted the second European Nations' Cup, the Cold War looked different. Berlin's future had been brutally decided by the construction of the Berlin Wall in August 1961. Plugging the final hole in the Iron Curtain paradoxically stabilised East–West relations in Europe. Outside the old continent, the Cuban Missile Crisis of October 1962 did something similar. Cold War brinkmanship over the stationing of US nuclear missiles in Turkey and Soviet nuclear missiles in Cuba brought the world to the cusp of nuclear war. Moscow and Washington drew back, withdrawing weapons from Cuba and Turkey, respectively, and establishing a direct line of communication. In August 1963 the two countries signed a Partial Test Ban Treaty, the first agreement to limit the testing of nuclear weapons.

The first leg of Spain's preliminary round match in the Nations' Cup took place on 1 November 1962, three days after the Cuban Missile Crisis ended. The hosts thrashed Romania 6–0 at the Bernabéu to all but secure safe passage into the round of sixteen. Like Spain, Spanish football was changing, though in seemingly different directions. From the early 1960s, under the leadership of Foreign Minister Castiella, the Franco regime looked outwards, seeking partners for its 1959

Stabilisation Plan, a series of reforms designed to guide Spain from autarky to economic liberalisation. The 'Spanish miracle', a period of rapid economic growth from 1959 to 1974, was underpinned by foreign investment, industrialisation and tourism. Western visitors flooded the country, bringing hard currencies and softer cultural influences. The grim Spain of the 1940s, epitomised by Camilo José Cela's 1950 novel *The Hive*, became the sun-kissed holidaymakers' haven of the 1960s. A quasi-fascist tyranny evolved into something closer to a development dictatorship. Modernisation, then, but for a regime that never lost its hatred of communism. The final speech of Franco's life, on 1 October 1975, railed against 'a masonic left-wing conspiracy … in indecent concubinage with Communist-terrorist subversion'.[22]

As Spain opened to the world, Spanish football turned, partly at least, inwards. Hopes had been high for the 1962 World Cup in Chile. Helenio Herrera's squad featured Gento and Suárez, plus four natural-ised Spaniards: Di Stéfano, Puskás, Santamaría and Barcelona's Paraguayan-born striker Eulogio Martínez. But Spain lost two of their three matches in Group 3, to finalists Czechoslovakia and Brazil, and were eliminated. Bad luck was as much to blame as bad play. Brian Glanville called Brazil's 2–1 win in Viña del Mar on 6 June 'a manifest injustice'.[23] The backlash, though, was immediate and the scapegoats obvious. In *Marca*'s words, 'Spain has been eliminated from the World Cup because our team was not sufficiently Spanish'. 'Foreign influence', the paper said, had gone too far. The national team 'no longer plays like a team of real Spaniards, with passion, with aggression, with courage, with virility, and above all, with fury'.[24]

So, Spanish football attempted to rediscover the fury. After the 1962 tournament, the DND banned the further import of foreign play-ers. Herrera was replaced as national team coach by José Villalonga, about as establishment a figure as you could choose: a young Francoist officer during the Civil War, later head of the Military School of Physical Education in Toledo, and manager of Real Madrid for the club's first two European Cup wins in 1956 and 1957. None of Di Stéfano, Puskás, Santamaría or Martínez played for Spain again.

If the players were re-nationalised, Spanish football continued to internationalise. Scarred by the 1960 boycott, sports officials and politicians sought contacts with the outside world, including the Soviet Union. After Stalin's death in 1953, the Soviet leadership increased international sports exchanges, as part of Khrushchev's commitment to peaceful coexistence. In 1952, the Soviets sent forty-four sports delegations abroad and received sixty-seven overseas delegations. By 1960, the numbers had jumped to 399 and 407, respectively. One official called sport 'one of the most important channels of international relations'.[25]

Spain, as we know, refused to join the Soviet guest list in 1960. But change was coming. The breakthrough arrived in Spain's second sport, basketball. Hardliners had long resisted contests with the communist superpower in the European Basketball Cup. Political and sporting caution went hand in hand: the Soviets won five of the six EuroBasket tournaments between 1951 and 1961. But DND officials, with support from Castiella and Saporta, lobbied hard for a basketball thaw. Saporta brought American players to the Spanish league, arranged tours to the United States and organised the first tour of Eastern Europe in 1968. Five years earlier, he helped persuade Franco to allow a Spanish basketball team to compete on Soviet soil. Real Madrid travelled to the Lenin Palace of Sports in July 1963 for the second leg of the final of the FIBA European Champions' Cup final against CSKA Moscow. Madrid lost the second leg (91–74) and a tiebreaking third game 99–80, but the trip marked a new era, 'the first step toward the normalization of sporting relationships with the main ideological enemy of Francoism'.[26] The path was open to a clash in the number one sport, football.

UEFA didn't rush to address Spain's no-show in Moscow in 1960. When the topic finally came up, at a meeting of the European Nations' Cup organising committee in January 1962, UEFA instructed Spain 'to refund to the USSR football federation the loss indicated'.[27] It was the lightest of slaps on the wrist. There was no tournament ban, no other sanctions. By 1964, as Juan Antonio Simón and Julian Rieck put it, 'UEFA seemed to have forgotten about what had happened in 1960'.[28] When Spain reached the last four of the second European Nations' Cup, UEFA accepted the RFEF's offer to host the semi-finals and the final.

UEFA's lenience wasn't surprising. Spain, like the Soviet Union, had been a founder member of UEFA in 1954. The men who built a continental federation after World War Two were serious about 'creating a United Europe of Football', as Swiss administrator Ernst Thommen described it at the founding congress in Basel. Unlike NATO, the EEC or the Warsaw Pact, UEFA sought to cross Cold War divides. It aimed to be, in Philippe Vonnard's words, 'something special', a pan-European body that could do more for integration than economic or military organisations constrained by geopolitics.[29]

Though the Soviet Union didn't join UEFA club competitions until 1966, it supported UEFA from the beginning. So did Spain. Both countries had leverage at FIFA – the head of the Soviet Football Federation, Valentin Granatkin, for example, was FIFA vice-president from 1955 to 1979 – and both sought similar influence at UEFA. Both countries, moreover, backed Henri Delaunay's brainchild, the European Nations' Cup. Spain's Agustín Pujol, who joined UEFA's executive committee in 1956, was part of the commission formed a year earlier to investigate the tournament's feasibility.

For these different authoritarian regimes, football offered a way around exclusion from European projects, a way to gain prestige and influence unattainable elsewhere. Pujol's position helped him make Spain's case in 1964, as did the fact the country had two of Europe's best stadiums, the Nou Camp and the Bernabéu. This time Franco's doves bested his hawks. Castiella and Solís convinced the Caudillo that the 1960 boycott 'had been a diplomatic failure' and that hosting the Euros would showcase Spanish hospitality.[30] UEFA gave the green light after the Spanish government promised to allow the Soviet team to enter the country. The turnaround looked dramatic: from European football pariah to European football respectability in four years. But Spain, like the Soviet Union, had always been part of the UEFA family, part of an organisation that emphasised sport's apolitical nature and, wherever possible, avoided getting embroiled in Cold War politics. The trick was getting estranged family members to talk. As the Franco regime granted visas to Soviet footballers in May 1964, it looked like mission accomplished.

The 1964 Nations' Cup followed the same format as the first edition: a knockout competition, with three rounds of home-and-away matches, beginning in June 1962, then the denouement in Spain in June 1964. Twenty-nine teams entered the competition, including big hitters like England and Italy who'd stayed home in 1960. The Soviet Union was one of three teams to receive a first-round bye.

Konstantin Beskov's side made impressive progress. A tough round-of-sixteen match-up against Italy was comfortably negotiated. A crowd of 102,000 in the Lenin Stadium watched the Soviets win the first leg in October 1963, thanks to goals from forwards Viktor

Ponedelnik and Igor Chislenko. A 1–1 draw in the return match in Rome – Italy's equaliser from Gianni Rivera arrived in the final minute – set up a quarter-final clash against Sweden. A 4–2 aggregate win in May 1964 punched the Soviet Union's ticket to Spain.

May was a busy month for the Soviet Union's star player, Dynamo Moscow's Lev Yashin. Between the matches against Sweden, the goalkeeper was in Copenhagen, representing a Rest of Europe XI against Scandinavia. Before a knee injury forced him off at half-time (a precaution, with the second leg against Sweden to come), Yashin had been in typically brilliant form. The previous autumn, representing a Rest of the World XI against England at Wembley, Yashin's performance was 'so wonderfully competent', wrote the *Liverpool Daily Post*'s Horace Yates, 'that he barred the way ... when the odds were a 100–1 on a score'.[31] Yashin ended 1963 with the Ballon d'Or, still the only goalkeeper to have won the annual prize for Europe's best footballer (see Figure 4.3).

Lev Yashin, like Alfredo Di Stéfano, Ferenc Puskás, Garrincha and Stanley Matthews, was born on the wrong side of football's armchair revolution. All these players peaked before television made football a mass global phenomenon. Still, there was no doubting the star attraction when the Soviet squad arrived in Spain for the 1964 Euros.

Figure 4.3 Djalma Santos (holding camera) with Lev Yashin and Eusébio, London, October 1963. © Ray Green/Keystone/Hulton Archive/Getty Images.

Yashin, like his contemporary, the cosmonaut Yuri Gagarin, combined international appeal with political reliability, 'a model of Communist propriety'.[32] In the previous decade, he'd revolutionised goalkeeping. Yashin was the prototype of the twenty-first-century sweeper-keeper: fast and aggressive off his line, a vocal defensive organiser. The Muscovite helped the Soviet Union win 1956 Olympic gold and the inaugural Euros in 1960. He was the talk of the tournament in Sweden in 1958, but, like Spain, had a World Cup to forget in Chile. Mistakes in a 2–1 quarter-final loss to the hosts 'marked an historic date', reckoned *L'Équipe*: 'the end of the greatest modern goalkeeper'.[33]

Yashin considered retirement on his return home, where irate fans left threatening notes on his car and – shades of Gusztáv Sebes in 1956 – threw rocks at his apartment windows. But this wasn't the end. After taking time off, Yashin returned to top form in 1963 and continued to play until 1970. Fans besieged the man in black (in fact, Yashin's goalie shirt was dark blue) when he got to Barcelona in June 1964. Ricardo Zamora, Spain's legendary goalie of the 1920s, was desperate to meet the 'Black Spider': 'I am sure that what I achieved in the art of stopping in other times is now a thing of the past for Yashin'.[34]

Spain, as we've seen, returned to old ways after the disappointment of Chile: no more international fancy-dans, instead the bread and butter of the 'fury', played by 'real' Spaniards. José Villalonga was the ideal coach for this back-to-basics approach. Villalonga was politically loyal ('a bit of a lackey') and no 'revolutionary strategist'.[35] In his new role, the ex-Real Madrid boss relied on youthful midfield energy from the likes of Fusté (23), Amancio (24) and Zoco (24), plus the talent still at his disposal. Notably Luis Suárez Miramontes. Born in 1935 in Galicia, Suárez was a less comfortable fit with the traditions of the fury than Villalonga. Not least because he'd played in Italy since 1961, when *El Arquitecto* ('The Architect') took his midfield skills from Barcelona to Inter Milan in a world-record transfer deal. Suárez's appearances for the national team were sporadic: just six games between 1961 and 1964 – the peak of his career – and thirty-two caps in total, a meagre haul for such a brilliant player. After the 1962 World Cup, even though Herrera dropped him for the Brazil game, critics accused Suárez of being 'anti-patriotic'. The Inter star seemed too cerebral and too detached to embrace the Spanish fury.

Luis Suárez didn't play in Spain's preliminary round clash with Romania in November 1962. He wasn't missed, as Villalonga's team eased past their communist opponents 7–3 on aggregate. Next up was Northern Ireland. After the underdogs snatched a 1–1 draw in Madrid in October 1963, the brilliance of the two Luises (Del Sol and Suárez) and Gento's sixty-fifth-minute strike at Belfast Park set up a quarter-final with the Republic of Ireland. Suárez, a pivotal figure in Inter's run to the 1964 European Cup final, was again absent for the fixtures in March and April. Again, it didn't matter. Villalonga's side won 7–1 on aggregate. 'Spain were great – much too good for us', admitted Irish captain Charlie Hurley after the 5–1 spanking in Seville.[36]

The semi-finals were set. In the first of a double header on 17 June, Spain would play Hungary at the Bernabéu, where else? This was effectively the national stadium in the Franco era, a showpiece construction, opened in 1947, that bore the name of the Real Madrid president who'd fought with the Nationalists in the Civil War and regularly boasted about his role in the 'reconquest' of Catalonia. The Soviet Union would then face Denmark at the Camp Nou. The Soviets swept past the Danes, winning 3–0 in front of 39,000 spectators in the Catalan capital. Two-up at half-time through Valery Voronin and Ponedelnik, the favourites eased up in the second half, as Denmark struggled to get out of their half. A late third from Valentin Ivanov ensured Beskov's side the chance to defend its European title.

Spain faced a stronger opponent. It wasn't the golden squad of 1953, the dazzling collective that we encountered in Chapter 2, but Hungary's 1964 team was exceptionally talented. None more so than Flórián Albert, the Ferencváros forward voted Young Player of the Tournament at the 1962 World Cup. On 17 June, though, the future (1967) Ballon d'Or winner gave way to the man who won the award in 1960: 'Delicate and effervescent, with the crowd chanting his name throughout, [Luis Suárez] conducted most of the best movements in the match', including the cross for Chus Pereda's opener in the thirty-fifth minute.[37] In the second half, injury slowed Suárez and the visitors came back into the game. They equalised six minutes from time, when José Ángel Iribar spilled a long shot and Ferenc Bene bundled home the rebound. That meant extra time in the Madrid gloaming. Some spectators got angry at 'a Hungarian official' who approached the touchline to advise his tired team. Bottles and cushions rained down from the stands, as police led away the alleged rule-breaker.[38] With eight minutes remaining, Fusté flicked on a corner and Amancio swept the ball into the net. Spain had defeated a second opponent from behind the Iron Curtain and were into the final. Could they complete a communist hat-trick in Madrid?

Back to Chus Pereda. A couple of weeks before the tournament, at Spain's La Ventosa training camp, José Villalonga, in the midfielder's recollection, gathered the team in a circle. He drew a small football pitch in the sand, populating one side of the field with pines and the other with rocks. The pines were the 'Russians', he explained, the rocks the Spanish. Villalonga then crushed the pines with the rocks. 'You are the rocks because you are stronger in mind and body'.[39] Perhaps Villalonga's posturing previewed Spanish anxieties? RFEF president Benito Pico felt under such pressure to beat the communists that he considered having the Soviet team poisoned.

Both sides, though, holstered their Cold War weapons in the lead-up to the final. Nobody was poisoned. The rocks and pines were nice to each other. People on the streets of Barcelona had greeted the Soviet players 'cordially' before the Denmark game, reported *Izvestia*, requesting autographs and trying out the odd word of Russian. Once the Soviets arrived in Madrid for the final, Spanish newspapers wanted to know 'the "secrets" of Soviet football' rather than stoke Cold War fires. The focus was sport, not politics. Luis Suárez gave a balanced view of the dangerous opponents his team would face on 21 June. 'I don't think the Russian team [is] very fast, but they are strong, and their energy is unceasing'. 'The USSR seem well prepared to retain their title', reckoned French newspaper *Minoir Sprint*. But beware 'the eclectic Spaniards'.[40]

It's a scorching June day in Madrid, but a pre-match downpour ensures a slippery surface, as English referee Arthur Holland leads the teams out for the final. The early play is nervy. Spain dominate possession, with the Soviets playing on the counter-attack. In the sixth minute, two Soviet defenders fail to deal with a speculative Suárez cross; the ball bounces off Eduard Mudrik to Pereda, who converts from close range (see Figure 4.4). Two minutes later, the Soviets are level. A long ball from Victor Anichkin finds striker Galimzyan Khusainov in acres of space. His weak shot dribbles under Iribar.

The game then settled down, as finals often do. Communism and Francoism cancelled each other out, as players struggled to stay upright in heavy conditions. 'Tight defensive marking', the *Daily Post* concluded, 'made the final something of a disappointment'. The crowd

Figure 4.4 Spain's Chus Pereda (far left) opens the scoring in the 1964 European Nations' Cup final. © Allsport Hulton/Archive.

was better than the football. Suárez remembered the 'special' atmosphere in the Bernabéu: 'the fans were in the right frame of mind to get behind us right from the start. That … helped us to stay calm'.[41] On 21 June, wrote Jimmy Burns, 'football and politics were in perfect synchronicity'. Villalonga's 'young, impassioned, aggressive, virile team' – and an audience that sang 'Arriba España!', 'Viva Franco!' and the fascist anthem 'Cara al Sol'.[42]

The match looks destined for extra time when, with six minutes left, Chus Pereda receives the ball on the right. He turns Anichkin, then sends a cross into the box – a cross missed on the initial broadcast, thanks to problems with the main feed, and not seen until decades later in foreign footage of the game. It's not a good ball, underhit and angling away from goal. No matter. Marcelino, the Real Zaragoza striker, somehow produces 'one of the all-time great headers'.[43] He gets enough power on a diving effort to send it into the bottom left-hand corner of the net. Yashin is rooted to the spot. The crowd erupts. A few minutes later, Holland blows the final whistle. Spain have won the 1964 European Nations' Cup.

In 2007, Daniel Gómez called Marcelino's goal 'the most important in the history of Spanish football'.[44] It was hard then to argue. This was a year before Fernando Torres' strike won Spain a second European Championship – and first international trophy in forty-four years – and three years before Andrés Iniesta got the biggest goal of all, the winner against the Netherlands in South Africa that gave Spain its first World Cup. Back in 1964, there were raucous celebrations on the pitch, before captain Ferran Olivella received the Henri Delaunay Cup from UEFA president Gustav Wiederkehr. Olivella paid due homage: 'We offer this victory first of all to Generalisimo Franco, who came this evening to honour us with his presence and energise the players'.[45] The much-maligned Villalonga was then chaired around the Bernabéu, trophy cradled in his arms. The next day, a delighted Franco officially received the Spanish squad at El Pardo, to drive home the symbolism of the moment. Sport and politics in lockstep, in the service of Francoist peace and 'national unity'.

Before the final, the Spanish press had been respectful of the Soviet team, repeating stereotypes about communist football – rigid, defensive, lacking in imagination – but emphasising its quality. The DND issued a statement on etiquette: 'The attention of the whole sporting world will be focused on this match, and therefore [the crowd] should demonstrate their good education, fair mindedness and sportsmanship'. All parties, from Franco and the Soviet players to the international press, agreed that the crowd behaved well. The Soviet anthem wasn't booed. Good Soviet play was applauded. 'I am sure', Franco told the nation, 'that the team of the USSR … took away from Spain an excellent impression'.[46]

Much of the caution went out of the window in the euphoria of Spain's victory. Media lines about 'the formidable Russians' now highlighted the scale of the Francoist David's achievement against the communist Goliath. An achievement built on the virtues of the Spanish fury, with not a foreign import in sight. This was a team of youthful vigour, reflecting the renewed 'greatness of Spain' under Franco. The fury with a liberalising 60s twist.

Less convincing were attempts to ascribe Spain's victory to *genio latino* ('Latin genius'), an impulsive Spanish individualism that trumped communist discipline. Suárez apart, the 1964 team was, in Pereda's words, 'a good unit', closer in spirit to Greece in 2004 than Spain in 2008 or 2024. The '64 side was less skilled than its 1962 predecessor, which featured Di Stéfano, Gento and Puskás. But, as Suárez concluded, 'it was a team, rather than a selection of top players, and this teamwork was the crucial element in our triumph'.[47]

How did the public respond to 21 June 1964? It's hard to separate the regime's projections from unfiltered reality. Spain's win caused an outpouring of joy that wasn't always an endorsement of Francoism – witness the celebrations in the outlawed Spanish Communist Party, barely a year after the regime had executed communist leader Julián Grimau. As in Argentina in 1978, when, as we'll see in Chapter 6, prison officers and political prisoners celebrated the country's first World Cup together, football in Spain in 1964 presented the façade of a strong, united country. To capitalise on the feel-good factor, state broadcaster TVE retransmitted the game on 29 June, allowing fans, as *ABC* explained, 'to relive the sensational Spanish triumph'.[48] But it's debatable how long the propaganda boost lasted. You could, in the words of Argentine poet Carlos Ferreira, 'sing the song of forgetting' – whether it was 'Arriba Espana!' in 1964 or 'Argentina, campéon' fourteen years later – but there was only so long you could forget the world beyond football. Perhaps that's why Spain's 1964 Euros victory, like the tainted victory of Argentina's junta in Buenos Aires in 1978, 'with those crazy sweating flags/with the world upside down', didn't linger in the popular memory.[49]

For the Soviet Union, defeat in 1964 was a bitter pill to swallow. Soviet newspapers focused on the match, praising the victors, but venturing no political conclusions. Those were drawn behind closed doors. Accusations that the English ref had favoured Spain (a viewing of the game suggests, if anything, that the opposite was true), like rumours that the Spanish team took performance-enhancing drugs, couldn't save Beskov. On his return to Moscow, he was sacked. Beskov went back to club management before returning to the national team in 1979. His second stint ended like the first – sacked after exiting a tournament (the 1982 World Cup) thanks to a politically charged defeat, this time to Poland, where Solidarity's rise the previous year fatally undermined communist supremacy. As Mikhail Yokhin concluded in 2013, 'the party didn't really trust Beskov'.[50]

The Soviet team remained competitive after 1964, finishing fourth at the 1966 World Cup, reaching the quarter-finals four years later in Mexico, and finishing runner-up to West Germany at the 1972

Euros. For *La Selección*, in contrast, 1964 quickly came to feel like lightning in a bottle. Many of the young players who defined Villalonga's team had short international careers. Left back Isacio Calleja won only thirteen caps, as did outside right Carlos Lapetra. The heroes of 21 June, Marcelino and Pereda, played fourteen and fifteen times, respectively, for their country.

Media boasts about winning 'the Spanish way' soon looked foolish. Spain performed poorly at the 1966 World Cup, eliminated at the group stage after defeats to Argentina and West Germany. The squad, as Jimmy Burns put it, 'had run out of luck'. As had Villalonga, whose emphasis on discipline was wearing thin. 'The military still wanted to rule the national squad', Barcelona midfielder Fusté complained.[51] Villalonga had never been a creative coach and, by 1966, his main creative force, Luis Suárez was past his best.

Villalonga was sacked after the 1966 tournament, but still the fury abated. Between winning the 1964 Euros, and reaching the final in France twenty years later, Spain's record was appalling. Spain didn't qualify for the World Cups of 1970 and 1974, exited at the group stage in 1978 and, even as hosts in 1982, won just one of five games, drawing with Honduras and losing to Northern Ireland. It was worse in the European Championship. Spain failed to qualify for the expanded finals of 1968, 1972 and 1976. 'We had a league with some great footballers', recalled José Ángel Iribar, 'but we just didn't seem to hack it internationally ... other teams were better than ours'.[52] Including the Soviet Union. The two countries only played two more competitive fixtures, in qualification for the 1972 Euros. The Soviets won 2–1 in Moscow on 7 June 1971 and then held Spain to a 0–0 draw in Seville in October, en route to topping Group 4 and, eventually, reaching the final.

You can see why 1964 has been called Spain's 'forgotten triumph'.[53] It didn't presage a golden age, but decades of under-achievement. When the national team finally fulfilled its potential, winning three Euros and one World Cup between 2008 and 2024, the Franco dictatorship, like the Caudillo himself, was long dead. Beating the Soviet Union on 21 June 1964 was an undoubted propaganda fillip for Francoism, challenging Duncan Shaw's claim that football under the dictatorship was merely a 'political soporific', alleviating the repression of the decades after the Civil War.[54] But that fillip didn't last long, and – aside from Real Madrid's 1966 European Cup win over Partizan

Belgrade – it wasn't repeated on the football field. So, it got harder for the regime to use Spain's most popular sport to sell rhetoric about the 'new Spain'. When Spain lost to the Soviet Union in June 1971, *Arriba* and *Marca* carried stories about the squad defiantly singing 'Arriba España!' and 'Cara al Sol' on departure from Moscow. But the singing, according to eyewitnesses, originated with *Arriba* and *Marca* journalists and was only taken up by DND and RFEF administrators. The players kept silent.

Perhaps the players' silence in June 1971 reflected a 'de-Falangisation' of Spain, and Spanish football, that began in the 1950s and gathered impetus in the 1960s. Perhaps it spoke to the fact that Soviet communism was no longer the mortal enemy. The 1964 final was the fiercest of Cold War battles, pitting the world's oldest communist regime against one of its most strident adversaries. What followed was more bridge than rampart. Under Franco and Brezhnev, wily operators who understood the weaknesses of their systems, Spain and the Soviet Union inched towards rapprochement. After Soviet clubs entered UEFA competitions in 1966, Spanish–Soviet clashes became a regular feature of European football. Spain's basketball team visited the Soviet Union in 1968 and toured Communist China four years later. Away from sport, Spain and the Soviet Union signed a Maritime Agreement in 1967, opening their seaports to each other. The agreement was extended in 1969, when the Soviet Union opened a de facto consulate in Madrid. The countries signed a trade agreement in 1972, three years after Franco's Foreign Minister Gregorio López-Bravo first visited Moscow.

L'Équipe called the 1964 final 'a lesson in solidarity', a reconciliation through football between countries that otherwise 'did not want to know each other'.[55] Spain and the Soviet Union never became friends; they never established full diplomatic relations. Mutual suspicion was too entrenched for that. But things improved after 1964, and football remained central to the story. When Real Madrid travelled to the Soviet Union for a European Cup quarter-final against Dynamo Kyiv in 1973, López-Bravo, a keen Real supporter, saw an opportunity to leverage sport for commercial gain, in the form of a permanent trading mission in Moscow. His message to the Real party was simple: play nice. So, Madrid players were more complimentary than usual about their hosts. Club president Santiago Bernabéu, a staunch anti-communist, pinned a Real Madrid badge on the lapel of Ukraine's Minister for Sport and Culture. In the match that followed, a 0–0 draw in Odesa, Real Madrid – scarcely believably – played in red shirts. The permanent trade mission was in the bag. By 1973, Spain and the Soviet Union had normalised relations to a degree impossible to imagine a decade earlier. Soviet officials would soon turn their attention to a football crisis involving another red-shirted team from another Spanish-speaking nation, Augusto Pinochet's Chile. But that's another story for another chapter.

5 # EUSÉBIO AND THE 'MYSTERY MEN OF THE EAST'
North Korea vs. Portugal, Liverpool, July 1966

'We want three!' 'We want three!' chant the delirious spectators in Goodison Park. Moments later, in the game's twenty-third minute, the North Koreans duly oblige. Having started a move on the left wing, striker Yang Song Guk picks up a loose ball in the Portugal box and slides it low into the net. Horrified, goalkeeper Jose Pereira puts his head in his hands. 'This is ridiculous', the BBC Television commentator David Coleman gasps in astonishment, 'the Portuguese are torn apart'. 'Easy!' 'Easy!' comes the call from the terraces. Everyone there is going wild. Few had given the communist minnows a hope. Now they are 3–0 up. The match looks like it will be one of the biggest upsets in World Cup history.

The quarter-final stages of World Cup finals have a habit of producing memorable matches. In the clash between Brazil and Czechoslovakia in France in June 1938 – better known as 'the battle of Bordeaux' – three players were sent off, another had his leg shattered, and the Czech keeper played for an hour with a broken arm. The game between Argentina and England in Mexico in June 1986 witnessed Maradona's infamous 'Hand of God' goal, followed four minutes later by his marvellous 'Goal of the Century'. England's quarter-final clash with Portugal in Germany in July 2006 will long be remembered for Cristiano Ronaldo's mischievous wink, following the referee's dismissal of his nettled Manchester United teammate Wayne Rooney. And in July 2010, football fans across the globe felt sickened when, deep into injury time, Uruguay's bad-boy striker Luis Suárez cynically blocked Ghana's passage to the semi-finals in South Africa by 'saving' a goal-bound shot with his hands.

If these matches provoked anger and controversy, the quarter-final clash between North Korea and Portugal in England in July 1966 conjures excitement and joy. Today, video footage and bubbly reviews of the game abound online. The game's popularity can be put down partly to people's enduring fascination with the Swinging Sixties – the age of revolution, sexual freedom and, for some in England, football's glorious peak. It also helps that the game turned out to be an eight-goal thriller, in which Portugal's great marksman Eusébio, who scored four, truly arrived as a superstar. Recently, rumours have added a dark, political twist to the game's status. These centre on stories claiming that, despite their achievements at the World Cup, the North Korean players were consigned to labour camps when they returned to Kim Il Sung's notorious 'hermit kingdom'.[1]

North Korea's game against Portugal in 1966 is a bona fide World Cup classic. But there's more to this thrilling game than first meets the eye. Conventional wisdom has it that football feeds aggression, that it heightens nationalist fervour and triggers violence both on and off the pitch. We have already seen how football could generate enmity and perpetuate divisions during the Cold War. Yet a deep dive into the Portugal–North Korea clash of 1966 shows the polar opposite: how the people's game could break down barriers between East and West, and in curious, enduring ways. Why, we might ask, was the Goodison Park crowd supporting the North Koreans so fervently? How had the communist underdogs managed to get so far in the tournament? And what did the British government make of the prospects of the Koreans playing – not to mention beating – England in the semi-finals?

The Portugal–North Korea match shines light on a quite different subject too, the legacy of which we still grapple with today – colonial racism. During the 1960s, Portugal's dictator António Salazar claimed he was on the front line of the Cold War in Africa. Determined to lead the West's fight against the global tide of communist-inspired decolonisation, Salazar devised a simple yet cunning strategy: to trawl Portugal's African colonies for footballing talent and use these gifted Black players as 'ambassadors for empire'. Stars like Eusébio would not only bring Portugal victory on the football field, strengthening Salazar's personal reputation and hold on power. By representing the mother country so proudly, they'd also help bind Portugal and its African colonies more tightly. Even better if, along the way, the Portugal team got the chance to represent the West and demonstrate their prowess against communist opponents.

The World Cup of 1966 is when football, to coin a phrase, 'came home'. England, the designers of the modern game, not only hosted the tournament but won it for the first and so far only time. The 1966 World Cup made history for other reasons too. It was the first and to date only World Cup to be boycotted, by over thirty African nations protesting against apartheid South Africa's recent readmission to FIFA and FIFA's refusal to guarantee at least one African nation a spot in the finals.[2] It was the first World Cup to have live television coverage that featured the use of slow-motion replays and guest pundits.[3] And it was also very nearly, lest we forget, the only World Cup without an actual World Cup. Four months prior to the tournament, the Jules Rimet Trophy was stolen in London, then found a week later by Pickles, a black-and-white collie later invited to England's celebration banquet as a reward. Pickles quickly went on to appear in *The Spy with a Cold Nose*, featuring a dog implanted with a listening device that MI6 sends as a gift to the Kremlin.[4]

If the British, as this movie indicates, always regarded Soviet Russia as their prime enemy during the Cold War, North Korea was one of Moscow's chief lackeys. Hundreds of British troops had died in the first hot war of the Cold War in Korea in the early 1950s. The Korean War had widened the East–West conflict beyond Europe and stimulated an arms race that irrevocably deepened it. With over three million dead, Korea itself was left permanently divided by the war – psychologically, ideologically and territorially. In the south, capitalism reigned supreme, backed by the American military. In the north, Kim Il Sung, hero of the guerrilla war against the Japanese during World War Two and a hard-core communist, ran the ruling Workers' Party and country with an iron fist. Kim's obsession with building a socialist command economy based on the concept of *Juche* (or self-reliance) increasingly cut off North Korea from the outside world.

At the time of the 1966 World Cup, North Korea was not the dysfunctional mess we think of today. The North then had much greater industrial capacity than the South and even a higher standard of living.

It enjoyed close relations with Leonid Brezhnev's Soviet Union and Walter Ulbricht's East Germany, and Kim Il Sung himself, now in his fifties, was in his political prime. Kim used the North's power to drive an ambitious foreign policy, based on the duty of socialist nations to unite against the West. He couldn't dare compete with Mao Zedong for the leadership of Asian communism – China had sixty times more people than North Korea and had just become the world's fifth nuclear power – but his ideological rhetoric could be equally as colourful. 'The peoples of the countries making revolution should join efforts to tear the left and right arms from US imperialism', Kim proclaimed. They should 'tear off its left and right legs and behead it everywhere it stretches out its crooked hands of aggression'.[5]

Although it's unclear whether Kim Il Sung was a fan, football was an integral part of his revolutionary world-view. It was the number one sport on the Korean peninsula and ripe for political propaganda at home and overseas. With Kim's support, North Korea qualified for the 1966 World Cup by thrashing Australia 9–2 on aggregate in the combined Africa, Asia and Oceania play-off group in neutral Cambodia. The Australian team, comprised largely of British ex-patriots, had been so confident about winning it had already ordered special ties for the England trip.[6] This was arrogant in the extreme. North Korean football benefited from a highly centralised structure, one that prioritised the production of elite athletes for the international stage. All of the national team's squad played for clubs in Pyongyang, had been trained to play in a fast-paced, attacking style, and, thanks to endurance training that included mountain climbing, were supremely fit. In 1961, a North Korean team on a tour of the Soviet Union had beaten Spartak Moscow. In 1965, the North Koreans had hosted and won a football tournament against China, North Vietnam, Guinea, Indonesia and Cambodia, without conceding a goal.[7]

Kim saw his team's first appearance at the World Cup as an unmissable opportunity to promote Asian anti-imperialism at a point when, in countries like Sukarno's Indonesia and Ho Chi Minh's Vietnam, the West was trying to destroy communism. It would also be a chance to get one up on the South Koreans, who in their only appearance in the World Cup finals to date in 1954 had shipped sixteen goals without response in matches against Hungary and Turkey. Addressing the squad personally in Pyongyang on the eve of their departure for England, Kim made the importance of their mission abundantly clear.

The players' aim should be to win at least one game and 'overturn the European domination of world soccer'. Goalkeeper Ri Chan Myong left the meeting with only one thought in his mind. 'If I conceded a goal, the reputation of North Korea would fail', he later put it, ominously. 'We would have failed in the task set by the Great Leader. Therefore, I guarded the goal with my life.'[8]

Britain's Labour government, led by Harold Wilson, a Cold War hardliner and well-known Huddersfield Town fan, didn't exactly roll out the red carpet for the North Koreans. At the time, Britain refused to recognise North Korea as a legitimate state and the Foreign Office warned that allowing the team to participate in the World Cup would seriously complicate relations with other 'rogue' regimes like East Germany, annoy the South Koreans and anger British Korean War veterans. The government drew up plans to refuse the North Korean team visas but scrapped them after concluding that, if England barred any qualified team from entering, FIFA would take the World Cup elsewhere. Wilson's government, with minister of sport and former Football League referee Denis Howell at the forefront, decided instead to try and downplay North Korea's presence by, among other things, restricting national anthems to the opening and final matches. Given the political and financial capital Wilson had invested in the World Cup, losing it at the eleventh hour would have been a huge own goal. In retrospect, it might also have deprived England of their victory.[9] Four years later, Wilson would famously claim that England's unexpected World Cup quarter-final defeat by West Germany in Mexico cost him the general election that took place just four days afterwards. He may have been right.[10]

When the North Koreans arrived in London in early July 1966 (after warm-up matches in East Germany),[11] they were greeted with a mixture of suspicion and derision. The scars of the Korean War were still raw, and for many British people all Asians (or Orientals) were the same: inscrutable at best, cruel and dangerous at worst. Reheated stories of Kim's regime having tried to 'brainwash' Western prisoners into becoming communists during that conflict blended with terrible memories of the Japanese maltreatment of British POWs in World War Two. Next to nothing was known about the Korean team, its coach or tactics. Many reporters simply dubbed them the 'Mystery men of the East'; 'so little known', Brian Glanville wrote, 'they might be flying in from outer space'.[12] Stories of the expensive camera equipment the Koreans had bought after arriving in England made the squad look like spies, while other reports about the players having been banned from smoking, alcohol and even sex for two years prior to the tournament typecast them as craven communist automatons.[13] The general assumption – which the British government shared – was that the Koreans would keep to themselves and, as rank outsiders, make little to no impact on the tournament.

But then something strange happened. The Koreans had been drawn in Group 4 of the tournament and would play their three scheduled matches at Ayresome Park, home of Middlesbrough FC, in the north east. A town whose steelworks had built the Sydney Harbour Bridge in the 1930s, Middlesbrough had recently fallen on hard times and was scarcely the best equipped venue for the World Cup. Its press centre, for instance, was squeezed into the town hall crypt.[14] As the North Koreans' seventy-five-strong party (including two chefs and four cameramen) took the train from the capital to the north east, the players entertained themselves with patriotic songs. Passengers looked on, initially bemused but gradually warming to the exotic sounds and the openness of players who behaved nothing like robots. Not one of the players or officials had ever set foot outside North Korea, but their excitement at representing their country in the West was palpable.[15]

The Koreans' sincerity, politeness and enthusiasm rubbed off on the people of Middlesbrough, who quickly adopted them. The Koreans played in red, like the local team. They averaged only five and half feet in height, which naturally made them underdogs. They impressed workers at the town's giant ICI chemicals plant, their training camp, with their technique and all-out attacking intent. And, though their official minders restricted the players' contact with outsiders, they cultivated friendship. Middlesbrough's mayor, Jack Boothby, was presented with an embroidered picture of a red-crowned crane, Korea's national symbol of longevity and peace. The town hall reciprocated by flying the North Korean Red Star flag. Photographs of the players joshing with journalists, signing autographs for teenagers, and laughing at Laurel and Hardy movies (see Figure 5.1) made them even more likeable.[16]

In the opening match of Group 4, on 12 July, the North Koreans played the mighty Soviet Union, recent European Nations' Cup runners-up. With its hoardings advertising everything from Brylcreem to Fyffes Bananas, the newly refurbished Ayresome Park looked resplendently capitalistic for the two communist sides. The game was a bad-tempered

Figure 5.1 Members of the North Korean World Cup squad watching *Towed in a Hole*, a Laurel & Hardy comedy, in their Middlesbrough hotel, before their match against the Soviet Union at Ayresome Park, 12 July 1966. © Central Press/Hulton Archive/Getty Images.

affair, with fists thrown. Despite being Cold War allies, the Soviets cut the diminutive Koreans no slack and bullied their way to a comfortable 3–0 victory – behaving, as a South Korean reporter at the game recalled, like 'sons of bitches'. The Middlesbrough crowd shouted their support for the Koreans but against the muscular, experienced Soviets they looked out of their depth. 'Not tough enough!' 'Tactically amateurish and naïve', the British press concluded.[17]

Three days later, the Koreans faced Chile, who'd come third in the 1962 World Cup finals but were fresh from a 5–2 pre-tournament mauling at the hands of East Germany. The South Americans went ahead through an early penalty, but with only three minutes of the game left, and the locals baying for an equaliser, midfielder Pak Sung Jin scored with a volley from twelve yards out. This was the first time an Asian team had ever scored a goal at the World Cup finals. The crowd's raucous reaction in the stands was enough to bring down the electric strip lighting in the press's refreshment room. The game ended 1–1. The fans 'haven't cheered Middlesbrough like this for years here', the BBC's excited commentator Frank Bough told his viewers. In the hullabaloo after the match, with his players still crying tears of joy, the North Korean coach thanked the spectators for their backing. 'Rarely have supporters taken a team to their hearts as the football followers of Middlesbrough have taken these whimsical orientals', *The Times*' correspondent wrote the next day.[18]

The Koreans' draw with Chile left them with an extremely tall order: needing to beat two-times world champions Italy to qualify for the quarter-finals. The *Azzurri* were one of the tournament favourites, with many of their rich and famous players hailing from AC Milan and Internazionale, clubs that had recently won the European Cup. After a slow start, the game turned on the half-hour mark when Italy's legendary captain Giacomo Bulgarelli was stretchered off the field after a clumsy challenge on Pak Sung Jin. With no substitutes allowed, this meant the Italians, who needed a draw to progress, were a man short for the rest of the game. Soon afterwards, in the forty-first minute, the Koreans sensationally took the lead. Pak Do Ik, a twenty-four-year-old former printer who played for the Moranbong Phenian club back home, struck a right-footed effort from the edge of the box beyond Enrico Albertosi's desperate dive and into the net at the Holgate End. The Middlesbrough crowd went crazy. The Koreans now had their poster boy for the World Cup. Pak Do Ik's life would never be the same again.

In the second half, the Italians frantically piled on the pressure, expecting their opponents to crack, but the North Koreans held on for victory. As the final whistle blew, pandemonium broke out in Ayresome Park. Local fans darted on to the pitch to celebrate with their tearful Korean heroes, the Italian superstars made a quick escape, and the press jabbered in disbelief. Football writer Arthur Hopcraft later recalled the comical sight of 'a tall British sailor lugging two Koreans off the pitch, one under each arm, like prizes'.[19] In the packed dressing room afterwards, the Koreans made merry by drinking lemonade; local dignitaries, on the harder stuff, smiled like Cheshire cats and patted them on the back. The communist side had beaten 'football's millionaires', as Pyongyang called the *Azzurri*, and pulled off what was seen instantly as the greatest giant-killing feat in the game's history. The next day, the 'fairytale' result was reported across the footballing world. For many football enthusiasts in Britain, especially on Teesside, the North Koreans were now the darlings of the World Cup.[20]

If it's fair to assume Kim Il Sung was the happiest man in the world on hearing of North Korea's qualification for the quarter-finals, António Salazar might have been a close second. The reclusive, fervently Catholic dictator of Portugal had for years invested heavily in turning his country from a football laughing stock into a force to be reckoned with. The night North Korea despatched the Italians, Portugal had themselves gone through to the quarter-finals by dumping the World Cup holders, Brazil, out of the competition. With North Korea rather than Italy in the way, the semi-finals now looked a relative formality. Portugal were in supreme form and surely lightning – in the shape of plucky communist upstarts – couldn't strike twice.

Almost forgotten today outside of Portugal, António Salazar was Europe's most resilient right-wing authoritarian leader of the twentieth century. A contemporary of Hitler, Mussolini and Franco, he ruled Portugal for over thirty years, between 1932 and 1968. Despite branding itself the *Estado Novo,* or New State, Salazar's regime was backward-looking in the extreme. It spent up to 40 per cent of the country's budget on the armed forces while keeping the mass of the nation's nine million population poor and illiterate. It muzzled the press and trade unions, and was strongly pro-Western. Salazar's Portugal was the only non-democratic founder of NATO – an indication of its strategically important bases like the Azores – and an enthusiastic member of capitalist, free trade organisations. Salazar banned Marxist parties and used the state's much-feared secret police, the PIDE, to stamp out any connections between political opposition and Moscow.[21]

Salazar's Portugal was also Europe's most stubborn opponent of decolonisation. After World War Two, the British, French and Dutch gradually bent to the 'winds of change' that swept the developing world, abandoning colonies in Africa, Asia and the Middle East. In the 1960s, Europe – the real cockpit of the Cold War in the conflict's early years – was effectively in geopolitical stalemate. As a consequence, leaders in both the East and West turned greater attention to winning hearts and minds in the developing world. This was now the Cold War's crucial battlefield and where, some believed, the conflict could be won or lost.[22]

Salazar resisted any calls for colonial emancipation. Like many of his compatriots, the dictator believed that the Portuguese had a unique talent for imperialism and for creating multiracial societies in the tropics owing to their ability to adapt to its environments and peoples. Equally importantly, his regime saw Portugal's African colonies as key to projecting power at home and overseas; if Portugal lost these colonies, Portugal's status would be damaged irreparably. Communist states not surprisingly labelled Salazar a racist, particularly when he began suppressing Marxist independence movements in Mozambique and Angola. Even the Americans tried to modify his colonial policies for fear of the harm they were doing to the West's reputation, but with little success.[23]

Football played a critical role in Salazar's quest to retain and rejuvenate Portugal's empire. From the early 1950s onwards, scores of talented players from Mozambique and Angola were persuaded to sign for top clubs like Benfica and Sporting Lisbon and to represent Portugal. The players' affluent lifestyles and celebrity status functioned as a showcase for the benefits that 'enlightened imperialism' could bring. Their prowess on the pitch helped strengthen the imperial project, bolster Portugal's sporting image and boost the country's overall reputation. Clubs like Benfica toured Mozambique and Angola with their African players to campaign against the Marxist 'terrorists' the Portuguese army was fighting and to raise funds for wounded Portuguese soldiers. Salazar's regime tasked the PIDE with keeping close tabs on any political views the African players expressed, especially when they played behind the Iron Curtain. The Salazarists took the threat of communist subversion in football so seriously they even tried to persuade Benfica's owners to change the club's famous red shirts because of that colour's leftist associations.[24]

In the 1960s, Benfica reached the European Cup Final four times, winning twice, with a team featuring a clutch of African stars. To many Portuguese, Benfica's multiracial makeup epitomised a combination of new-found national togetherness and manly resurgence. The team's victory over Real Madrid in the 1962 European Cup Final – after which state medals were bestowed on the whole squad – took Portuguese football to unheard-of heights. Alongside this, the national team, having been terrible for years, suddenly became serious contenders for honours. Gone were the days of the late 1940s and 1950s, when Salazar's regime was rocked by 10–0 and 9–1 drubbings by England and Austria, respectively. Instead, Portugal's multicultural team could now compete with the best. African players like the defender Hilário, midfielder Coluna and attacker Fernando formed the spine of a world-class side that mixed stern defence with flamboyant forward play.[25]

In what is now regarded as one of the greatest Portugal teams of all time, one player stood out above the rest: Eusébio da Silva Ferreira.

Born in the slums of Maputo in Mozambique, Eusébio smashed goal-scoring records for Benfica and Portugal in the 1960s and 1970s. Nicknamed the Black Panther or *o Rei* (the King), he was renowned for a blistering right-foot shot and became the first African to leave a major mark on the world game. In Portugal, Eusébio was an important 'unifying' figure for the Salazar regime, a living example of social mobility, patriotism and racial integration. He was as popular with white Portuguese as he was with Black African immigrants. Eusébio carefully avoided political comments, knowing that the PIDE closely monitored him and other African footballers for seditious behaviour. The footballer's global iconic status belied his lack of true freedom: being classed as a 'national asset' by Salazar meant that Eusébio was forbidden from transferring abroad. When the great Italian club Juventus and others came knocking, the door was shut firmly in their faces.[26]

In contrast with North Korea, Portugal eased their way through the first round of the 1966 World Cup finals, despite being in the 'group of death'. In their first match in Group 3, they beat the reigning Olympic champions, Hungary, 3–1, with goals from José Augusto and José Torres, both of whom played for Benfica. In their second, they won 3–0 against communist Bulgaria. Torres scored again and Eusébio opened his tournament account with a first-time low shot across the goalkeeper from near the penalty spot. In their third match, Portugal beat Brazil, World Cup champions of 1958 and 1962, 3–1. Eusébio again scored, twice, the second a trademark right-foot volley from an acute angle that was past goalkeeper Manga before he'd had the chance to move. The match soon attracted notoriety for the rugged treatment Portugal's defenders meted out to Pelé, who had to leave the pitch injured.[27] The truth is Pelé was carrying an injury and on the day Brazil's golden team were out-fought and outplayed by a superior outfit. After this third consecutive victory, Portugal topped the tournament's scoring charts and were many people's tips to take the trophy.

Portugal's quarter-final match with North Korea took place on Saturday 23 July 1966 at Goodison Park in Liverpool, home of Everton FC. The venue put Portugal at a distinct advantage. The team were already based in the north west of England and knew the Goodison pitch well from having just played Brazil on it. The North Koreans had to up sticks from the bosom of Middlesbrough and move 150 miles south to, of all places, a Roman Catholic seminary, which the Italians had booked but no longer needed. Being surrounded by Christian iconography apparently caused some of the players, all strict atheists, sleepless nights. At Ayresome Park the Koreans had played in front of around 20,000 spectators. The attendance at Goodison would be 51,000 – a frightening prospect for a team whose base back home was a cigarette factory. As the Koreans took the train to Liverpool they again buoyed themselves with patriotic songs, and, as befitting their new-found celebrity status, with signing autographs for dozens of well-wishers. Accompanying them and on other trains were upwards of 4,000 supporters from Middlesbrough. 'Pak Do Ik – Crown Prince of the Orient', declared one teenager's banner.[28]

As the Teesside contingent led the Mersey-siders in chants of 'KO-RE-A' before the start of the quarter-final, not one of them could have predicted the barmy spectacle about to unfold (see Figure 5.2). The Koreans came flying out of the traps. Adopting their usual 4-4-2

Figure 5.2 Portugal (left) and North Korea wave to the crowd before kick-off, Goodison Park, 23 July 1966. © Popperfoto via Getty Images/Getty Images.

formation and relentless attacking style, they quickly dispossessed their ambling opponents after kick-off. The Koreans flooded forward and, with less than a minute gone, Pak Sung Jin, the scorer against Chile, bagged another courtesy of a beautiful shot with the outside of his left foot from the edge of the Portugal box. Pak turned to the crowd and clasped his hands above his head, as if thanking them for their support.

In the twentieth minute, José Pereira, Portugal's normally dependable goalkeeper, entirely misjudged a cross from Yang Song Guk, and Li Dong Woon made it 2–0. 'We want three!' cried the crowd and Yang Song Guk gave them it a few minutes later after dummying a defender and coolly slotting past Pereira from eight yards. Smart-suited Korean officials in the stands danced with delight. Shouts of 'Easy!' from the supposedly neutral crowd ridiculed the Portuguese 'world-beaters'.

Portugal were in a deep hole. They didn't look complacent. It was more that the Koreans, highly energetic and harrying in numbers, were playing better. Portugal had created chances. José Augusto had struck a rising shot from twenty-five yards that the gloveless Ri Chan Myong had saved with aplomb. The keeper had also acrobatically tipped over a header from Torres, stretching every sinew in his five-foot-seven-inch frame to reach the bar. But the Koreans had so far matched their taller, more muscular opponents. Defenders Lim Zoong Sun and Oh Yoon Kyung were even beating the six-foot-four-inch Torres, nicknamed the Kind Giant, in the air.

What is more, the Koreans were being rewarded for their all-out attacking strategy. This didn't look methodical, robotic, 'communist'. It looked 'free' and it captivated the crowd. It's not difficult to imagine what António Salazar thought of it – nor of how his country would cope with such a degrading defeat. On hearing that Portugal were 3–0 down, Britain's sports minister Denis Howell nervously envisaged North Korea's 'dreaded national anthem' being played after all, despite his efforts to avoid such an outcome, in the tournament final.[29]

A lesser team might have wilted under this sort of pressure, but Portugal were an extremely tight unit. Four of the players – Vicente, Hilário, Coluna and Eusébio – came from Mozambique. Five of the players were teammates at Benfica, three others at Sporting Lisbon. Portugal had class and steel. They had a fluidity in defence most other national teams craved, and in captain Mario Coluna, nicknamed the Sacred Monster, one of the most imposing and physical midfielders of his generation. Above all, they had Eusébio, voted European footballer of the year in 1965 and, alongside Pelé, then widely regarded as the best player in the world.

Cue one of the greatest comebacks in World Cup history. With half an hour gone, José Augusto played a slightly wayward pass through to Eusébio in the Korean box and, as the defence hesitated, the striker stabbed the ball home. Eusébio, ever the gentleman, immediately picked up the ball from out of the net and raced with it all the way to the centre-spot. Two minutes before half-time, Oh Yoon Kyung clumsily brought down the gangly Torres seven yards from goal. While Torres received treatment just off the pitch to the left, next to the schoolboys sitting in front of the Gwladys Street End, Eusébio smashed the penalty kick past Ri Chan Myong's desperate dive.

At the start of the second half North Korea rallied, enjoying good periods of possession. The Koreans were tiring, however. At one point, the referee rebuked someone on their trainers' bench for throwing what looked like sweets onto the pitch. Only a few players had had the chance to pick them up when, in the fifty-eighth minute, Portugal equalised.[30] Eusébio ran onto a slide-rule pass from left-winger Simoes and, without even looking at the goal or breaking stride, hit an unstoppable right-foot shot into the top left-hand corner of the Korean goal. 'Well, that's the man we thought could win the match for Portugal', uttered the BBC's David Coleman, a little gloomily.

No sooner had Portugal regained possession, Eusébio picked up the ball in his own half, beat two men with pace, strength and a step-over down the left wing, and ran into the penalty box. There, two Koreans scythed him down, one from the back, the other from the side (see Figure 5.3). Though limping heavily, Eusébio coolly side-footed in the penalty, putting Portugal into the lead with his fourth goal of the game.

For the final thirty minutes of the game, Portugal slipped into their customary, commanding gear. Coluna and Jaime Graça controlled the midfield and Eusébio warmed Ri Chan Myong's hands several times more. Ten minutes from time, the striker took an in-swinging corner to the far post, where Torres headed the ball back to the unmarked José Augusto, who nodded it into the net. The Koreans' resistance was broken.

The match ended 5–3 to Portugal. After the final whistle, on the pitch the visibly relieved Portugal players mobbed a still-limping

Figure 5.3 Eusébio wins his side a second penalty in the quarter-final to put Portugal 4–3 up. © Staff/Mirrorpix/Getty Images.

Eusébio. One intrepid teenager managed to break the police cordon and persuaded the man-of-the-match to autograph his match programme. For the majority of the crowd, though, the real stars of the show had been the Koreans. Spectators saluted them as they left the pitch, clapping and cheering the players for having, as Coleman put it, 'played their hearts out'. Away from Goodison Park, Denis Howell's relief at hearing of Portugal's comeback and victory was palpable. 'Disaster had been averted,' he said years later.[31]

Three days after their remarkable victory over North Korea, Portugal played the hosts England in the World Cup semi-final at a packed and partisan Wembley Stadium. Though Eusébio again scored, Portugal lost 2–1 thanks to goals by midfielder Bobby Charlton. Many Portuguese would forever dispute the result of this match. FIFA had 'fixed' the game in England's favour by switching it from Goodison Park to Wembley at the last minute, they and others claimed, meaning England wouldn't need to travel away from London and their supporting crowd would be larger. On top of this, the Portuguese argued that Eusébio was cynically man-marked out of the game by England's enforcer, Nobby Stiles, whose physicality even the English FA's top brass found embarrassing. Portugal's defeat to England would always be known as the Game of Tears, owing to the heartbroken state Eusébio was in after the final whistle.[32]

Ever the professional and patriot, Eusébio dusted himself off and two days later scored again in Portugal's 2–1 third place play-off victory. Because this was against the Soviet Union, the result meant far more to the Salazar regime than it did to the players. Beating his regime's arch-enemy was the 'best gift we gave Salazar', the Mozambican defender Hilário claimed afterwards. Like Francisco Franco, the dictator had for years forbidden games against the Soviets on ideological grounds. In 1966, Portugal was effectively at war with the Soviet Union – as well as Mao Zedong's China and Fidel Castro's Cuba – owing to their military and financial support for Marxist guerrillas in Portugal's African colonies.[33]

When the Portugal team returned home, the Salazar regime milked this victory over the Soviets and the team's overall performance at the World Cup to the full. Doing so was easy. For a country to have finished third in its first World Cup finals was a major achievement. The team's goal-getting, entertaining style had also enthralled millions at home and overseas. Both of these feats reflected well on Salazar. Soon after their return to Lisbon, the Portugal players were feted in a parade through the city's main streets and given full state honours for promoting 'Portugal's good name and prestige'. Salazar's government lavished attention on the African players, especially Eusébio, who by scoring nine goals had won the World Cup's prestigious Golden Boot. Later that summer, the dictator invited the players to the inauguration of the recently completed Salazar Bridge, connecting Lisbon to the southern shore of the River Tagus. Because Eusébio was overseas, trying in vain to arrange a transfer to Italy, pride of place went to the team captain, Coluna, who sat beside Salazar and helped him cut the ceremonial ribbon.[34]

Portugal's success at the 1966 World Cup was in many ways the last hurrah for Salazar. Two years later, the despot suffered a massive brain haemorrhage after falling from a deckchair while having his hair cut. He would never fully recover and died, aged 81, in July 1970. Even while he was incapacitated in hospital, Salazar still cast a political spell over many of the nation's footballers. Famous players regularly demonstrated their fealty by paying him highly publicised well-wishing visits. Others, feeling that times were changing, could be less deferential. At the 1969 Cup Final between Academica de Coimbra and Benfica, the former's players entered the field wearing scholars' gowns. What now looks on film like a bizarre fancy-dress parade was a deeply subversive act that expressed solidarity with the students at Coimbra University who were in open war with the *Estado Novo*.[35]

Five years later, the *Estado Novo* passed into history. In April 1974, a group of leftist army officers, disillusioned by the dirty, unwinnable counter-insurgency campaigns in the African colonies, rebelled. Their actions prompted the Carnation Revolution that swept away Portugal's authoritarian regime. Shortly afterwards, Portugal's African colonies were granted independence. A number of prominent African footballers returned home, including the great Coluna, who went on to develop coaching programmes in Mozambique. Eusébio finished his career in North America and Mexico, but went back to Lisbon. A national treasure in Portugal, he would later describe Salazar as his and the whole country's 'slave master'.[36]

Given North Korea's extraordinary performance at the World Cup, we might expect its players to have been set for life when they returned home. This was far from the case. Contrary to long-standing rumours, many pedalled by Western propagandists using partisan South Korean sources, the squad were not immediately imprisoned for having lost their 3–0 lead to Portugal. On their arrival from England at Pyongyang Airport, the players were treated as national heroes and carried aloft by celebrating supporters. Like their Portugal counterparts, they also received official honorary titles. Kim Il Sung used the players' feats in England as evidence of the power of North Korean people's sport and of the superiority of socialism. He could also justifiably lay claim to having put Asian football on the map and given a historic boost to the sport across the continent. Very soon, however, the Korean players became collateral damage in a terrifying, high-ranking political purge.[37]

The year after the World Cup, Kim faced a rare challenge to his authority. The Gapsan faction, a disgruntled group within the Workers' Party, questioned his cult of personality and economic strategy. Kim acted ruthlessly by charging the faction leaders with crimes against the state, expelling them from the party, and despatching them to the countryside or prison. Members of the Gapsan faction had for many years helped nurture football in North Korea and had close connections with the national squad. This put the World Cup heroes in Kim's crosshairs. To make things worse, stories circulated that some of the songs the players had been charming the locals with in England had extolled members of the Gapsan faction. As a result, most of the players were shipped to remote collieries or labour camps, on trumped-up charges that they'd been drinking and womanising on the eve of the quarter-final against Portugal. Pak Sung Jin, North Korea's top scorer in England, was later imprisoned on spying charges and allegedly reduced to living off insects in solitary confinement. Pak Do Ik, the conqueror of Italy, was compelled to work as a forest labourer for a decade, before being 'rehabilitated' as national team coach and a torch-bearer for the 2008 Beijing Olympics.[38]

The effect of all of this is that North Korean football nosedived. Though Kim's son, Kim Jong Il, sought to revitalise the sport in the 1980s and after his father's death in 1994, the country wouldn't participate in another World Cup until 2010. Ironically, the greatest impact of North Korea's 'miracle' in 1966 was on South Korea, where the shock effect of their rival's success prompted a massive effort by the government, assisted by big business, to improve the quality of elite players and the national team. South Korea, alongside Japan, hosted the World Cup in 2002 and finished fourth in the tournament.[39]

The end of North Korea's football dream was not the end of the love affair between the team of 1966 and the people of Middlesbrough, though. Memories of the bond they'd forged during the World Cup remained strong on both sides in the years and decades ahead. After Ayresome Park was demolished to make way for a housing estate in 1997, a bronze cast of an imprint of a football boot was set among the homes, marking the exact spot from where Pak Do Ik had struck his winner against Italy. Having previously never even recognised an art-work outside North Korea, Pyongyang soon declared the bronze boot a national historic monument.[40]

Shortly after this, in 2001, North Korea's authorities granted British film-maker Daniel Gordon privileged access to the country, to produce a documentary about the eight surviving members of the World Cup team. *The Game of Their Lives* was a hit. Off the back of this, a year later, the Korean players made an emotional return trip to England, financially supported by Middlesbrough FC and the town council. After first being given a rousing reception before a game at Goodison Park, the site of their match against Portugal, the players received a heroes' welcome at the Riverside, Middlesbrough FC's new ground, where they paraded on the pitch before a Premier League match against Leeds United (see Figure 5.4). When Pak Do Ik re-enacted his legendary World Cup goal, he was greeted with a deafening roar. 'They were back where they belonged in the hearts and minds of Boro fans', the club's fanzine affirmed. In turn, the Koreans thanked the locals for having helped them so much on their World Cup odyssey thirty-five years earlier.[41]

The warm feelings expressed on both sides were genuine and testified to the way that the World Cup of 1966 had helped break down Cold War divisions. The people of Middlesbrough hadn't of course converted to communism back in the 1960s. But they'd softened their hostility towards North Korea and, through friendship with the country's footballers, realised that even in the communist 'hermit kingdom' people were just people. For their part, the North Korean players had learned that what they'd initially called 'the alien land of Britain' was not an aggressive, class-based enemy of the proletariat but a country that embraced outsiders. Though the players had less opportunity than the citizens of Middlesbrough to question their country's foreign policy,

Figure 5.4 Members of the North Korean team from the 1966 World Cup prior to the 2–2 draw between Middlesbrough and Leeds United at the Riverside Stadium in Middlesbrough, 26 October 2002. © Ross Kinnaird/Getty Images.

they could still, in Pak Do Ik's words, use football as a means of promoting peace.[42]

Taking Pak Do Ik at his word, some in Middlesbrough sought to build on the players' return visit by formalising the special relationship between North Korea and Middlesbrough. A twinning of towns was discussed, as was, absurd as it might seem, the idea of holding an annual North Korea Day in Middlesbrough. Nothing came of these schemes, but people-to-people contacts continued. When North Korea decided to establish an embassy in Britain in 2003, a senior member of Middlesbrough town council was invited to open it. When the British embassy in Pyongyang wanted to mark a decade of diplomatic ties with North Korea in 2010, it made perfect sense to use the Middlesbrough football connection.

The result was two women's football games played in Pyongyang between Middlesbrough Ladies FC and local club sides. In contrast with Dynamo Moscow's visit to Britain in 1945, Middlesbrough Ladies FC's mini-tour was a resounding success. The host teams won in front of millions of North Korean television viewers, the tourists felt the affection of the friendly spectators, and the Ladies' coach gushed publicly about football's power to break down cultural barriers. As if history was repeating itself, the Ladies also entertained the locals by singing, in this case verses normally confined to the Riverside's terraces. We can bet their songs sounded as mysteriously exotic as those the North Korean team sang in England back in 1966.[43]

6 THE GAME OF SHAME
Chile vs. Soviet Union, Santiago, November 1973

Anyone coming across the faded footage of the match today would think everything looks perfectly normal. Or at least initially. It's a gloriously sunny day and we are in the Estadio Nacional in Santiago, Chile in late November 1973. The Chile players – red shirts, blue shorts, brown sideburns – are lined up in the centre of the pitch. Each of them has his right arm raised and is turning to salute the fans before kick-off. We might expect the crowd to be larger given it's a winner-takes-all World Cup qualifier, but perhaps the spectators are dwarfed by the vastness of the arena.

As the camera retreats, however, it's clear there's something very, very wrong: Chile's opponents, the Soviet Union, haven't turned up. Absurdly, the game is going ahead anyway. Austrian referee Erich Linemayr blows his whistle and several Chile players tentatively jog forward into the empty half, passing the ball between themselves towards the would-be Soviet goal. The rest of their team oddly stays in defensive formation. Are they expecting a Soviet counter-attack, perhaps?

When Chile's captain, Francisco 'Chamaco' Valdés, takes possession of the ball in the penalty box, he knows he must score. After all, if his shot goes high or wide, there's no Soviet player to restart the game and the match will be in a bizarre, nil–nil limbo. Slowly, very deliberately, Valdés dribbles the ball to less than a yard out from the goal line, then blasts it into the net past the invisible goalkeeper. The final whistle goes. Game over. Chile are going to next summer's World Cup finals in West Germany.[1]

As football curios go, it's difficult to beat the match between Chile and the Soviet Union on 21 November 1973. The game begs all sorts of questions. Given that it featured only one team and lasted all of seventeen seconds, should it even be classed as a match? Who or what was responsible for this encounter, which looks even more farcical than the foggy Arsenal–Dynamo Moscow game of November 1945? Why had the Soviet team failed to show up, throwing away any chance of playing at the World Cup finals in West Germany? And what has any of this got to do with the Cold War?

The answer to the last question is quite simple – pretty much everything. In late 1973, Chile was briefly at the very centre of the Cold War. In Santiago in September, the Chilean armed forces carried out a bloody coup against President Salvador Allende. The leader of the first Marxist government ever to come to power at the ballot box was now dead, thanks, many suspected, to the guiding hand of America's Central Intelligence Agency. A military junta, led by General Augusto Pinochet, took Allende's place. Pinochet's henchmen went on to imprison, torture and murder thousands of left-wingers without impunity. Chile's right-wing dictatorship would outlast the Cold War.

The onset of General Pinochet's reign of terror in late 1973 might have passed much of the world by but for one thing: the caudillo's decision to turn Chile's most famous sports ground, the Estadio Nacional in Santiago, into a detention-cum-death camp. Intended to showcase the junta's ruthlessness and stamp out domestic opposition, the decision prompted outrage overseas, especially in the communist world. The Soviet Union doubled down on the controversy by leading a vociferous campaign calling for their November World Cup qualifier away to Chile, due to take place in the Estadio Nacional, to be moved to another country on humanitarian grounds. It failed but, in refusing to play the 'game of shame', the Soviets' actions made World Cup history. The peculiar affair of the Chile–Soviet Union match is an important illustration of how football could be used as a powerful tool of political protest during the Cold War. It also reveals, on close inspection, how political grandstanding could sometimes hide something more mundane – the fear of losing on the pitch.

The Cold War cast a terrible pall across Latin America. The United States had long claimed policing rights in the Americas, dating back to the Monroe Doctrine of the 1820s. After World War Two, Washington's fixation on the threat of communism in its own back-yard – particularly after Fidel Castro's socialist revolution in Cuba in 1959 and the proliferation of KGB field officers in the region – led to the United States allying itself with right-wing military regimes all over the continent. The callous caudillos that dominated Latin America in the 1970s had little in common politically, writes historian Odd Arne Westad, except their hatred for leftists and general references to 'order' and 'Christian civilization'. The military regimes could get away with terrorising their citizens and killing their leftist opponents because they knew the United States would not break its ties with them, despite their human rights abuses.[2]

As warm as Washington's embrace was, the Latin American caudillos still needed to curry favour at home and abroad. Sports – especially baseball, basketball, boxing and football – were as popular a political tool for doing this as in other parts of the world. In the 1970s, several Latin American military dictatorships excelled at weaponising football. Brazil, the continent's largest country and most powerful military regime, wrote the playbook. Its chief author was General Emilio Garrastazú Médici.

A fan of Rio de Janeiro's famous club Flamengo, Médici became Brazil's president in 1969. Brazil's military had already been in power for five years at this point but was faced with increasing unrest, culminating in the recent kidnapping by left-wing guerrillas of the US ambassador. Médici's dual stabilisation strategy was to order even more arrests, interrogations and executions while playing the populist card, principally by demonstrating his government's support for the nation's one true passion: football (see Figure 6.1). The dictator pumped funds into the coffers of the national football confederation and ordered a massive stadium-building scheme that would help modernise the game. Médici also started religiously attending Flamengo matches at the Maracanã Stadium, to show the people their leader was just like them; before long he was helping pick the team. Secret CIA reports paid tribute to the myriad ways in which Médici cleverly associated his regime with football. Bewildered field agents unfamiliar with football crowds wrote in awe of the bedlam created by spectators at the

Figure 6.1 Pelé receives the Emilio Garrastazu Médici Cup to celebrate scoring 1,000 goals in his career, 3 January 1970. He is with João Havelange, President of the Brazilian Sports Federation. © Pictorial Parade/Archive Photos/Getty Images.

Maracanã and of football's unique ability to unify a country that was so socially and racially divided.[3]

Under Médici's watchful eye, Brazil waged a meticulous, no-expenses-spared campaign to win the World Cup in Mexico in 1970. Médici publicly fell out with maverick team coach João Saldanha, a well-known communist, over his refusal to select the dictator's favourite striker, Flamengo's Dario. Saldanha was replaced by Mario Zagallo, as keen as his predecessor on playing 'artful' football but whose regimented management style better suited the military's ethos. Senior officers held key positions in the national team's World Cup delegation. Its head of security was Major Roberto Ipiranga Guaranys, later identified as one of the regime's cruellest torturers. The squad's fitness trainer was Captain Claudio Coutinho, who utilised aerobic and stress-relieving techniques he had learned at NASA. State-of-the-art science was applied in other ways, too. Handmade boots were made for every player from special casts, and their kit was redesigned to cope better with the energy-sapping heat and humidity of Mexico. A fortnight before it departed for Mexico, the Brazil squad went on a Central American sleeping-and-eating schedule.[4]

These preparations paid off handsomely. Brazil didn't just win the World Cup in 1970. They were the first team to win all their games at a finals; the first to have a player, Jairzinho, score in each match; and the first to become three-times world champions and therefore keep the Jules Rimet trophy. In Mexico, Brazil served up some of the most beautiful, inventive football ever seen, televised across the globe in colour for the first time. Their 'Five Number 10s' – Jairzinho, Gerson, Rivellino, Tostão and, of course, Pelé – played with a freedom and ebullience that, akin to the Magical Magyars in 1954, belied their country's authoritarian reputation. The team's victory in the final over Italy was widely seen as a triumph for South America's artful modernity over Europe's out-of-date defensive-mindedness. Brazil's fourth and final goal in the final, scored with a first-time rocket by right-back Carlos Alberto, would pass into history as one of the greatest team goals ever.[5]

Just a few months after Brazil's victory at the 1970 World Cup, Salvador Allende won power in Chile. Allende had been a gifted athlete in his youth and a member of the Everton de Viña del Mar sports club (named after the English football club). Now in his 60s, Allende was an avowed socialist who, in spite of the CIA's efforts, had secured the Chilean presidency as head of a radical, leftist coalition through democratic elections. The surprise result sent shockwaves through Washington. When Moscow started supporting Allende financially and militarily, things went from bad to worse. President Richard Nixon feared the Soviets now had a 'Red Sandwich' between Havana and Santiago, which could swamp all of Latin America. National security adviser Henry Kissinger was even more alarmist, arguing that Allende's peaceful, electoral triumph could act as an 'insidious' model for communists not only in America's backyard but even in Western Europe.[6]

Kissinger and the CIA became obsessed with getting rid of Allende. The adventurist statesman and indefatigable agency did their utmost to sabotage the Chilean economy and create the conditions for a military coup. Emilio Médici chipped in by supplying intelligence to dissident officers in Santiago plotting Allende's violent removal. On 11 September 1973, the Chilean military overthrew the Allende administration, using maximum force. With the crucial support of its commander-in-chief, General Augusto Pinochet, the army launched an all-out attack on the presidential palace. As the building went up in flames, Allende ordered his allies to surrender, then committed suicide using the AK-47 Fidel Castro had given him while visiting Chile two years earlier.[7]

Fuelled by the belief that Chile faced an existential threat from foreign communists and internal subversives, Pinochet's new government rounded up thousands of alleged traitors in the weeks following the coup. Once the jails were full, the junta showed it really meant business by turning ten football stadiums into makeshift detention camps. The largest and most high profile of these was the 75,000-seater Estadio Nacional in Santiago. Chile's 'monument to national sport' had hosted the World Cup final in 1962. It was also the home of the club side Universidad de Chile, the team of Santiago's intelligentsia.

Over a two-month period that ended in early November 1973, Pinochet used the Estadio Nacional as a base for crushing opposition to his regime (see Figure 6.2). As many as 40,000 people were interned there. Military guards herded prisoners onto the terraces, where they'd nervously await their fate at gunpoint. Tragically, some prisoners initially thought they'd been brought to the stadium to watch a surreal

Figure 6.2 A Chilean Army guard watches prisoners in the stands of the Estadio Nacional in Santiago, 22 September 1973. © Bettmann/Getty Images.

football match. The groundsmen were, after all, bizarrely still tending the pitch. After sitting on the terraces for days, some brave souls tried to keep their spirits up by shouting 'goal!' whenever a groundsman's mower passed between the posts. Below, in the stadium's vast complex of rooms, and in the adjacent velodrome, internees were interrogated, starved and tortured. Accompanied by the sounds of the Beatles and Rolling Stones, their bones were broken, they faced mock firing squads, or they were executed. News of these crimes soon spread across Chile and internationally.[8]

Into this Cold War cauldron, as if by fate, dropped a pair of ideologically charged football matches. In recent qualifications for the 1974 World Cup finals in West Germany, the Soviet Union had topped European qualifying Group 9, while Chile had come top of South American Group 3. However, because they were the group winners with the worst records, under FIFA's complex rules for the tournament, the Soviet Union and Chile – friends under Allende but now sworn enemies under Pinochet – had to compete for the last spot at the finals in a two-legged, intercontinental play-off. The dates of the two games had been set a month before Pinochet's coup. The first match was to take place on 26 September in Moscow's Lenin Stadium. The second was scheduled for 21 November in the Estadio Nacional in Santiago.

In contrast with his ally in Brazil, Emilio Médici, Augusto Pinochet was highly suspicious of football. Amateur football in Chile had a strong left-wing bent and several players in the professional game, including internationals Leonardo Véliz and Carlos Caszely, had actively supported Allende's Road to Socialism. Véliz feared for his life on the day of Allende's death and hid his Marxist books and music cassettes in the attic in case the military came calling. Soon after seizing power, Pinochet publicly accused Caszely, whose family members were well-known communists, of treason. Despite this, recently declassified documents reveal the dictator effectively ordered professional football to be left alone. Attacking the number one sport in the country, and especially its star players, would, he realised, make his regime deeply unpopular.[9]

Pinochet's anti-communist instincts told him to outlaw the World Cup play-off games against the Soviet Union, just as Franco had refused to engage with the same mortal enemy in the European Championship quarter-finals back in 1960. But these were tempered by the views of the Chile Football Association and especially its vice-president, Retired Admiral Carlos Chubretovic, who argued, like Franco's football advisors in 1964, in favour of the matches' propaganda potential.[10] Henry Kissinger, who had contacts with Pinochet, likely took the same line. A lover of football since playing it as a boy in Bavaria, Kissinger consistently used the game as a diplomatic or intelligence-gathering tool. In 1969, he'd learned Moscow was secretly building a submarine base in Cuba thanks to seeing U2 spy-plane photographs of football fields designed for off-duty Soviet seamen. At a Moscow summit in late 1973, Kissinger chewed the fat with Leonard Brezhnev about the skills of Brazilian winger Garrincha. A few years later, he helped arrange Pelé's move to New York Cosmos as part of a broader plan to improve relations between the US and Brazil.[11]

The Chile football team didn't have a strong track record. Its high point to date had been third place in the 1962 World Cup finals, thanks in part to a historic victory over the Soviet Union in the quarter-finals, mentioned in Chapter 4. Since then, the Chilean team had achieved little but its form had improved in the early 1970s. Confidence was also boosted by the club side Colo-Colo's recent success in becoming the first-ever Chilean team to reach the final of South America's most prestigious club tournament, the Copa Libertadores. Beating the Soviet Union again was not, it seemed, beyond the realms of possibility.[12]

The Soviet Football Federation initially had mixed feelings about playing Pinochet's Chile. On the one hand, agreeing to the games ran counter to the Kremlin's efforts to ostracise Pinochet's regime. Moscow and its Eastern bloc satellites had severed diplomatic relations with Santiago soon after Allende's overthrow. On the other hand, Brezhnev loved football ('I play the left side', he once told US President Gerald Ford, jesting perhaps) and refusing to play the games obviously risked jeopardising the Soviet Union's World Cup place. On paper, the Soviets were among the favourites to win the World Cup in 1974. In 1972, they'd reached the final of the European Championship in Belgium and come third, alongside East Germany, at the Munich Olympics. The only downside was the Soviets' recent form. In their last four home games the team had managed to score only one goal, while its usually sturdy rearguard had conceded five. The Federation decided to go ahead with the two games, probably confident in the belief that an experienced Soviet side was odds on to beat Chile over 180 minutes.[13]

Coming as it did only a fortnight after Salvador Allende's death, the first meeting between Chile and the Soviet Union, in Moscow on

26 September, was always going to be a tense affair. On landing at Moscow Airport, the Chilean players felt like they'd entered a lion's den. No Chilean or Soviet diplomats greeted them, and the immigration authorities temporarily detained two players, Carlos Caszely and defender Elías Figueroa, for alleged irregularities in their passports. During their stay downtown, Muscovites treated the Chile delegation with thinly veiled contempt. True stories of Pinochet's attacks on Soviet citizens in Santiago may have been behind this. Rumours also got around of the KGB's plans to hold the Chilean players as hostages in exchange for the release of communist prisoners held by Pinochet's regime. Soviet psychological warfare or not, the Chilean team could have barely felt more unsettled before its most testing game in years.[14]

Come the day of the game, the two teams were well-matched. The Soviet side had Yevhen Rudakov in goal, a Ballon d'Or nominee in 1971 and 1972; defender Revas Dzodzuashvili, named in the team of the 1972 European Championship; midfielder Arkady Andreasan, from Soviet league champions Ararat Yerevan; and a clutch of Dynamo Kyiv legends including midfielder Volodymyr Muntyan and striker Oleg Blokhin. The Chile team boasted central defender Elías Figueroa, three times South American player-of-the-year in the 1970s; Leonardo Véliz, a left-winger (in both senses of the word) who played for Colo-Colo; Caszely, a forward nicknamed 'king of the square metre' for his ability in the penalty box; and Francisco Valdés, midfield general and, to this day, the top scorer in the history of the Chilean league.

As Chile strode onto the field in the imposing Lenin Stadium, they were greeted by the deafening sound of 60,000 high-pitched whistles. Before kick-off, highly abnormally, no anthems were played and no pennants exchanged. Once the game started, it was clear to everyone that Chile had travelled 8,000 miles to do just one thing: park the bus. Under strict instructions from their coach Luis Alamos, Chile's defenders rarely left the edge of their penalty box, let alone their half. In the first forty-five minutes, Chile barely got into Soviet territory at all. When they did, Caszely's job appeared to be to either get fouled or commit a foul, wasting as much time as possible. Counter-attacks didn't seem to be part of Alamos' plans at all. Bustling and bruising did.

The second half was much the same as the first. The Chileans played attritional football, the Soviets got frustrated, and tempers flared. The Brazilian referee, Armando Marques, didn't help matters by appearing to favour Chile; Véliz would later claim this was because he hated communism. The Soviets did create the odd chance. Blokhin came closest, hitting the post from close range after a typically brilliant run. But otherwise, the Soviets ran into a wall engineered by the centre-halves Figueroa and Alberto Quintano, the real stars of the match. The longer the game went on, the more desperate the Soviet players and fans grew. Soviet coach Yevgeny Goryansky pushed his players further up field and threw on more forwards as substitutes. It made no difference. The game ended 0–0.[15]

For the Soviets, the result was a disaster. They had not only failed to score, meaning they had no cushion to take to Santiago for the second leg. They hadn't looked like scoring either, against a team that, given the political turmoil at home, should have been a pushover. For the Chileans, it was mission accomplished. Pinochet publicly congratulated the team 'on behalf of the people of Chile'. The draw in Moscow was 'the most important result in the history of Chilean soccer', proclaimed *Estadio* magazine, and, it added, proof of the junta's restoration of national discipline.[16]

The bad-tempered stalemate in the Lenin Stadium only upped the Cold War ante. This spelt trouble, especially for FIFA. A fortnight after the scoreless draw, on 12 October, at a meeting of FIFA's World Cup organising committee in West Germany, the Soviets threw a spanner in the works: they wanted the return leg, scheduled for late November in Santiago, to be moved to a neutral venue owing to the political situation in Chile. Chilean officials firmly rejected this request. Its new government, they said, could assure everyone that the match was playable and that the Soviet team would be safe on Chilean soil. The organising committee, chaired by FIFA's veteran president Sir Stanley Rous, who'd first crossed swords with the Soviets during Dynamo Moscow's tour of Britain back in 1945, decided to send a two-man delegation to Santiago to investigate matters on the spot. Initially, Abílio d'Almeida, FIFA's Brazilian vice-president, and Helmut Riedel, East Germany's FIFA delegate, agreed to go. When, perhaps under Soviet pressure or afraid that he'd be manipulated by Pinochet, Riedel withdrew, FIFA's Swiss general-secretary, Helmut Käser, took his place.[17]

Why did the Soviets call for a change of venue? We can't know for sure due to an absence of documentation, but for many people over the decades the answer has been simple enough: disgust at General Pinochet's conversion of the Estadio Nacional into a hellhole.[18] This was certainly a factor but it's far more likely the Soviets were driven not by principle but politics. In 1960, Moscow had railed against Francoist Spain for boycotting matches against the Soviet Union and thereby bringing Cold War politics into sport. Now the tables were turned. The Kremlin wanted to exploit the propaganda value of opposing Pinochet's regime. Highlighting the junta's barbarous actions in the Estadio Nacional and the Soviet Union's refusal to play there fitted in with this perfectly.[19] In fact, a week before the Moscow match, at a meeting at FIFA's headquarters in Zurich, Soviet officials had raised no objections to playing in the Estadio Nacional, despite widespread reports, including in the Soviet press, of the atrocities being committed there. After failing to beat Chile in Moscow, however, the officials changed their tune. Years later, several members of the Soviet squad, including defender Evgeny Lovchev, claimed that their coach and government officials feared defeat was likely in Santiago.[20]

Billed as a fact-finding mission, Käser and d'Almeida's two-day visit to Santiago in late October was a political and diplomatic whitewash. It resembled a similar FIFA mission Rous had spearheaded to apartheid South Africa in the early 1960s.[21] Santiago was a frightening and frightened city after six weeks of state-sanctioned terrorism but there was not a hint of this in the FIFA men's report. Ordinary people on the streets 'looked happy', they said. Vice-Admiral Patricio Carvajal Prado, the new Minister of National Defence, assured Käser and d'Almeida personally that the Soviet team would be given 'a warm welcome' and that the Estadio Nacional would be empty of detainees by early November. In the stadium itself, where the hundreds of remaining prisoners had been hidden from view for the day, nauseating photographs showed Käser and d'Almeida laughing and joking with journalists. Their report stated that the Estadio Nacional was nothing like Dante's Inferno but merely a 'clearing station' for detainees whose political activities before and after the recent coup had yet to be established. The terraces were clear, a grandstand was being repainted, and, the FIFA duo said rosily, the pitch was in perfect condition. Käser and d'Almeida concluded that there was nothing whatsoever to stop the match planned for 21 November going ahead in Santiago, where 'life is back to normal'.[22]

This wasn't FIFA's finest hour. Many football writers have since heavily criticised the organisation for colluding with Pinochet's regime in giving the Estadio Nacional a clean bill of health.[23] In early November, by a large majority vote, FIFA's World Cup organising committee accepted

Käser and d'Almeida's report. Käser notified the Soviets of this and drew their attention to FIFA's rules, which stated if a team refused to play a scheduled World Cup match it would be disqualified from the tournament. The Soviet football federation reacted to this 'warning' by launching a public assault on FIFA. Designed to generate international support for its cause and shame FIFA into changing its mind, its statement declared that an atmosphere of 'bloody terrorism' existed in Pinochet's Chile. The whole world knew that the Estadio Nacional had been turned into 'a concentration camp', it said, and Soviet footballers could not possibly play at a venue 'stained with the blood of Chilean patriots'.[24]

This rhetoric failed to force FIFA into giving the Soviets what they wanted but it did add to the international controversy over the game. The world's press now started to crawl all over the FIFA quarrel, with many newspapers in both the East and West taking Moscow's side.[25] Embarrassed by this, FIFA suggested a compromise. In strict secrecy, Käser asked Chilean and Soviet officials whether they would agree to play the final eliminator in another Chilean city, like Viña del Mar. In a long, angry telex accusing the Soviets of political blackmail, the Chileans refused. The Soviets disdainfully wrote a single sentence to FIFA, saying a match in Chile would be 'impossible'. On 12 November, FIFA informed the news media that the Soviet Union had excluded itself from the match and would therefore not be taking part in the 1974 World Cup finals.[26]

If FIFA hoped this ruling now put the painful Chile–Soviet Union issue to bed, they were wrong. International football had entered uncharted territory, and an issue that was already enmeshed deeply in the Cold War became even more politicised. As the *New York Times*, not a newspaper known for its interest in football, correctly pointed out, this was the first time a team had disqualified itself from the World Cup for political reasons since the start of the competition in 1930. The Soviet Union didn't take FIFA's decision lying down. Soviet papers expressed outrage at FIFA's siding with Chile's 'executioners'. East Germany's news agency castigated FIFA for flouting 'all moral principles' and called for a rescinding of the Soviet ban. Rumours quickly spread that the Soviet bloc would boycott the World Cup unless FIFA changed its mind. Letters of complaint the organisation received from football federations across Eastern Europe, Africa and Latin America suggested other countries might follow suit.[27]

It was amidst this furore that the long-disputed match between Chile and the Soviet Union in the Estadio Nacional on 21 November finally took place. Or kind of. Everyone knew the Soviets weren't going to be there, but technically Chile still needed to take to the field to qualify for the World Cup finals. FIFA told the Chile team it should treat the game like any other: don kit, line up on the pitch, kick-off, and score a goal, after which it would be awarded a 2–0 walkover. This might appear risible (and it did), but it would hopefully, so FIFA thought, put a line under everything.

An estimated crowd of 17,000 turned up to watch the non-match. The spectators were not, as some have since argued, prisoners. Two weeks earlier, all of the remaining detainees in the Estadio Nacional had been transferred to a salt-mining town a thousand miles away in the Atacama Desert. Leonardo Véliz thought the spectators had merely come along to laugh at him and his teammates but they made little noise. This might have been out of respect for those who'd recently been tortured in the impromptu holding pens below. It could also have been due to the soldiers ringing the touchline. FIFA and the Chilean football association presumably wanted as many spectators there as possible, to help lend the match credibility. To boost numbers, the 'ghost-match' was followed immediately by a real one, a friendly between the Chile team and the great Brazilian club Santos. Pelé, still Santos' number one attraction, was injured and not there.[28]

Immediately before the World Cup match kicked off, the stadium announcer explained that the Chilean team would score a 'goal of honour' – no irony intended – in compliance with FIFA's rules. It had been arranged beforehand that the scorer would be Chamaco Valdés. An odd choice, in some respects. Valdés was a member of the footballers' trade union and had recently helped free a fellow union activist and former footballer, Hugo Lepe, from the Estadio Nacional after bravely meeting with General Pinochet. As a leftist, he just might have been tempted to blaze his precious shot over the bar in a grand gesture of defiance, leaving the match in an embarrassing void. But, crucially, Valdés was also the team captain, a man who was trusted not to screw things up. He couldn't take his teammates down with him. If he did, who knows what Pinochet might do to them all?

Véliz and others hated playing the match, for being used, as they saw it, as political pawns by the Pinochet regime. The footage suggests that not all of the Chile players felt this way, though. Valdés' goal was greeted by genuine excitement by some of the players, a recognition perhaps that, after all the shenanigans, they had booked their places at the World Cup finals. Quite why the players quickly grabbed the ball and headed back to the halfway line to place it on the centre spot for a restart is anyone's guess. Instinct perhaps, but the match was over and done. Minutes later, the scoreboard high above the stadium terraces confirmed the result. The cheery slogan immediately above it – 'Youth and Sport United in Chile Today' – was as questionable as the game itself.[29]

In the friendly against Santos, Chile were thrashed 5–0. This might have put the dampeners on the celebrations for some people there. It was a result that certainly didn't augur well for the next summer's World Cup. The Chilean press had no doubts about what the day meant, however. The dispute surrounding the match had already justified the junta's overthrow of Moscow's Marxist ally, Allende, it said. Now, their nation had defeated 'Goliath' at home and, more importantly, scored a moral victory over international communism.[30]

The Soviet Union had gambled. It had put all its chips on red, tried to hassle FIFA into taking away Chile's home fixture, and lost. Desperate to still go to the World Cup finals, it now took things to a new level, largely by playing the man rather than the ball. During the Cold War, the Soviet authorities often galvanised support for the national team by portraying it as the victim of pro-capitalist bias within world football. In the days that followed the ghost game in Santiago, the media in the Soviet bloc accused Stanley Rous of engineering a gigantic conspiracy. The FIFA president had insisted that the match be played at the Estadio Nacional, TASS and others claimed, in the hope that the Eastern bloc would retaliate by boycotting the World Cup finals. This would allow Rous' England, who had failed to qualify, a backdoor entry into the tournament. No evidence of this was produced and none has been found since.[31]

When this tactic failed, the Soviet media accused Rous of double standards. Due to the Troubles in Northern Ireland, FIFA had recently switched the venue of a World Cup qualifier between Northern Ireland and Bulgaria from Belfast to Sheffield in England. If Rous had no qualms about holding matches at neutral stadiums in times of political upheaval, *Soviet Sport* asked, what kept him from putting pressure on the Chileans in this case? Rous' legitimate answer to this was that the initiative for the recent switch had come from the Northern Irish and that both countries and FIFA had agreed to it. As a consequence, he argued, Moscow's demand for a special meeting of FIFA's World Cup organising committee to hear the Soviet Union's case was groundless.[32]

FIFA came under extraordinary pressure to replay the Chile–Soviet Union match in other ways too, including hundreds of angry letters. An East German youth football organisation compared the situation at the Estadio Nacional to the Nazi death camps and asked if Rous would have approved of a match at Dachau or Sachsenhausen. British boys' teams challenged FIFA's decision-making, as did several West European football federations such as the Netherlands, one of the favourites for the World Cup. Ordinary football fans from countries like Austria and West Germany sent FIFA copies of newspaper cartoons depicting hooded Chilean executioners playing keep-ups with skulls and guillotines being rigged to the goals in the Estadio Nacional. Helmut Käser took time out to respond personally to many of these missives. He received death threats and the Swiss police gave him instructions on how to deal with suspect bomb packages.[33]

For all the media speculation and Moscow's rumourmongering, the Soviet Union seems not to have tried seriously to organise an Eastern bloc boycott of the World Cup finals. To have done so, and met with opposition from its satellites, risked publicly exposing the bloc's weaknesses. Moscow would have had to push its fellow communists extremely hard indeed to agree to a boycott. East Germany had qualified for the finals for the first time ever and Poland for the first time since 1938. Bulgaria, in contrast, had been at every World Cup finals since 1962 and so thought of itself as a permanent fixture at the tournament. This all spoke to the limits of Cold War bloc solidarity in the face of football's overwhelming popularity and national importance.

On 5 January 1974, at a long-scheduled meeting in Frankfurt, FIFA's World Cup organising committee confirmed officially that Chile had qualified for that year's finals. Later that day, the draw for the tournament was made. This, finally, put an end to the whole affair.[34] The Soviets were livid; this was another 'shameful' decision, they said, that violated 'the ideals of sport'. Six months later, the Soviets exacted a measure of revenge by helping ensure Stanley Rous lost the FIFA presidency to the Brazilian former Olympic swimmer João Havelange. Revolutionary change ensued, though not to Moscow's liking, as

Havelange, an ex-arms trader, turned FIFA into a vast, commercially oriented corporation.[35]

From Pinochet's perspective, Chile's sporting and political struggles to win itself a place at the World Cup finals in 1974 had doubtless been worth it, but his team had a dismal time in West Germany. Pinochet's efforts to use the tournament to boost his regime's image came to little. Chile lost their opening match to the hosts 1–0, thanks to a long-range effort from Bayern Munich's maverick defender Paul Breitner, who boasted of having read the works of Marx, Lenin and Mao. In the game, Carlos Caszely achieved infamy by becoming the first player to receive a red card at a World Cup finals. Chile then drew 1–1 with East Germany and, crucially, 0–0 with the little-fancied newcomers Australia, and so were eliminated from the World Cup with only two points.

Off the pitch, things weren't so good either. Anti-Pinochet protesters targeted Chile's team at the World Cup as a way of publicising the plight of Chilean political prisoners. During Chile's matches, exiles and European activists conspicuously waved socialist banners. In the game against Australia, a handful even managed to break the police cordon and run onto the field in front of the television cameras (see Figure 6.3). Hostility towards the Chilean delegates in West Germany was so intense that they always travelled in a group with thirty security guards. At first, Chile's players refused to answer journalists' questions about Pinochet's regime, which led to speculation they had been threatened or brainwashed. When, in response to this, they started charging fifty dollars an interview, the hostility increased. None of the players dared to criticise the junta openly. Prior to the team's departure for West Germany, Carlos Caszely had boldly refused to shake hands with Pinochet, allegedly in response to the regime having tortured his mother with burning cigarettes. But he was not about to put his family at further risk while he was playing in West Germany. After the World Cup, Caszely could escape to Spain, having signed for Levante a year earlier.[36]

Outside of Chile, few people nowadays will probably have heard of Carlos Caszely or any of his 1974 World Cup teammates. Not so Daniel Passarella, Osvaldo Ardiles or Mario Kempes. Today, their names instantly conjure the excitement of the spectacular 'tickertape' World Cup in Argentina four years later. Argentina won that tournament and in so doing scored a massive propaganda coup for General Jorge Rafael

Figure 6.3 In heavy rain, anti-Pinochet demonstrators disrupt Chile's match against Australia in Berlin, 22 June 1974. The game ended goalless. © Rolls Press/Popperfoto via Getty Images/Getty Images.

Videla, the country's dictator. It's open to debate whether, as David Winner and others claim, the 1978 World Cup is the beautiful game's ugliest moment. But there's no doubt it put a cap on the Cold War caudillos' sports-washing successes of the 1970s.[37]

The dull but sadistic Videla ruled Argentina from 1976 to 1983. For most of this period, Buenos Aires was the operations centre for Plan Condor, a US-organised, anti-communist alliance between the dictatorships of Argentina, Bolivia, Brazil, Uruguay, Paraguay, Peru and Pinochet's Chile. Using American intelligence and counter-insurgency support, Videla conducted a 'dirty war' that made Pinochet's regime look almost benign. His junta targeted not only left-wing guerrillas but trade unionists, priests, Jews, psychoanalysts and schoolchildren, together with the relatives of real and imagined subversives. An estimated 30,000 people were 'disappeared' and tens of thousands were tortured, raped and imprisoned without trial. Victims were thrown alive out of aircraft into the South Atlantic. Pregnant women were murdered after giving birth and their babies adopted by the families of childless generals.[38]

Videla's use of the 1978 World Cup to bolster domestic support and massage his unsavoury international image bore more than a passing resemblance to Hitler's hosting of the 1936 Berlin Olympics. The dictator was inadvertently helped by João Havelange, who was eager to expand tournament participation by Global South countries and signed up corporate sponsors to buttress his financial influence and political power. Many of the same human rights groups that had carried anti-Pinochet banners in West Germany in 1974 called stridently for an international boycott. Videla retaliated by hiring an American public relations firm to polish his junta's public profile, stirring up Argentinians by telling them all foreigners hated them, and claiming that his country was playing for the 'Christian West'. Paul Breitner and three-time European footballer-of-the-year, Holland's Johan Cruyff, sat out the tournament. Thirty years later, Cruyff denied any political motives and attributed his action to his family having recently been a victim of a brutal kidnap attempt.[39]

With supreme irony, Videla's Argentina won their first World Cup with a communist manager, César Luis Menotti. *El Flaco* – the skinny one – who came from a Peronist family, never spoke publicly about politics during the tournament but encouraged his team to play the sort of 'left-wing', emancipatory football favoured in the country's shanty towns. Into this free-flowing 'fútbol villero', Menotti injected a greater intensity and discipline in the hope that the Argentinian game would be better equipped to compete with European giants like the Netherlands and West Germany. His approach paid off, but that's only half of the story.[40]

Argentina's progress through the World Cup was pockmarked by allegations of cheating. The hosts' early victories over Hungary and France were tarnished by dubious refereeing decisions around penalties and sendings off. In the second round, Argentina overcame Poland thanks partly to striker Mario Kempes diving full length to palm away a certain Poland equaliser. Crucially, needing to then beat a strong Peru team by at least four goals to reach the final, Argentina won 6–0. The jury is still out on why the Peruvians played so abysmally. Many put it down to the Argentine junta bribing some of their players and negotiating a deal with Peruvian officials over grain shipments. Others claim Peru's government agreed to throw the match as part of the Condor Plan: in exchange for Videla's regime torturing troublesome Peruvian dissidents. General Videla is said to have visited the Peruvian dressing room before the match (with Henry Kissinger, who'd recently retired as US Secretary of State) and lectured the players on the need for Latin American solidarity.[41]

The final between Argentina and the Netherlands in the Estadio Monumental in Buenos Aires on 25 June was a masterclass in Argentine gamesmanship. The Dutch were brought to the stadium by a scenic route through the city's raucous backstreets and once there were kept waiting on the pitch by the hosts for nearly ten minutes as the crowd howled at them. The Argentinians then protested over the protective arm cast worn by René van de Kerkhof, despite his having worn it in earlier games without objections, infuriating the Dutch players and delaying kick-off for another fifteen minutes. During the match, the occasional pieces of flair were heavily outnumbered by misdeeds by both teams but especially the hosts: handling, time-wasting, and nasty fouls, including Argentina's captain Daniel Passarella laying out Johan Neeskens with a punch to the face. Argentina eventually won 3–1 after extra time, with Kempes scoring twice (see Figure 6.4).

As Videla presented the World Cup to Passarella, across Argentina people poured on to the streets to celebrate with a nationalistic fervour

Figure 6.4 Mario Kempes (arms aloft) scores his second goal to give Argentina a 2–1 lead in extra time against the Netherlands in the Estadio Monumental in Buenos Aires, 25 June 1978. © STAFF/AFP via Getty Images.

perhaps unmatched in the history of the World Cup. Sickeningly, among the delirious throng in Buenos Aires were inmates of the junta's nearby torture centre, the infamous Naval Mechanics School. Overcome by Argentina's victory, the centre's torturer-in-chief had ordered a handful of his prisoners into a car so they could drive around the city and celebrate. One of them, Graciela Daleo, asked if she could put her head through the car's sunroof. 'I stood up and looked out', she recounted years later. 'I couldn't believe what I was seeing. Rivers and rivers of people singing, dancing, shouting. I began to cry, because I remember thinking if I start shouting "I'm disappeared," no one's going to give a damn. This was the most concrete proof I ever had that I had ceased to exist.'[42]

7 US AGAINST US, OR US AGAINST THEM?
West Germany vs. East Germany, Hamburg, June 1974

Saturday 22 June 1974. A warm Saturday night at the Volksparkstadion in Hamburg. It's just after 9 p.m. and a crowd of 60,000 is watching a bad game of football between two local rivals. But this is no ordinary derby. It's East versus West, communism versus capitalism, dictatorship versus democracy: the first and only time that the two halves of divided Germany, the German Democratic Republic (GDR) and the Federal Republic of Germany (FRG) – separate nations since 1949, partitioned by the Berlin Wall since 1961 – play a FIFA-accredited match. And it's happening at the World Cup. In West Germany. The political stakes could hardly be higher.

As the game drifts towards a scoreless draw, East German goalkeeper Jürgen Croy gathers the ball after another West German attack founders. He arcs it to the right-hand side of the field, where it finds substitute Erich Hamann. The midfielder is in space and ambles into the West German half. He's under no pressure. Freeze-frame the game here, and it looks like a half-paced friendly, not a World Cup clash for the ages. Hamann looks up and lofts a pass towards the penalty area, where it finds striker Jürgen Sparwasser. The FC Magdeburg man chests the ball down and charges into the box, past the uncharacteristically flailing figure of Franz Beckenbauer. As goalkeeper Sepp Maier rushes out, Sparwasser lifts the ball over him and into the roof of the net (see Figure 7.1). Sparwasser does an ungainly forward roll, then celebrates

Figure 7.1   Jürgen Sparwasser scores the winning goal for East Germany vs. West Germany, Hamburg, 22 June 1974. © STAFF/AFP via Getty Images.

with his teammates. Fifteen minutes later, Uruguayan referee Ramón Barreto Ruíz blows the final whistle. The underdogs have defeated the hosts and favourites in their backyard. The *Bruderduell* ('brothers' duel') has gone the way of socialism.

Saturday 9 January 1988. Another West German city, another East German team. The veterans of FC Magdeburg are in Saarbrücken for an indoor tournament. Among the old pros are members of the GDR's 1974 World Cup squad: Wolfgang Seguin, Joachim Streich and Jürgen Sparwasser. On the morning of the 9th, the squad are sightseeing, when Sparwasser disappears in a department store. He's still missing when the squad meets for lunch. Back at the team hotel, Seguin discovers all Sparwasser's possessions are gone, bar his FCM tracksuit. There's a note from Sparwasser and his wife, Christa: 'Forgive us ... We have decided not to return to the GDR ... It is difficult for us to separate from you, but there was no other choice.'[1] The truth is clear. The GDR's most iconic footballer has committed the treasonous act of *Republikflucht* ('flight from the Republic') to seek asylum in West Germany.

Fourteen years separated the greatest night of Jürgen Sparwasser's career from his final act as a GDR citizen. When he retired in 1979, he'd represented East Germany 49 times, scoring 14 goals, and played 298 games for FC Magdeburg, notching 133 goals. Sparwasser won the East German Cup four times and the East German league three times. He was integral to the Magdeburg team that beat AC Milan in May 1974 to win the European Cup Winners' Cup, the only GDR team to claim a UEFA trophy. Sparwasser, though, never escaped that moment in the Volksparkstadion. 'You'd only have to write "Hamburg '74" on my gravestone and everyone would know who it is', he once remarked. He later told journalist Thomas Blees that the goal against West Germany 'damaged me'.[2] After such an historical moment, heavy lies the socialist crown. In the end, it was too heavy for Sparwasser to bear.

Jürgen Sparwasser's story shows the political and human complexities of Germany's ultimate Cold War football match, a game in which not everything was as it seemed, on or off the pitch. West Germany lost on the night, but won the tournament, while East Germany didn't win another game. West Germany's star players would scale further heights, while, for most of the GDR squad, 1974 was as good as it got. In the age of détente, there were signs that East–West relations were thawing, in sport as in politics. But that didn't stop the GDR's secret police, the Stasi, from placing the 1974 game under blanket surveillance. The Stasi's solicitude reflected a wider truth. The 'us against us' game in Hamburg meant more to East Germans than it did to their West German frenemies. In the glorious history of West German football, the Sparwasser goal is an awkward footnote. In the old East Germany, it's a nostalgic touchstone in a faded football landscape – a reminder of the importance sport once had in shaping a divided nation.

The draw for the 1974 World Cup took place on 5 January in Frankfurt. Compared to the protracted celebrity razzmatazz that accompanies this event in the twenty-first century, it looks quaint. Football's biggest tournament was then on the cusp of modernity, six months before João Havelange replaced Sir Stanley Rous as FIFA President. A freckled kid in a suit, plucked from a boys' choir in West Berlin, is the only helping hand for the FIFA delegates, as the sixteen qualified teams are placed into groups of four. It's all very low key. There is, though, one exciting moment, when shocked silence yields to loud applause. It's when East Germany is placed alongside the seeded hosts, plus Australia and Chile, in Group 1. *Die Neue Fußballwoche* was unsure about the draw. West Germany, the 1972 European champions, were 'the hot favourites', reported chief editor Klaus Schlegel, but the GDR, making its finals debut, wasn't there to make up the numbers: 'Our football doesn't need to hide!' On the West German side, ex-national team striker Uwe Seeler spoke for the confident majority: 'For me, the matter is perfectly clear. We're going to the second round!'[3]

East and West Germany weren't football strangers. The two countries had met at the 1972 Olympics. Eighty thousand people in Munich's Olympic Stadium watched the GDR defeat the FRG 3–2 to reach the semi-finals, thanks to a late goal from striker Eberhard Vogel. But the game was misleading, as were the two previous all-German encounters, in qualifying matches for the 1960 Olympics in Rome and the '64 Games in Tokyo (one win apiece). A glance at the lineups on 8 September 1972 tells us why. The 'amateurs' in the East German eleven include many of the subsequent World Cup squad: Croy, Sparwasser, Streich, Seguin, captain Bernd Bransch and Dynamo Dresden striker Hans-Jürgen Kreische. The only familiar names in the West German lineup are the two goalscorers and later Bayern Munich legends, Uli Hoeneß and Ottmar Hitzfeld, only one of whom, Hoeneß, had a noteworthy playing career. Hoeneß and Hitzfeld, like their team-mates, were amateurs, as professional athletes were barred from the Olympics. As the East German authorities privately conceded, this wasn't the real West German team. The 1974 game would be the first proper game between the divided halves of a football-mad nation.

The contest took place against an uncertain political backdrop. In the Bonn Republic, the comedown from the 1960s, a decade of economic growth and political reawakening, was in full effect by 1974, as West Germans grappled with the aftershocks of the 1973 oil crisis. The 'new sobriety' wasn't just about belt-tightening. The World Cup came two years after the Munich Olympics, an expensive spectacular ruined by tragedy, when Palestinian terrorists kidnapped and killed eleven Israeli athletes. The scars of Munich, notably the botched West German hostage rescue at Fürstenfeldbruck airfield, meant few people were in the mood for another sporting jamboree. Security measures were tight, with one Munich newspaper calling the 1974 World Cup 'a police sports festival'.[4] Fittingly, in this age of reduced expectations,

West Germany had a new leader. The magnetic former mayor of West Berlin, the Social Democrat Willi Brandt, had resigned in May after an East German spy was found to be working in the Chancellor's office. Brandt's replacement was the quintessential safe pair of hands, former Finance Minister Helmut Schmidt.

There was new leadership in East Berlin too. In May 1971, Erich Honecker, the former head of East Germany's youth organisation, ousted died-in-the-wool Stalinist Walter Ulbricht as party leader. The new boss initially presented himself as a reformer, announcing a lavish programme of welfare spending. Perhaps more grudgingly, the ruling SED (Socialist Unity Party of Germany) 'made its peace with jeans and long hair'.[5] Cultural liberalisation created space for a socialist Woodstock, the World Youth Festival in East Berlin in 1973, and films and novels that criticised socialism and frankly depicted sexuality and gender relations.

On the international stage also, East Germany appeared to be loosening up. Working with Willi Brandt and Egon Bahr, the West German politicians who sought rapprochement with the communist world via *Ostpolitik*, the SED leadership signed the Basic Treaty in December 1972. The FRG and the GDR now recognised each other as separate, sovereign states. Both countries joined the UN in September 1973. Leading Western nations, including the United States, Britain and France, finally accepted the GDR's existence. The Basic Treaty increased contacts with West Germany, in sport and elsewhere. Like currency, pensioners and tourists, athletes could now cross the inner-German border more easily. In May 1974, the two German sports federations signed an agreement for up to eighty annual sports contests.[6] The World Cup clash in Hamburg could hardly have arrived at a more auspicious moment.

Yet 'change through rapprochement', in Bahr's phrase, was easier said than done. Mutual suspicions were deep. West Germany's conservative party, the Christian Democratic Union, had promised not to ratify the Basic Treaty if elected in 1972. Even after the Social Democrats returned to power, and ratified the Treaty, many West Germans queried East Germany's claims to legitimacy. In the West, the GDR remained 'the so-called GDR' long after 1972.

In East Germany, distrust of the 'other' Germany was even more pronounced. Honecker's liberal credentials didn't bear much scrutiny. He'd been heavily involved in the decision to build the Berlin Wall in

1961 and, later in the decade, in repressing Western influences on Beatles-loving youth. The GDR's opening to the world in the early 1970s was accompanied by a huge increase in surveillance. When Honecker came to power in 1971, the Stasi had a full-time staff of just under 49,000. When he was ousted in 1989, the Stasi had more than 91,000 full-time employees, in a population of 16.4 million – plus 180,000 'unofficial informers'. That's one informer for every sixty adults in the country.[7] On Honecker's watch, East Germany became the world's biggest police state.

Stasi expansion very much applied to sport, which became in the 1970s the GDR's most reliable international calling card. As the country racked up Olympic medals by fair means and foul, its leaders sought to regulate sporting contacts with the West, even as they were encouraged. With the next two major international sporting events scheduled for West Germany, the Stasi issued a directive in 1971 that envisaged saturation coverage of elite athletes who ventured across the Iron Curtain.

Football was dangerous to the socialist status quo: an unpredictable, popular and global sport, in which the world's strongest nations, including West Germany, were political enemies. When Oberliga champions Dynamo Dresden hosted Bundesliga champions Bayern Munich in the European Cup in 1973, a huge Stasi offensive kicked into gear. 'Operation Advance' deployed more than 3,000 Stasi staff, countless informers in thirty-six locations, and border, transport and regular police to minimise the exposure of GDR citizens to enemy influences. For the 1974 World Cup, in which East Germany would play at least three matches in West Germany (including one in the still-contested city of West Berlin), Stasi plans were even more smothering. The national team's forty-nine-person delegation included thirteen Stasi operatives.[8] The 1,500 'tourists' permitted to support the team in West Germany were strictly vetted. Genuine fans had no chance of getting tickets. Of the 141 people in the World Cup delegation from Potsdam, 123 were SED members.[9] Some of them, we can safely assume, were Stasi spies.

The shroud of security didn't seem to weigh too heavily on the GDR team, which entered the 1974 World Cup on a thirteen-match unbeaten run. Coach Georg Buschner had a settled team and some outstanding players. There was Jürgen Croy, from Sachsenring Zwickau, who Bayern Munich coach Udo Lattek called 'one of the world's best goalkeepers'. The defence was marshalled by the captain, Hallescher FC Chemie's Bernd Bransch, like Croy a member of the GDR all-time XI voted for by readers of *Die Neue Fußballwoche* in 1989. Also in that team was Bransch's centre back partner, Konrad Weise, of Carl Zeiss Jena, in Johan Cruyff's words 'as snappy a terrier as [Berti] Vogts'.[10] The midfield options were more prosaic, but up front Buschner was spoilt for choice. Forwards included Hans-Jürgen Kreische (Dynamo Dresden), four-time winner of the Oberliga golden boot; Peter Ducke, in the twilight of his career but once named by Pelé as one of the world's ten best strikers; the national team's record goal-scorer, Joachim Streich; and Jürgen Sparwasser. Sparwasser was one of four Magdeburg players in the squad, and they came to the World Cup in especially fine fettle. A month before the tournament, an FCM team featuring Sparwasser, Martin Hoffmann, Jürgen Pommerenke and Wolfgang Seguin beat AC Milan 2–0 in Rotterdam to win the European Cup Winners' Cup. The underdogs were all local boys, who grew up in the small *Bezirk* (county) of Magdeburg. Sparwasser cut his teeth at Lokomotive Halberstadt, just along the road from Pommerenke at Aufbau-Traktor Wegeleben.

As was often the case, however – whether it was cars, currency or the world's game – whatever the GDR could do, the FRG could do better. West Germany entered the 1974 finals as hosts and European champions, with the strongest team in its history. The 1972 Euros quarter-final win over England ('football from the year 2000', gushed *L'Équipe*) was orchestrated by a playmaker, Günter Netzer, who would barely get a game in 1974.[11] Helmut Schön's squad was dominated by Bayern Munich, who, like Magdeburg, were fresh from a continental breakthrough: the club's first European Cup, secured after a 4–0 replay victory over Atlético Madrid on 17 May. Fresh might be the wrong word. Six of Bayern's line-up at the Heysel Stadium in Brussels – Sepp Maier, Paul Breitner, Franz Beckenbauer, Hans-Georg Schwarzenbeck, Uli Hoeneß and Gerd Müller – would play the GDR in Hamburg barely a month later. Fatigue may have contributed to West Germany's lethargic performance on 22 June, but nobody thought about that before the game. The mood in the West German camp was confident, even over-confident. Günter Netzer wasn't alone in dismissing 'East German robot football'. On the morning of the game, West Germany's biggest tabloid, *Bild*, published an article titled 'Why we'll win today', in which Sparwasser was called 'wooden'.[12]

Yet, all was not well behind the scenes. Sequestered at Malente, the tightly policed training camp sixty kilometres from Hamburg, the squad got embroiled on the eve of the tournament in a dispute with the West German FA (the DFB) and team coach Schön about bonuses. This was a form of the generational conflict that happened in many parts of Western society in the long 60s. The older generation, like Schön, born in 1915, found it hard to grasp the material demands of the younger generation, children of the post-war economic miracle: 'All I ever hear from you', he complained at one team meeting, 'is money, money, money!' The squad's most outwardly rebellious player, 'Red' Paul Breitner, was one of the Malente ringleaders. Breitner was a complicated guy. He sported a revolutionary-looking afro and beard and once brought Mao's *Little Red Book* to training, but later signed for Real Madrid, Franco's favourite team, and did ads for McDonald's and Volkswagen. Breitner and his fellow players, led by captain Franz Beckenbauer, demanded 75,000 DM per head for winning the World Cup. The DFB was reluctant to agree.[13] The gulf between the earning capacities of the German squads was wide. East German players received 6,000 M apiece, half in West German DM and half in the GDR's less valuable Ostmark, for their appearances at the 1974 World Cup.[14] The West Germans eventually agreed to a maximum 70,000 DM per player.

While money reared its ugly head in Malente, the GDR training camp at Quickborn appeared to be an open, happier place. The players' long hair and blue jeans, and willingness to talk to the media, belied the 'robot' stereotype, as even conservative West German newspapers noted. But outward appearances could be misleading. The pressure on the East German squad was as great as its freedom of speech and movement was limited. For all the talk of 'just another game', few doubted that the looming match against the class enemy would have political ramifications – for the socialist republic and for its diplomats in football boots.

The 1974 World Cup wasn't a great tournament. Apart from the losing finalists, the Netherlands, whose 'total football' was on fluent display, the football was defensive. No previous World Cup had a lower goals per game average (2.55). Defending champions Brazil, the glorious attacking team of Mexico 1970, finished fourth in 1974, scoring six goals in seven games. The tournament structure didn't help. A second round of group games meant that, with wins worth only two points, teams could play cautiously and advance.

The misfires in 1974 weren't confined to the pitch. The opening ceremony on a rainy day in Frankfurt's Waldstadion was so lame that the crowd chanted for the organisers to get on with the football. After watching Brazil's 0–0 draw with Yugoslavia, attendees might have had a rethink. Perhaps East German pop star Frank Schöbel emerging from a giant plastic football to croon 'Freunde gibt es überall' ('There are friends everywhere') wasn't so bad after all?[15] The game set the tone for an uninspired tournament, played against a nervy political backdrop and in poor weather. Attendances were uneven: the three games in West Berlin's Olympic Stadium sold only 47.3 per cent of their ticket allocation. After Munich '72, security was the priority, not fun or wasteful expenditure. Only two stadiums, in Dortmund and Gelsenkirchen, were purpose-built for the tournament. All venues bar Dortmund's Westfalenstadion were ringed by athletics tracks, which stifled the atmosphere. The 1974 World Cup took place just before football began its journey towards global commercial and cultural ubiquity. Hence the tournament's slightly kitschy, provincial feel: the dull opening and closing ceremonies, the naff marketing designs and the lack of football fever. In contrast to the 2006 World Cup, Germany in 1974 seemed underwhelmed, even abashed by its hosting role. A frustrated DFB chairman Hermann Neuburger asked after the tournament: 'Why couldn't people take the second World Cup win to their hearts?'[16]

The early games in Group 1 reflected the tournament Zeitgeist: low-quality football, political tensions and patchy attendances. With the financial standoff at Malente resolved, West Germany began with a 1–0 win over Chile on 14 June, courtesy of Paul Breitner's superb thirty-five-yard strike. The performance suggested all was still not right in the camp. Boos rang around Berlin's Olympic Stadium, as the hosts struggled against defensive opponents. The most notable occurrence was in the stands, as exiled Chileans unfurled banners against the dictatorship of Augusto Pinochet, who, as we saw in Chapter 6, had seized power from the socialist Salvador Allende the previous September. This previewed the bigger protest at Chile's final group game against Australia in West Berlin, when eight anti-Pinochet protestors entered the field of play after half-time, with a large banner proclaiming 'Chile socialista': the first political pitch invasion in World Cup history.

There were no political dramas at the GDR's opening game, as the debutants secured a comfortable 2–0 victory over fellow newcomers Australia in Hamburg. Just 17,000 people were there. The East Germans took the lead in the fifty-eighth minute, when Colin Curran kicked Jürgen Sparwasser's goal-bound shot into his own net. The highlight of a forgettable game came fifteen minutes later, when substitute Martin Hoffmann's cross was smashed into the net on the half-volley by Joachim Streich. *Die Neue Fußballwoche* warned that better teams would punish the GDR's midfield weaknesses.[17] Still, it was a first World Cup win, even against technically weak, defensive opponents, and not to be sniffed at.

The GDR's performance in its second match against Chile was better, even if the result, a 1–1 draw, was not. Sergio Ahumada cancelled out Martin Hoffmann's close-range header, before Hoffmann and Hansi Kreische hit the woodwork in the final ten minutes. The draw took the East Germans through to the second round, where they were joined by West Germany, 3–0 victors over Australia in Hamburg. A brilliant long-range shot from Wolfgang Overath, under fire after a poor performance against Chile, set the hosts on their way. Bernard Cullmann and Gerd Müller then clinched an easy win. Easy, but unimpressive. There were whistles in the stadium as the West Germans failed to add to their lead after Müller's header in the fifty-third minute. When an angry Franz Beckenbauer misplaced a pass, he spat (or, in Beckenbauer's telling, made 'a derogatory motion') towards the crowd.[18] Rumblings of discontent still swirled around the team, despite its 100 per cent record: Schön was unhappy with his players; Netzer was frozen out because the Bayern nucleus preferred Overath. In contrast, the GDR camp seemed in good spirits. With qualification secure, the East Germans entered the final group game in a relaxed mood. They were, in Georg Buschner's words, 'complete outsiders': 'Nobody expected us to win.'[19]

The stage was set for one of the biggest matches in German football history. Politically, it was far more significant than the World Cup final three weeks later between West Germany and the Netherlands. Both sides made goodwill gestures before the game. The West German government cancelled its annual commemoration of the popular uprising in the GDR on 17 June 1953, a date known provocatively in the West as the 'Day of German Unity'. In return, Erich Honecker allowed an East German bride from Cottbus to join her husband in the West. The match on 22 June marked the first public appearance of the GDR's new 'permanent representative' to Bonn, Michael Kohl. Kohl was joined in the stands by various West German dignitaries, including Chancellor Helmut Schmidt (no football fan, he arrived late); the Minister-President of Rhineland-Pfalz and future Chancellor, Helmut Kohl (a big football fan); and Günter Gaus, the Federal Republic's first permanent representative in East Berlin.

In contrast to the miserable weather that dogged much of the tournament, Saturday 22 June 1974 was a warm, sunny day in Hamburg, with the temperature an ideal 22° for the 7.30 p.m. kick-off. A crowd of 60,341 filled the Volksparkstadion. Millions more watched on television. The live audience included 1,500 East Germans, waving hammer and sickle flags and class-consciously chanting '7-8-9-10-*Klasse* (great)'. The wholesome appearance of the visiting crowd, seemingly dressed in standard-issue clothing from the state-owned department store, told its own story. Communist directives described the tourists as 'normal people' who liked a beer and were under no 'gagging order'. This wasn't true. The 250-strong delegation from Halle, for example, included thirty communist functionaries, 212 SED members, only seven people under the age of twenty-four and just three women. Before departing for West Germany, they'd attended a training course on topics like 'the class struggle between the GDR and the FRG' and 'the current situation in West Berlin'. The exclusionary nature of such touring parties didn't go unnoticed. Workers at a factory in Vetschau near the Polish border questioned the selection process and asked why so few people could go to the World Cup.[20]

With both teams qualified for the second round, the game's political importance outweighed its sporting significance. This created problems for West Germany, who required only a draw to win Group 1. The players knew how much Helmut Schön wanted to win: Schön had played and coached with great success in Dresden before departing for West Germany in 1950 and still had family there. No doubt they wanted to win too. But they didn't *need* to win and that can play tricks on players, particularly when tiredness creeps in. Perhaps this explains the strangely flat approach of the hosts, who, in journalist Ulrich Hesse-Lichtenberger's words, seemed 'like men playing a game they didn't know the rules of'.[21] The East Germans, in contrast, had a clear game-plan. Buschner's team set out to be well-organised, defensively strong and dangerous on the counter-attack. And so, on all three counts, it proved to be.

There's a warning sign in the first minute for the West Germans, when Georg Schwarzenbeck underhits a back pass and almost lets in a sharp-looking Sparwasser. After that, the favourites take tentative control of proceedings. FC Cologne's Heinz Flohe, in his first start of the tournament, fires a long shot over Croy's bar. After slick approach play from Gerd Müller, Jürgen Grabowski drags the ball wide from close range, when perhaps he should have scored. There's no perhaps about the next big chance, at the other end after thirty-two minutes. Reinhard Lauck's cross from the left finds Hansi Kreische unmarked six yards out. But Kreische leans back and volleys over the bar, with the goal gaping. The ever-dangerous Müller has the last opportunity of the half, turning in the box and directing a mishit shot against Croy's left-hand post. At half-time, the West Germans have been the better side, but not by much. Despite a lively atmosphere, the game feels cautious and sterile.

That feeling grows in the second half, as the tension increases and the football gets worse. The game at times seems reduced to a series of misplaced passes, poor crosses and pot shots. The GDR look comfortable at the back and threatening on the break. The hosts, meanwhile, are unravelling. Beckenbauer screams for the ball, but no-one is listening. When Schön calls for Günter Netzer to replace Wolfgang Overath in the sixty-ninth minute, the Real Madrid star is as far from the bench as he can be, hoping he doesn't get the nod. Ten minutes later, Sparwasser latches on to Hamann's through ball and puts the GDR ahead. On East German television, commentator Heinz Florian Oertel ('Sparwasser! Sparwasser! Und Tor!') sounds quietly delighted. There are twelve minutes left and the GDR hold out comfortably. West Germany force some corners and free-kicks but run repeatedly into a dark blue defensive wall. The closest to an equaliser is a Hoeneß long shot that the excellent Croy saves easily. At the final whistle East German players celebrate with their goalkeeper ('a great game from all our players!', enthuses Oertel), while their opponents walk quickly to the dressing room. The television camera shows the man of the hour, Sparwasser, before cutting to Schön as he leaves the pitch alone. For the West German coach, so strongly tied to his hometown of Dresden, this was a most painful defeat (see Figure 7.2).

In East Germany, reactions to the 1–0 victory were joyful but restrained. Georg Buschner captured the mood nicely: 'We've won an

Figure 7.2 The final score, 22 June 1974. © Herbert Kronfeld/ullstein bild via Getty Images.

important match, no more'. Wolfgang Hempel, in *Die Neue Fußballwoche*, cautioned that the Federal Republic remained 'title favourites', while the GDR would again be underdogs against 'the big fish' of Argentina, Brazil and the Netherlands in round two.[22] But there was pride that the GDR's win had been well-earned, as West German defender Georg Schwarzenbeck admitted. Praise for Buschner came from unexpected quarters. Even the anti-communist *Bild* admitted that 'the ice-cool tactician' had got things right.[23]

How did ordinary East Germans feel? Electrician Helmut Klopfleisch supported West Berlin's top team, Hertha BSC, and was known to the Stasi as an enemy of socialism. For him, 22 June 1974 was 'a day of mourning ... The worst of it all was the 300 Party bosses in the stands, waving their little flags with the East German sign, clapping at all the wrong moments because they knew nothing about football'. Klopfleisch's reaction, however, was untypical. As he grudgingly admitted, the GDR's 'lucky win' sparked 'big celebrations' in East Berlin.[24] Many GDR citizens welcomed the underdogs' triumph. It was always nice to give West Germany 'a bloody nose' in sport, one Dynamo Berlin supporter later claimed. Sandra Dassler, thirteen years old in 1974, recalled meeting boastful West Germans on holiday in Hungary, 'with their Mercedes and our Trabant standing next to them', and so joined in the celebrations in her hometown of Meiningen.[25] In Thomas Brussig's 2001 novel *Leben bis Männer* ('Life Until Men'), the narrator, a football coach in Magdeburg, proudly notes an upsurge of interest in football after June 1974: 'We were overrun by kids who wanted to be Sparwasser.'[26]

East German responses to the Sparwasser goal rejected the either/or declarations of loyalty that both German states wanted. They suggest that, in the East at least, a sense of shared identity had survived almost thirty years of Cold War division. Thirteen-year-old Marion Spröte celebrated East Germany's win in Hamburg at her holiday camp in Usedom, but her favourite player remained West German captain Franz Beckenbauer. Frank Leonhard, a Union Berlin supporter, was happy when Sparwasser scored but equally pleased when Paul Breitner and Gerd Müller did the same a few weeks later to give West Germany victory over the Netherlands in the final.[27] Many East Germans, in other words, happily supported two teams in 1974. This wasn't to the communists' liking. Stasi reports from July 1974 gloomily recorded 'national chauvinist' support for West Germany among soldiers in the National People's Army.[28]

Happiness was in short supply in the West German camp on the night of 22 June (see Figure 7.3). Conspiracy theorists have suggested West Germany threw the game against their rivals to get the easier second round draw (Poland, Sweden and Yugoslavia, as opposed to Argentina, Brazil and the Netherlands). The reaction of players, coach and media tells us what an absurd theory this is. *Bild* wasn't the only newspaper lamenting 'the serious mistakes' of the head coach ('Not like that, Mr Schön!' was its headline). Schön himself, deeply upset, appeared to be on the brink of resignation or a breakdown – or both. As for the players, their first response to a humiliating defeat was to get drunk, prompting another weary response from Schön: 'This is not going to help'.[29]

But perhaps it did. What happened next has become the stuff of German football legend. Schön was pulled back from the brink and Franz Beckenbauer took charge, organising the team's move to a new training camp at Kaiserau near Dortmund. The pair shared press conference duties on 23 June, but it was the captain not the coach who did

Figure 7.3 The downcast trio of Uli Hoeneß (left), Paul Breitner and Franz Beckenbauer leave the pitch at Hamburg's Volksparkstadion after West Germany's 1–0 loss to East Germany, 22 June 1974. © Schirner/ullstein bild via Getty Images.

the talking. It's an exaggeration to say that Beckenbauer replaced Schön after the GDR defeat, but the twenty-four hours after the game marked a turning point, one that demonstrated Schön's ability to move with the times. As he'd write in his autobiography: 'A national team coach had a different kind of authority in the Nazi period than the national team trainer in the democratic 60s and 70s.'[30] Beckenbauer, the son of a Bavarian postal worker, had none of Breitner's political radicalism. But he was a more astute politician and businessman, and the ideal representative of the new generation of skilled, marketable and wealthy Bundesliga footballers.

'Shaken awake in time', as Beckenbauer put it, West Germany didn't look back. Uli Hoeneß and Heinz Flohe were dropped, and, despite outside clamour, Günter Netzer jettisoned entirely. Into the team for the second round came Rainer Bonhof, Dieter Herzog and

Bernd Hölzenbein. A 2–0 win over Yugoslavia in Düsseldorf (with goals from Breitner – another screamer – and, inevitably, Müller) was followed by an impressive 4–2 win over Sweden on 30 June. Back at Düsseldorf's Rheinstadion, in sodden conditions, the hosts trailed at half-time but scored four second-half goals to win the game of the tournament. Two goals in two minutes from Overath and Bonhof seemed to have set the West Germans on their way before Roland Sandberg equalised a minute later. Jürgen Grabowski restored West Germany's lead in the seventy-ninth minute. Hoeneß's last-minute penalty, after a dive from Müller, sealed the deal.

Success against Sweden set up a winner-takes-all clash with a strong Polish team, who'd also won their first two second round matches. The prize, thanks to the vagaries of format, was a place in the World Cup final. In the so-called *Wasserschlacht* ('battle in the rain') in Frankfurt's Waldstadion – yes, it was tipping it down again – players struggled to pass the ball, even the great technician Beckenbauer. Poland, led by the tournament's golden boot winner Grzegorz Lato, were the better team, but Sepp Maier was inspired. And the hosts had Gerd Müller, whose typically opportunistic seventy-sixth-minute strike decided the match. After financial feuding, squad divisions, embarrassing defeat and near managerial meltdown, West Germany were one step away from a second World Cup.

Could the GDR make it an all-German final? The ultimate Cold War rematch was, alas, never likely. East Germany's prize for topping Group 1 was the most murderous 'group of death' in World Cup history: defending champions Brazil, a strong Argentinian side (who'd lift the trophy on home soil four years later), and the Netherlands, by common consent the best team in 1974. The GDR opened with a 1–0 defeat to Brazil, courtesy of Rivelino's low freekick in the sixtieth minute (see Figure 7.4). Defensively 'a lot went right', reflected Buschner, but 'only after the game was lost did we remember our attacking qualities'.[31] Sparwasser again looked sharp, while Martin Hoffmann missed a good chance late on.

The result meant East Germany needed at least a draw against the Dutch, who'd just thrashed Argentina 4–0, to avoid elimination. It was a bridge too far. With its core of Ajax players and Rinus Michels as coach, the *Elftal* were too good for the *Auswahl*. In a high-press masterclass in Gelsenkirchen on 30 June, goals from Johan Neeskens and Robbie Rensenbrink secured a 2–0 win. *Die Neue Fußballwoche*

Figure 7.4 Jürgen Sparwasser swaps shirts with goalscorer Rivelino, after Brazil's 1–0 win over East Germany in Hannover, 26 June 1974. © Horstmüller/ullstein bild via Getty Images.

raved about the victors – a reminder that Cold War politics was no barrier to appreciating great football – but was proud of the GDR's efforts. Konrad Weise had marked Cruyff out of the game, but the GDR had lost the ball too easily, played too cautiously, and been ineffective on the counter. The superlatives coming the Dutch team's way, the newspaper concluded, were 'fully deserved'.[32]

After closing with a 1–1 draw against Argentina, the GDR team returned home with a spring in its step. The East German FA's report for 1974 was cautiously optimistic. With a sixth place finish in West Germany, the national team had fulfilled 'realistic expectations', performing well on the pitch and behaving well off it. GDR football, the report concluded, was part of a broad 'international middle class', though still deficient in numerous areas – technique, tactics, speed, heading, tackling and world-class individuals – that would take it to the top of the tree.[33] The head of East German sport, Manfred Ewald, disliked football, preferring the 'discipline and rationalism' of Olympic sports to the 'individualism and fanaticism' of the people's game. And Ewald wasn't impressed at having to attend a reception for the national team after its return from West Germany. 'I have never', he said, 'welcomed a team that didn't win any medals'.[34] Even at the height of its success, in the golden year of 1974, East German football couldn't escape doubts about its value to the communist system.

West Germany and the Netherlands met in the World Cup final in Munich on 7 July 1974. These were two well-matched teams with no great animus for each other: the bitterness came later, as did the sense, in the Netherlands and elsewhere, that the 'wrong' team won the final. If this were true, the Dutch had themselves to blame. They took the lead in the second minute from the penalty spot, Neeskens converting after Hoeneß's foul on Cruyff. Rather than pressing home the early advantage, the total footballers showboated. Breitner equalised from the spot after twenty-five minutes, following Bernd Hölzenbein's swan dive. And just before half time, the ultimate predator, Gerd Müller, did what he did best, turning in the penalty area to give West Germany the lead. The Dutch dominated the second half but found no way past Maier or their inaccuracies with the final pass or shot. West Germany were world champions again.

As both the left-wing Dutch newspaper *De Volkskrant* and East Germany's *Die Neue Fußballwoche* argued, this was a deserved victory over worthy opponents. Rinus Michels praised his team's 'surprisingly good performance' in the tournament, as did many Dutch fans and commentators. Celebrations in West Germany, meanwhile, were muted, especially compared to the euphoria that followed the miracle of Bern in 1954. Sepp Maier complained that 'Germans can organise a World Cup perfectly ... But we don't have the faintest idea about holding a party'.[35] His comment followed the DFB's refusal to allow the players' wives to attend the post-final banquet at Munich's Hilton Hotel. Why wasn't 1974 like 1954 or 2006? An antiquated, protocol-obsessed governing body was part of the problem. Fingers can also be pointed at the bad weather, the ghosts of Munich '72, the egoism and materialism of the players, and a 'denationalisation' of public life following the upheavals of the 60s and détente. We might throw another factor into the mix. In the biggest match of the tournament, the one with the most emotional and political resonance, West Germany had fluffed its lines. How could there be national celebration when your team wasn't even the competition's best Germany?

On 30 April 2018, Munich's Olympic Stadium hosted an unusual football game. 'Re-Enactment of the 1974 East Germany–West Germany Match' featured just two players. The Swiss artist Massimo

Furlan, the man behind the idea, was Sepp Maier. The German actor Franz Beil was Jürgen Sparwasser. Everyone else on the pitch – the other twenty players, the referee and the linesmen – was imagined. For the next ninety minutes, the original commentaries from East and West German television were broadcast in the stadium, as a small audience watched the surreal spectacle of East playing West twenty-eight years after German reunification. As in 1974, not everything went to plan: Beil got injured in the first half. As spectators checked to see whether this was part of the football theatre (someone apparently asked Siri if Sparwasser went off injured in 1974), Furlan carried on alone. After what must have seemed like an interminable wait (performance art, like football matches, can be dull), the ghost of Sparwasser once again scored past the prone figure of Maier. Unlike the real Maier in 1974, though, Furlan as Maier left the field in 2018 to warm applause and flowers.[36]

In the world outside Massimo Furlan's 'Re-Enactment', East and West Germany never met again. The communists were in no rush to put the GDR's 100 per cent record on the line, but it was inadequacy more than avoidance that ensured we never got round two of the fraternal duel. West Germany's 'decline' after 1972 and 1974 included runners-up finishes at the 1976 European Championship and the 1982 and 1986 World Cups. East Germany, in contrast, failed to qualify for another international tournament. Snatching defeat from the jaws of victory became a specialty, earning *die Auswahl* various unkind nicknames: 'the qualification failures', 'the world champions of friendlies', 'the beautiful losers'.

Given performance discrepancies, it's not surprising the two countries didn't play again. The closest they came, ironically, was when the socialist republic no longer existed. A 'festival of German football' in November 1990, organised to celebrate unification a month earlier, was meant to feature a match between East and West Germany in Leipzig. Fears of crowd trouble, however, led to the game's cancellation, with 25,000 tickets already sold. Nostalgists had to be content with a more modest coda: a benefit game between 'Team East' and 'Team West' in 1993, featuring veterans from both 1974 teams. It ended 4–4. Jürgen Sparwasser once more scored the opening goal.

Sparwasser remains the central figure in the Cold War drama in Hamburg on 22 June 1974. Other players went on to greater fame or notoriety: Franz Beckenbauer, for example, became in 1990 only the second man, after Brazil's Mário Zagallo, to win the World Cup as a player and a coach, when West Germany beat Argentina 1–0 to claim the trophy for a third time. After hanging up his boots, Uli Hoeneß had a long, successful and controversial career as general manager and president of Bayern Munich, which ended when he went to prison for tax evasion in 2014. On the East German side, the post-1990 opening of Stasi files revealed that members of the 1974 squad, including Erich Hamann, captain Bernd Bransch and coach Georg Buschner, had been secret police informers.

But it's Sparwasser's story, and goal, that remain etched in collective memory. After the game, rumours swirled that his reward for smiting the class enemy was a house and a West German car. 'This was all rubbish', Sparwasser later recalled. 'There was no big honour and no special bonus'. The goal arguably did him more harm than good. Ex-teammate Martin Hoffmann suggested in 2004 that Sparwasser's moment in the sun 'soon became awkward to him'.[37] It's easy to see how Sparwasser felt caught between two stools. He was no poster boy for the communist regime, but he was the author of one of its most glorious sporting moments. In a department store in Saarbrücken in 1988, the pressures came to a head and Sparwasser chose asylum in the West over fame in the East.

In 1997 the left-wing Berlin newspaper *Jungle World* began interviewing people for a feature titled 'Where were you when Sparwasser scored?' In the first column, the former chairman of the West German Communist Party, Herbert Mies, recalled his reaction: 'I was immediately convinced that this would be the beginning of an easing'.[38] For Mies, 'easing' meant relaxing anti-communist measures in West Germany and the first steps towards a radical leftist collaboration between East and West. The fact that such hopes were pie in the sky is less important than the fact that Mies had them because of a football match. He wasn't alone. The game and goal left their mark on Germans on both sides of the Iron Curtain. Some, like Mies, thought politically. West Germany's permanent representative to East Berlin, Günter Gaus, reflected on a result that 'temporarily' boosted East Germany's self-confidence, while André Brie, a reform-minded SED member, lamented the fact that 'a sporting victory over the FRG was a wretched substitute for the ability to effect real change'.[39] Younger interviewees remembered the game more personally. Music journalist Christoph Gurk, who lived near East Germany's training camp, recalled getting the autographs of the players, including the one he really wanted, Sparwasser. The young East German Marion Spröte was conflicted about the result because she liked Franz Beckenbauer so much.[40]

In the political struggle between East and West, as in the 1974 World Cup, West Germany had the last laugh. German unification in October 1990 incorporated the socialist East into the structures of the West German state. Now the scoreboard read 'Germany 1 GDR 0'.[41] In the decades since the *Wende* ('turn') of 1989–90, the old *Bundesländer* have dominated the political, economic and sporting landscapes of the new Germany. A glance at the Bundesliga since 1991 shows how few East German clubs have played in the division, let alone been competitive there. FC Magdeburg, the local boys made good in 1974, finished fifth in Germany's 2. Bundesliga in 2024/25, after languishing further down the pyramid for much of the previous thirty years. Carl Zeiss Jena, who provided four of the GDR's starting lineup in Hamburg on 22 June 1974, currently play alongside several other ex-East German clubs in the North-East Regional League, the semi-professional fourth tier of German football.

To younger generations, Germany's Cold War division now appears a distant historical event, and the GDR a state they've heard about but never knew. To older *Wessis* ('Westerners'), the forty-year division of their country ended, effectively, in continuity: the same political system, the same football structures, extended in 1990 to the five new *Länder* in the East. For West Germans who love football, the Sparwasser goal might be a blot on a proud national record, but it's easily counterbalanced by the triumphs of 1954, 1974 and 1990, the success of the Bundesliga, the excellent record of West German clubs against East German clubs in UEFA competition or the European Cups of Bayern Munich – not to mention the many, Western-driven football successes since unification. For older East Germans, the Sparwasser goal understandably means more. It's a marker of shared *and* divided national identities ('us against us' was also 'us against them'). It's a nostalgic beacon for a lost country, with all its light and darkness, and lost sporting culture. It's a golden moment in an otherwise modest football history. It's a badge of pride for *Ossi* ('Easterner') identities that have often vanished since unification. And it's an underdog story that can still be 'rubbed in the faces' of West Germans.[42] In the most symbolic match of Germany's football Cold War, there were many winners and many losers. And it's not always been easy to tell one from the other.

8 LEOPARDS ON TRIAL
Zaire vs. Yugoslavia, Gelsenkirchen, June 1974

We're back at the World Cup finals in Germany in June 1974. Just hours before the *Bruderduell* in Hamburg. Zaire, the first Black African nation to reach the World Cup finals, are playing reigning champions Brazil in one of the last games of Group 2. It's the eighty-fifth minute and we're about to witness an incident that will enter into folklore as one of the oddest in football history.

Brazil are already 3–0 up and have won a free kick outside Zaire's penalty box. As Rivelino and Jairzinho stand over the ball, Zaire form a five-man wall. When the referee blows his whistle, right-back Mwepu Ilunga rushes out from the wall and, before any Brazilian has touched it, hoofs the ball long and high into the opposition's half. The Brazilian players look bemused. The crowd jeers. BBC Television commentator John Motson calls it 'a bizarre moment of African ignorance'. Zaire, losers in their first two matches in the tournament, don't just play football badly, it seems. They don't even know the game's basic rules. In the decades ahead, footage of Ilunga's free-kick infringement will be replayed for laughs countless times on television and the internet, with he and his teammates derided as clowns or halfwits.[1]

This chapter shows that the truth behind Mwepu Ilunga's infamous 'moment of madness' can be found in the murky world of Africa's Cold War. In 1974, Zaire, nowadays the Democratic Republic of the Congo, was ruled by Mobutu Sese Seko, a murderous, anti-Soviet dictator bankrolled by both the Americans and Chinese. Taking advantage of this peculiar, dual support, Mobutu had spent vast sums on football for national and personal aggrandisement. He had 'Africanised' the game, partly to distance himself from his early abettors, the CIA. He had hired a top-notch coach from communist Yugoslavia to teach 'his' team, the Leopards, how to win. And he'd triumphed: the Leopards had become champions of Africa. Mobutu had great expectations in the run-up to the 1974 World Cup finals and a lot riding on his team's success.

As things turned out, Zaire's first and only World Cup campaign was a story of misplaced optimism, greed, humiliation and fear. Before playing Brazil, Zaire were first beaten 2–0 by Scotland and then, on 18 June 1974, comprehensively put to the sword by their coach's Yugoslavian compatriots, losing 9–0. This historic trouncing is the key to unlocking Chapter 8. The ease with which Yugoslavia took Zaire apart suggested that, nineteen years on from their controversial friendly in Dublin, the highly rated *reprezentacija* could make history by becoming the first communist country to win the World Cup. To the Leopards, however, the 9–0 stuffing spelt disaster. The rout not only crushed Zaire's flimsy team spirit. It came amid anarchy in the Leopards' camp, centred on fights about money, witchcraft and managerial betrayal. More sinisterly, the 9–0 debacle prompted an incensed Mobutu to issue threats even darker than those Kim Il Sung had delivered to his players before the 1966 World Cup. If they lost to Brazil by more than three goals, the Leopards were told, they would never see their families again. Football defeats can often have serious consequences, but rarely as dire as this.

The Cold War produced more than its fair share of posturing despots, but Mobutu Sese Seko was among the most egregious. A journalist-turned-army chief, Mobutu emerged as a political player in the Congo soon after its independence from Belgium in 1960. The Congo then looked to be on the road to democracy through the leadership of the pan-Africanist Patrice Lumumba. When Lumumba's socialism and links with the Soviet Union grew apparent, however, Mobutu and the Belgians engineered a coup that led to Lumumba's torture and murder. The CIA, who feared Lumumba was another rabble-rousing Castro, assisted. The United States, like the Belgians, saw the Congo as a strategic asset in the Cold War's African battleground and a valuable cash cow. Its vast natural resources included the uranium used in the atom bombs dropped on Hiroshima and Nagasaki.[2]

Mobutu visited President John Kennedy in the White House in 1963. Kennedy thanked him for saving his country from communism;

Mobutu told the president his highest wish was to undergo parachute training at Fort Benning. With the help of CIA-funded mercenaries, Mobutu officially took office as President of the Congo in 1965. He then eliminated his opponents through a Machiavellian combination of patronage, bribery, detentions and public executions – sometimes in football stadiums. By 1970, Mobutu had become 'President for Life'. He renamed the Congo the Republic of Zaire and changed his own name from Joseph-Desire Mobutu to Mobutu Sese Seko Koko Ngbendu Wa Za Banga, or The Warrior who Goes from Conquest to Conquest Leaving Fire in his Wake.[3]

The late 60s through to the mid-70s were halcyon days for Mobutu. They coincided with a period of intense Cold War competition in Africa, in which East and West felt the continent was up for grabs and victory might just tip the balance of the conflict in its favour. Washington, frightened by left-wing coups in countries like Libya, Somalia and Ethiopia that the Kremlin either supported or exploited, granted the strongman his political and financial wishes. In the wake of the split between the Soviet Union and China, and President Richard Nixon's famous visit to Beijing in 1972, Mobutu also successfully curried favour with the Chinese. Money from Beijing poured into Zaire, partly in exchange for Mobutu's support for anti-Soviet forces in Angola, which gained independence from Portugal in 1975. Angola showed how complex the Cold War fight for Africa had become by this stage. Moscow and Havana sponsored one side; Washington and Beijing, backed by North Korean and Romanian technicians, the other. Mao Zedong believed Angola was on the frontline in a Soviet imperialist campaign to snuff out Chinese socialism and destroy the only existing socialist state in the world.[4]

Playing the Cold War game in this way paid off for Zaire, at least in the short term. It also made Mobutu, who simultaneously looted his nation's mineral-rich coffers, a billionaire, with lavish properties around the world. The dictator's crowning glory was the 'African Versailles' built at his jungle-village birthplace in Gbadolite, boasting three palaces and an airport runway long enough for Concorde.

While lining his own pockets took priority, Mobutu also siphoned off millions to fund Zairian sport. This was for customary purposes: to unite a new and ethnically diverse nation, to assert his new country's sovereignty and to boost his own reputation. But it was also part of Mobutu's muscular 'authenticity' programme, a cultural revolution designed to promote a traditional African identity and to sell his country as a successful example of black liberation from colonialism. This 'Africa for Africans' programme sought to counteract Mobutu's image as a CIA tool, and was tied to the dictator's mission to make Zaire a beacon of sport in Africa. Nothing illustrated this mission better than Zaire's spectacular, $20 million staging of the 'Rumble in the Jungle' fight between boxers Muhammad Ali and George Foreman three months after the 1974 World Cup finals. An estimated one billion television viewers watched Africa's first heavyweight title fight. Ali won against the odds, rope-a-dope style; Foreman would forever claim his water had been drugged.[5]

Mobutu invested in football more than any other sport, reflecting its popularity in Africa. Egypt had sent Africa's first football team to an Olympics as early as Antwerp in 1920 and to a World Cup finals in Italy in 1934. During this period, though swift and intense, the game's take-up across the continent had been patchy and sometimes curbed by crass colonialism. Both the French and Belgians demeaned their subjects in some countries by forbidding Black players from wearing boots, ostensibly to limit on-field violence. Participation took off after World War Two, mingling with and often in synch with nationalist movements across the continent. In 1957, Egypt beat Sudan 2–0 in the final of the inaugural African Cup of Nations. Between 1957, when it was established, and the Mexico World Cup of 1970, membership of the Confederation Africaine de Football (CAF) grew from four to thirty-four countries. In Mexico in 1970, Morocco took Africa's first point at a World Cup finals courtesy of a draw against Bulgaria.[6]

As a child, Mobutu had learned football from Catholic missionaries and then been a goalkeeper in the army (though never team captain, despite later claims). In power, Mobutu's football model was Ghana, whose African Cup of Nations victories in 1963 and 1965 boosted the prestige of President Kwame Nkrumah. Following his national team's chastening defeat to Ghana's Black Stars in Kinshasa soon after becoming president, Mobutu bought out the contracts of Congolese players in Belgium, then prevented them from leaving their home country. These professionals, along with the best young local players, formed the basis of a new national squad, the Leopards, named after Mobutu's trademark leopard-skin hat. Mobutu splashed out on improving training facilities for the squad, and in 1967 raided state funds to pay for Pelé's Santos to play a friendly in front of 75,000 in Kinshasa. The great man scored, of course, in a 2–1 victory, before hobbling off with another injury. In 1968, the Leopards won the African Cup of Nations, beating Ghana 1–0 in the final. Mobutu's financial and technical support for the game in Zaire was increasingly seen as a template for the development of African football as a whole.[7]

By the time of the 1974 World Cup finals, in which Africa was still only allowed one place, Zaire's prospects were looking good. The team became the first sub-Saharan outfit to get to a World Cup finals, by beating Togo, Cameroon, Ghana, Zambia and Morocco in qualifications. Mobutu celebrated this achievement in the best way he knew how: by announcing that every Leopard would get a car, house and holiday.[8] In March 1974, Zaire won the African Cup of Nations for a second time, beating Zambia 2–0 in a final replay. At the tournament, their centre-forward Ndaye Mulamba proved he was the best striker in Africa, scoring nine goals in six games, a record that still stands today. Central defender Tshimimu Bwanga also oozed class, confirming his reputation as 'the Black Beckenbauer', while Kazadi Mwambe showed why he was regarded as Africa's top goalkeeper.

Even after the African Cup of Nations final, many observers struggled to identify any coherent tactical pattern to the Leopards' play, often using the vague term 'hybrid' to describe their style. But on the eve of the World Cup many Zairians had every confidence in the team's chain-smoking coach, Blagoje Vidinić, who had been appointed in 1971. The former Yugoslav keeper was famous for having taken Morocco to the Mexico World Cup finals in 1970, where his team came close to beating West Germany in the tournament's opening game before the historic draw with Bulgaria. In truth, Vidinić's job at Zaire was hampered by Mobutu's ban on players moving to European clubs, which deprived them of valuable international experience. Pre-tournament training in Switzerland was no substitute for this, and losses to local club sides in friendly warm-up games suggested problems lay ahead.[9]

Still led by Josip Broz Tito, Yugoslavia was a subtle but major player in political and footballing spheres in the 1970s. Tito's early pursuit of a Third Way in the Cold War via his leadership of the Non-Aligned Movement had paid off handsomely over the decades. Yugoslavia benefitted from strong links across many parts of the world, while visits from President Nixon and the Queen of England solidified Tito's reputation as one of the West's favourite communists. In the late 60s, Yugoslavia became the first communist country to open its borders to all foreign visitors and abolish visa requirements. To the soft power of Western tourism was added Tito's new friendship with China, which for years had branded the marshal a revisionist. Tito never overlooked the power of international propaganda, even during the détente era. Few other political leaders could have persuaded Hollywood superstar Richard Burton to play them, in the 1973 Partisan war epic *Battle of Sutjeska*.[10]

Blagoje Vidinić's coaching role for Zaire testified to the key part that football had played since the 1950s in Yugoslavia's efforts to spread the gospel of socialism by nurturing close diplomatic ties with decolonising countries. Yugoslavia enthusiastically supported several communist liberation movements in Africa during this era. When Patrice Lumumba was found murdered in the Congo in 1961, protesters in Belgrade had been so outraged they'd ransacked the Belgian embassy.[11] Mobutu had such a tyrannical reputation in the early 70s, he'd no fear of a Yugoslav or any foreign communist exploiting their role as Zaire's football manager to foment revolution. The dictator hired Vidinić to lead his team to glory because Yugoslavs had an excellent record of coaching in Africa. It also helped that the Yugoslav national side of the late 60s and early 70s was nicknamed the 'Brazil of Europe'. The team's renowned technical skills explain why Pelé chose to play them in his final game for Brazil in the Maracanã Stadium in July 1971.[12]

Was the Yugoslav national side really that good? Given that the team didn't even qualify for either the 1970 World Cup or 1972 European Championship, definitely not. But under their celebrated coach Miljan Miljanić, who after the 1974 World Cup took up the reins at Real Madrid, the side was capable of bold, imaginative football. It also boasted high-class players in bulky, left-footed midfielder Branko Oblak, athletic centre-forward Dušan Bajević, defender-cum-playmaker Vladislav Bogićević and captain Dragan Džajić, Red Star Belgrade's marvellous, goalscoring left-winger who Pelé described as the most natural footballer he'd ever seen.[13] The 'Magic Dragan' epitomised the new generation of openly professional footballers in Yugoslavia, whose huge salaries sat uneasily with the country's socialist principles. Yugoslavia were regarded as the most exciting attacking team in Europe on their day. Having been Europe's serial under-achievers, in the run-up to the 1974

Figure 8.1 Josip Broz Tito and his wife Jovanka visit the Yugoslav national team in Dusseldorf, 26 June 1974. © Associated Press/Heinz Ducklau/Alamy.

World Cup many experts tipped them to lift the trophy. Marshal Tito (see Figure 8.1) certainly fancied his side's chances. 'Today, I am the captain of our national team!' he joked when visiting the squad during the tournament.[14] The pressure was on the Yugoslavs as well as the Zairians.

On 13 June 1974, Yugoslavia had the privilege of opening the World Cup finals against the holders Brazil in Frankfurt. Though, as noted in Chapter 7, the game ended goalless, they impressed. Brazil, still ruled by a military dictatorship but without the retired Pelé, Gerson and Tostão, were clearly not the force they'd been in Mexico. But the *reprezentacija*, playing 4-3-3, dominated large parts of the game, looking compact, lively and skilful. Oblak and Jovan Aćimović were a double-barrelled powerhouse in midfield, while Džajić delighted the crowd with his usual graceful touches.

Before the tournament, doubts had been raised about Yugoslavia's ability to lift the trophy because of repeated failures to translate their superiority in matches into goals.[15] Feeble finishing cost them victory here. In the second half, Aćimović and right-winger Ilija Petković each missed gilt-edged chances. Fifteen minutes or so from the end, an unmarked Bogićević hit the post with a point-blank header from a Džajić corner. If the Yugoslavs were as profligate against their next opponents, Zaire, they would likely be going home early.

The second match of Group 2, between Zaire and Scotland in Dortmund, took place a day later. Scotland's squad was the strongest they'd had at any World Cup to date. Built around players from Leeds United and Celtic, the English and Scottish champions, it boasted Billy Bremner, Kenny Dalglish, Danny McGrain, Peter Lorimer and Denis Law. 'We can wipe the floor with this lot', Scotland's manager Willie Ormond told the press brashly before the game.[16] The Scots won 2–0, with goals by Lorimer and Joe Jordan, but it wasn't easy.

Zaire played a conventional 4-4-2 yet surprised Ormond's side with their unpredictable movements and rapid one-touch passing. Tshimimu Bwanga brought the ball out of defence at speed, and the swerving runs of Etepe Kakoko on the left wing and the thrust of Ndaye Mulamba through the middle caused the Scots problems. The Zairians created enough chances to level the scoreline and the German section of the crowd noisily took to them, akin to the way Middlesbrough had adopted the North Koreans in 1966 (helping drown out the sound of the Scottish fans' bagpipes in the process). The Leopards' one obvious weakness was their 'collective vertigo', as *The Guardian*'s David Lacey put it, when the ball came at them in the air, the cause of both Scotland goals.[17]

After the final whistle, despite their loss, the Zairians felt good. They'd responded positively to those, like the Italian and West German captains Giacinto Facchetti and Franz Beckenbauer, who'd doubted their right to play in the World Cup. Confidence was high for the game against Yugoslavia, set for 18 June.[18]

At this point, things started to go badly wrong in the Leopards' camp. Zaire's delegation to West Germany was a rag-bag of players, football and state officials, politicians, military officers and assorted hangers-on. Mobutu had even paid several practitioners of witchcraft a fortune to accompany the Leopards. Blagoje Vidinić clashed regularly with these assorted figures, especially the witch doctors, who each had their own ideas about tactics and match preparations. The coach was also pressurised by Mobutu's sports minister, whose entourage would push their way into the dressing room after practice or before games. This was far from the orderly way Vidinić was used to working in the communist system. The tensions, rivalries and back-biting were the last thing he and the players wanted.[19]

On top of this was the issue of money. The Leopards had arrived at the World Cup having seen nothing of a $100,000 collective bonus Mobutu had promised them for qualifying for the tournament. The players expected to be paid handsomely in West Germany for representing their country against the world's toughest opponents. However, in the days after the Scotland game, the Leopards learned not only that they'd effectively be getting nothing for that match, but that Mobutu's friends and officials had pretty much bled the squad's kitty dry for the entire tournament.[20] This swindling could have been linked to the financial problems Mobutu was experiencing. Just recently, he'd nationalised economic assets owned by foreigners, causing a catastrophic decline in Zaire's productivity and wealth.[21] Rumours later circulated that the players' kitty and pre-tournament bonus had been raided to help pay for the 'Rumble in the Jungle'.[22]

The Leopards were furious. Some wanted to call a strike, meaning the game against Yugoslavia would be called off, but then changed their minds. Why is unclear. Threats of imprisonment when they returned home? Or because FIFA offered to pay each of the players 3,000 Deutsche Marks to take to the field and save the tournament's reputation? Either way, the Leopards approached the Yugoslavia match in a completely different frame of mind to the Scotland game. Aggrieved, downhearted, demotivated, even rebellious perhaps. They were ripe for the taking.[23]

The match between Zaire and Yugoslavia kicked off at 7.30 p.m. on Tuesday 18 June in the Parkstadion in Gelsenkirchen, in the heart of the Ruhr. A good many of the 31,000 crowd were Yugoslavian *Gastarbeiter* who worked in the coalfields and factories nearby.[24] Raucous and wearing jaunty red, white and blue caps, they'd wave their nation's flag throughout. There were few Zairian spectators. Among the advertising hoardings for Tic-Tac Mints, C&A and Martini was another near the half-way line sponsored by the Mobutu regime. 'Zaire-Peace', it said simply, if incongruously.

As their teams warmed up, neither bench looked particularly confident. Newspapers later reported that after his latest run-in with Mobutu's witch doctors, Vidinić had been accused of selling Zairian secrets to his compatriots and pulled from the match, leaving the Leopards at the mercy of the improvised directives of Zairian officials.[25] Yet there the coach was in the dugout, bedecked in his bright green-and-yellow Zaire tracksuit, puffing on a cigarette as usual. The Yugoslavs, considerably taller than their opponents, wore their all-white away kit. Emblazoned across the front of the Zairians' green shirts was a big picture of a leopard mauling a football. Ominously, all the press photographers had taken position behind Zaire's goal. They were in for a very busy night.

Miljan Miljanić switched from 3-4-3 to 4-4-2 for the Zaire match. This allowed him to use his two wingers, Petković and Džajić, to maximum advantage. It also meant he could bring in the tall Dušan Bajević, Yugoslavia's leading scorer that season, who'd been unavailable for the Brazil game owing to suspension. In the eighth minute, Bajević and Džajić combined to exploit the Zairians' aerial weakness. The left-winger did what he always did, beat his marker, floated a cross to the far post, and his unmarked centre-forward headed home. A few minutes later, Kakoko had a chance to equalise but fluffed a one-on-one with the Yugoslav keeper, Enver Marić. Had the winger scored, the match scoreline just might have been quite different. As it was, by the eighteenth minute, the Leopards were 3–0 down (see Figure 8.2). Džajić

Figure 8.2 Zaire defender Lobilo Boba clears with an acrobatic overhead kick from Yugoslavia's Dušan Bajević early in the match at the Parkstadion in Gelsenkirchen, 18 June 1974. © Rolls Press/Popperfoto via Getty Images/Getty Images.

scored a free kick through an onrushing, five-man non-wall, given after a Zairian rugby tackle on the edge of the box. Then, after a smart move, Ivica Šurjak, Yugoslavia's second striker, neatly turned in the box and shot underneath goalkeeper Mwambe's body.

The experienced Mwambe had hardly covered himself in glory so far, not having moved a muscle for the first two goals. But whoever decided to replace him – we don't know whether it was the Zairian officials or Vidinić – with Tubilandu Ndimbi after twenty minutes seems to have panicked. This was the first time a goalkeeper had been substituted in a World Cup finals for any other reason than injury. Ndimbi was only five feet six inches tall and hardly likely to restore confidence in his team by dominating his box. The new goalkeeper's first task was to pick the ball out of his net after defender Josip Katalinski, completely unmarked at the back post, had had the time to bring down a lofted free-kick before smashing it past him. Ndimbi would go on to have a shocker. Stories told much later suggested he'd been brought on as he was a favourite of one of Mobutu's senior cronies, who had been pressing for his inclusion in the starting line-up.[26]

The Leopards reacted angrily to this fourth goal. Believing the scorer had been offside, a group of them surrounded Omar Delgado, the portly Colombian referee. Right-back Mwepu Ilunga surreptitiously kicked him up the behind, only for the referee to give a red card to the one man who was best qualified to reduce Zaire's deficit, Ndaye Mulamba (see Figure 8.3). There was no fourth official or video assistant to help spot this case of mistaken identity, so Mulamba trudged off the pitch. He, not Ilunga, would be out of the next match against Brazil. That the Leopards were so infuriated by Katalinski's goal seems to disprove the later theory that the players had deliberately thrown the Yugoslavia match to get back at the officials who'd stolen their money. The Leopards' anger was more likely swollen by being out of pocket and by wounded pride at conceding so many goals in front of a global audience.[27]

Any team 4–0 down and reduced to ten men after less than a quarter of the game played would find it difficult to keep going. This was especially so for a team at their first World Cup finals who, as champions of Africa, had believed they could, if not beat, at least compete with the best. But the Leopards did not throw in the towel. They kept their shape, tackled hard, pressed forward and soon won

Figure 8.3 Referee Omar Delgado erroneously sends off Zaire player Ndaye Mulamba (13) in the twenty-second minute of the game in Gelsenkirchen, 18 June 1974. © Horstmüller/ullstein bild via Getty Images.

a couple of corners. These efforts came to nothing though and by the thirty-fifth minute they were down 6–0.

The Yugoslavs were not playing particularly well, often mis-controlling the ball, hitting wayward passes and failing to dictate the game's tempo. But space inevitably opened up for them. From yet another cross, Bajević beat two defenders in the air to bag his second goal of the game. Then, with another header, Bogićević scored from a corner. First, Ndimbi and a defender got in each other's way when trying to win the cross. Then, instead of clearing Bogićević's header off the line with his left foot, Ilunga acrobatically sliced it into his own net with his right. This came just after Kakoko had wasted another great chance to open Zaire's account by thrashing the ball over the Yugoslavs' bar from close range.

The match now threatened to turn into a momentous rout. The Yugoslav players had stopped kissing each after scoring, suggesting they were easing off somewhat. But their compatriots in the crowd were loving it and clamouring for more. As the Leopards huddled in their penalty box for an impromptu team talk, Vidinić sat impassively and carried on smoking. Apart from raising cigarettes to his mouth, he'd barely moved a muscle since kick-off.

Having had a relatively quiet match so far despite setting up two goals, Dragan Džajić decided it was time to start enjoying himself. A beautifully disguised under-foot roll-cum-step-over beat two defenders near the by-line, only for his cross to be caught low down by Ndimbi. Bajević joined in, trying to put a teammate through on the edge of Zaire's box with an audacious back-heel. It was largely one-way traffic through until half time. Oblak missed a chance to score after intercepting a sloppy back pass and Bajević nearly completed his hat-trick with a near-post volley. In the forty-first minute, a Zairian player finally won a header in his own penalty box. When the whistle for the interval blew, Yugoslavia led 6–0.

Both Yugoslavia and Zaire showed no signs of letting up or time-wasting in the second half. Bajević irritated his manager by missing a sitter soon after the restart. The Leopards made inroads the longer the half progressed. In the fifty-fourth and fifty-seventh minutes, the Yugoslavs twice committed blatant professional fouls to stop Zaire breaking through to score. First, left-back Enver Hadžiabdić cynically caught the ball to prevent a one-on-one with his keeper. Then the long-haired Marić came storming out of his box to close down a Zaire move, got his timing all wrong and knocked the ball away from his opponent with his hands. The keeper wasn't even yellow-carded. Except for a snap shot by substitute Mayanga Maku late on in the game, these turned out to be Zaire's only real chances to reduce their deficit.

In the sixty-first minute, Yugoslavia made it 7–0. Oblak struck a decent free kick from twenty-five yards out, the Zaire wall – as was now routine – parted to let the ball through, and Ndimbi, trying to catch it as he dived to his right, fumbled the ball into the net. Shambolic. The next day, a photograph of Ndimbi pounding the turf in frustration appeared in newspapers around the world and would become the defining image of Zaire's ineptitude. Vidinić, finally, moved, wiping his hand across his mouth. Ndimbi's error seemed to knock the stuffing out of the Leopards, who just might have been hoping to keep a clean sheet in the second half or at least not give away any more cheap goals. A couple of minutes later, Ilija Petković scored with a neat strike from just inside the box to make it 8–0.

There were still twenty-five minutes to go. This must have seemed like an eternity to the Zairians, and the crowd, sensing something really special, got louder. Surely the Yugoslavs were going to reach double figures, never seen before at a World Cup finals. In the eighty-first minute, Bajević completed his hat-trick with a scruffy shot at the far post after a corner. Congratulating him, some of the Yugoslav players could be seen sniggering behind their hands. The score was now 9–0.

Thereafter the goals dried up. The game didn't exactly fizzle out. If anything, the Yugoslavs upped their tempo and threw more men forward, looking for that magic tenth goal. Each time they got anywhere near the Zaire goal the crowd's horns and shouts reached a crescendo. Yugoslavia had several chances, and Bajević missed another two sitters. But the Leopards held their shape and stuck at it. When the final whistle blew, the television cameras and journalists thronged around Blagoje Vidinić. The coach looked dazed and didn't say a word to anyone as he escaped down the tunnel.

Yugoslavia's 9–0 thumping of Zaire briefly set the 1974 World Cup finals alight. The scoreline was reported globally and classified as historic, equalling Hungary's demolition of South Korea at the 1954 World Cup finals. The fact that two communist countries shared the record for the biggest victories in World Cup history was not lost on some Western observers. It could be linked, several British newspapers and coaches argued, to Eastern European players being less greedy and less cosseted than many of their counterparts in the West. This viewpoint was obviously connected to the West German players' recent, highly publicised demands for more money. But it also reflected a general feeling among many in Britain and elsewhere that footballers were acting more like rock stars than athletes and an ignorance in the West of just how wealthy some players behind the Iron Curtain, like Dragan Džajić, were. West Ham's manager Ron Greenwood, soon to be England's boss, attributed the communist teams' success to their 'iron discipline', greater fitness and all-round more professional approach to playing football.[28] All four teams from Eastern Europe competing in West Germany – Poland, Bulgaria, East Germany and Yugoslavia – would make it through to the second round, equalling the number that'd qualified for the equivalent stage in 1962.

In Yugoslavia itself, the press marvelled at the scale of their team's victory over Zaire.[29] In the team's camp, euphoria soon gave way to caution and restraint. Having drawn with Brazil and beaten Zaire, all the Yugoslavs needed now, assuming Brazil beat Zaire, was a draw against Scotland to guarantee passage into the next round. Before the Scotland game, Miljan Miljanić was the height of professionalism. 'There are only three main points in football', he told journalists. 'To take the ball away, to make tactical moves, and to finish. We have players who can do all three.'[30] During the Scotland game, which took place on 22 June, Yugoslavia played cautious, possession football. Showing a different side to their game, they were also physical, or 'ugly' as some Scottish observers put it.[31] Scotland were desperate for a win but never really looked like getting it. Yugoslavia scored ten minutes from time, a simple header by substitute Stanislav Karasi from a Džajić cross. Joe Jordan equalised but too late, in the eighty-eighth minute. The match ended 1–1. Yugoslavia were through.

Having lost against Yugoslavia in Gelsenkirchen, the Leopards knew they were now out of the tournament. They had no points from two games. But this was the least of their concerns. If the defeat against Scotland had cost them money, that against Yugoslavia threatened a much higher price. Europeans had for years treated African footballers with an arrogant, neo-colonial disdain, lazily stereotyping them as exotic curiosities who lacked technique and discipline. The 9–0 drubbing reinforced this typecasting, turning Zaire into a global laughing stock: World Cup interlopers who were completely out of their league.[32]

Mobutu had been annoyed with his team's defeat to Scotland, despite their widely applauded performance. But the dictator was infuriated by the Yugoslavia result. To him, the thrashing represented a national disaster and personal humiliation. Accounts differ slightly about exactly what happened next but the gist is that, via officials within the Zairian camp, Mobutu issued the players with threats about their performance in the next game, against Brazil. According to Mwepu Ilunga, the central figure in the Brazil game free-kick incident, Mobutu sent his presidential guards to menace the Leopards. 'They closed the hotel to all journalists and said that if we lost 0–4 to Brazil, none of us would be able to return home'. Another player, Adalard Mayanga, supports Ilunga's story. 'They said to us the Brazil match was about honour. We had to come out with honour: three goals or less'.[33]

It's not difficult to imagine what the Zaire players were thinking as they took to the field a few days later to play Brazil. The match was in the Parkstadion in Gelsenkirchen, scene of their recent abasement, and taking place at the same time as the Yugoslavia–Scotland game. Brazil hadn't exactly been pulling up trees so far at the World Cup, having drawn 0–0 twice, to Yugoslavia and Scotland. But this made things worse. Had the world champions already qualified for the next round, they could have rested their best players and taken things easy against Zaire. As it was, Brazil knew that to escape the indignity of failing to get out of the tournament's first group stage, they had to beat Zaire by at least three goals. Blagoje Vidinić tried to calm the Leopards before the game, telling them that it would be his last as their coach and that, because Brazil had a similar style to theirs, they'd be easier to play against. Go out and enjoy it, he said. It's doubtful whether this helped much.[34]

Surprisingly, Vidinić, who now appeared to be back in full charge of the Leopards, didn't make sweeping changes to his team for the Brazil game. He chose instead to give the majority of those players who'd turned out against Yugoslavia a chance to redeem themselves. This included Mwepu Ilunga, whose foolish kicking of the referee had almost certainly added to the humiliating scoreline. Kazadi Mwamba was back in goal and Ndimbi wasn't even on the bench. Mwamba would have a great game – except for one crucial slip. Zaire packed their defence, a strategy designed to protect their penalty area and, ultimately, themselves.

This siege mentality was understandable given what was at stake, but after only twelve minutes Brazil scored. Jairzinho hit a rasping shot low into the bottom left corner. Mwamba stood no chance. The Brazilian team and their thousands of fans went wild, probably thinking another landslide was in the offing. This might have come about but for Mwamba (see Figure 8.4). The keeper saved a barrel-load of shots in the first half, including one brave, double-save on the edge of his six-yard box soon after Brazil had gone into the lead. His defenders helped out by scything down any Brazilian who threatened to get into the penalty area (obvious red-card offences today) and by spectacularly clearing things off Mwamba's goal-line. The referee, Nicolae Rainea from Romania, should have given at least one penalty to the Brazilians for Zaire's rough stuff, and Jairzinho, also generously, missed a sitter. Zaire got to half time one-nil down. This was a triumph in itself. By the same stage in the Yugoslavia match the Leopards had conceded six.

Figure 8.4   Zaire's goalkeeper Kazadi Mwamba punches the ball away from Brazilian forward Jairzinho during the match in Gelsenkirchen, 22 June 1974. © STAFF/AFP via Getty Images.

The second half wasn't a whole lot different to the first. Brazil continued to pressure but rarely in the air, and therefore failed to exploit Zaire's prime weakness. This was perhaps what Vidinić meant when he'd told his players about the Brazilians' style of play. In the sixty-sixth minute, Rivelino scored Brazil's second with an unstoppable left-foot strike from twenty-five yards out. Less a trademark banana shot, it arrowed past Mwamba into the top left-hand corner. No goalkeeper could have saved it. Brazil's manager Mario Zagallo punched the air in delight. Ten minutes later, Mwamba made another double-save, diving courageously at the feet of Mirandinha, who accidentally kicked the keeper in the head.

By this point, Brazil looked to have run out of ideas. The game had slowed down, the crowd had quietened, and the World Champions were looking desperate. In the seventy-ninth minute, however, Brazil scored a third. Right-winger Valdomiro hit a harmless cross-cum-shot from an acute angle and Mwamba, perhaps still feeling the effects of his head injury, allowed it to bounce over his shoulder at the near post and into his net. Was this deliberate, evidence, as some Leopards later claimed, that Zaire had agreed to the Brazilians' half-time request to let in a goal?[35] Surely not given Mwamba's sterling performance in the match. But it was a terrible mistake, especially in the circumstances. The Leopards now had ten minutes or so to stop a dreaded fourth goal.

As Zagallo's aides listened on the radio for news of the Yugoslavia–Scotland scoreline, his players looked for more goals. The three they'd scored already would not be enough to qualify for the next round if Zaire scrambled a goal of their own. In the eighty-first minute, Brazil's blond left-back Marinho Chagas was tripped in Zaire's box but Rainea unaccountably interpreted it as a dive. Then, in the eighty-third minute, Mirandinha was hacked down in a central position twenty-seven yards out from Zaire's goal. The referee, correctly, gave a free-kick.

The Brazilians were widely celebrated as the world's set-piece specialists. This was classic Rivelino territory and he'd already demonstrated his lethal shooting prowess from the same position a little earlier. The Zairians, for their part, had shown complete incompetence throughout the tournament in defending free-kick shots, their walls disintegrating when the whistle was blown. As Rivelino and a bunch of other Brazilians debated who was going to take the free-kick, the Zairians formed a jittery five-man wall, just inside their penalty box. The referee edged the wall back and when a Brazilian player demanded it went back even further, the players in the wall pushed him away. The crowd started heckling and the referee had to intervene to quell the players' row. By this point, a full two minutes had passed since the free-kick had been awarded, long enough for the Leopards to think about the potential enormity of what may be about to transpire.

At long last, Rainea stepped away from the wall and blew his whistle for the free-kick to be taken. As he did so, time seemed to almost stand still, allowing right-back Mwepu Ilunga to vacate his position in the wall, sprint to the ball and kick it as far away from Zaire's goal as possible. What was going through Ilunga's mind? Lots of things. He was nervous, like any player would be at a tense point of a game in the World Cup. He was scared that if the Brazilians scored another, fourth goal he'd be exiled and his family could fall prey to Mobutu's hit-squads. On top of this, he was angry at being robbed of his pay and dignity. Ilunga later claimed he was wasting time or even angling to get sent off. The red card would've been a protest against the cronies that had deprived the Leopards of their rightful earnings.[36]

The referee didn't dismiss Ilunga but yellow-carded him instead. Ilunga respectfully bowed to him, as if apologising for his impetuousness but not, as some pundits would later erroneously say, for being ignorant of the game's rules. When Rainea again whistled for the free-kick to be taken, the Brazilians, perhaps expecting another Zairian to come running out of the wall, rushed it, shot into the wall and the ball was cleared.

Weirdly, the free-kick incident seemed to take the sting out of the game. Zaire spent the last five minutes of the game pinned in their own half, but Brazil didn't create any chances. The Leopards didn't panic either; at one point, to waste time Ilunga himself started playing keep-ups before passing the ball back to his goalkeeper. The game ended 3–0 to Brazil. The result put Scotland out on goal difference and saw the reigning champions go through to the next round by the skin of their teeth.

Tito's Yugoslavia side had looked good in the World Cup's first round. It was their first World Cup finals in twelve years, but they'd topped Group 2 and relegated the World Champions Brazil to second spot. Their historic victory over Zaire had shown they could translate control into goals, at least against poor opposition. And in Oblak, Bajević and Džajić they possessed three of the most impressive players so far in the tournament. Back home, expectations were high. Many felt that this team could now get beyond the fourth place achieved in 1962 and even win the trophy. The pre-tournament favourites, West Germany and Brazil, didn't look that strong. Maybe the collective strength of the Eastern European teams that progressed into the second stage indicated the time had come for a communist nation to prove they were the best at the people's game.[37]

It wasn't to be. In the second stage of the tournament, Yugoslavia had to play West Germany, Poland and Sweden. The team that topped the group would go through to the final. Yugoslavia lost all three of their games: 2–0 to West Germany, and 2–1 to Poland and Sweden. Poland, graced by the presence of two of their all-time greats (both future exports to the West), Kazimierz Deyna and Grzegorz Lato, went on to finish third in the tournament. A communist country would, in fact, never win the World Cup during the Cold War. Hungary and Czechoslovakia came closest, as runners-up in 1954 and 1962, respectively.

Once again, for all their qualities, the *reprezentacija* had failed to do themselves justice. Yugoslavia would go to only two more World Cup finals during the Cold War and before the country's dissolution in 1992, coming sixteenth and fifth in 1982 and 1990, respectively. The country did benefit politically and financially from hosting the 1976 European Championship but Tito's hopes that home advantage on that occasion would help lead to victory were dashed. Instead, fellow communists Czechoslovakia took away the trophy, thanks to the rare genius of Antonin Panenka's chipped penalty over West Germany's Sepp Maier in the final. Yugoslavia came fourth out of the four teams that competed.

Looking to explain Yugoslavia's failure at the 1974 World Cup, at the time some commentators, like Liverpool FC's legendary manager Bill Shankly, attributed it to the team simply being too nice. 'They play for fun, not for keeps', Shankly witheringly stated. 'They play cards for money and then give you your money back.'[38] Ironically given the players' austere reputation in the West, years later critics would blame Yugoslavia's shortcomings in West Germany on creeping Westernisation. Rather than playing as a team, the critics argued, the players had focused instead on marketing themselves to Western teams, going shopping and arguing about bonuses. A good many of the Yugoslavia squad did move to Western Europe and the United States soon after the 1974 World Cup. Džajić played for SC Bastia in France, and Oblak for FC Schalke and Bayern Munich. Bogićević went on to become a cult hero at New York Cosmos. Bajević played and then managed in Greece. Hadžiabdić played in Belgium for Charleroi, managed Iran, then took up arms for Bosnia in the Yugoslav Wars of the 1990s.[39]

The Zaire team's humiliation in West Germany in 1974 demonstrates that despots like Mobutu Sese Seko didn't always get their own way on the football field during the Cold War. They still left victims in their wake, however. Unlike Blagoje Vidinić, who, after threats, evacuated his family from Kinshasa and never set foot there again, the Leopards were at least able to return to Zaire.[40] Once there, though, the state treated the players as pariahs. After their African Cup of Nations triumph back in March 1974, the Leopards had been feted as heroes in a ceremony at Kinshasa Airport and been driven away in a luxury coach. When they touched down from West Germany just four months later in July, virtually no one was there to greet them and the players had to pile into the back of an army truck. Mobutu then publicly summoned the squad to his private office, where he railed against their abysmal performance (fourteen goals conceded, none scored) and excoriated them for 'rebelling' against his wishes and threatened them with jail if they ever did the same again. Terrified, the players didn't dare mention the salaries and bonuses they were owed. Days later, under the headline 'The Leopards on Trial', alarming photographs appeared in the local press of the players atoning for their actions in West Germany by doing punishing, military-style training.[41]

Zaire's embarrassing record at the 1974 World Cup, and the 9–0 defeat to Yugoslavia in particular, damaged the image of African football immensely. During the tournament, Sir Stanley Rous, FIFA's retiring president, argued that the performances of Zaire (and Haiti, who'd also lost all of their games) devalued the currency of the World Cup and called for future World Cup qualifying rounds to be held on an intercontinental rather than geographical basis, thereby separating the 'sheep from the goats' in the early stages. Rous didn't get his way, but there were others, including the boss of UEFA and probably lots of ordinary football fans, who, after watching Zaire get pummelled by Yugoslavia, questioned the right of developing countries to have automatic representation at the World Cup finals. Things were made worse, of course, by the sports media's condescending treatment of teams like Zaire in large parts of the world. When Morocco reached the second round of the 1986 Mexico World Cup, Africa's reputation started to recover. When Cameroon beat the trophy-holders Argentina and made the quarter-finals in Italy in 1990, as the Cold War was ending, African football looked to have finally turned a corner. To date, Morocco's 2–0 defeat to France in the semi-final of the 2022 Qatar World Cup is Africa's best performance.[42]

The Leopards' performance in West Germany also inflicted damage on Mobutu's image, making him look a fool in front of millions for thinking his team could compete with the best. Consequently, like a spoilt child with a defective toy, he cast the team aside. After the World Cup, Mobutu cut funding to the national team, and the Leopards fell swiftly from grace. They were eliminated in the first round of the 1976 African Cup of Nations, never again became continental champions, and never made it to another World Cup finals. Football in Zaire slowly calcified in the years ahead. By the end of Mobutu's chaotic reign in 1997, the game was on its knees, with virtually no money to pay players and match officials. Senior administrators, the game's supposed guardians, stole it to build their private villas.[43]

All of this had a devastating effect on the squad of 1974. Shamed and ostracised, their international, and for some, domestic, careers were almost instantly over. Several players might have expected, like the Yugoslavs, to pursue lucrative careers overseas, but Mobutu prohibited the squad from making such 'dishonorable' moves. Most of the one-time celebrities faded into obscurity, scratching a living alongside most of the population as Zaire plunged into decades of economic crisis and political tyranny. Striker Ekofa Mbungu used the Volkswagen that Mobutu had given him for qualifying for the 1974 World Cup to become a taxi-driver. Kazadi Mwamba and others died prematurely in poverty. Ndaye Mulamba's death was announced at the 1998 African Cup of Nations, only for the ex-striker to be discovered penniless and drunk in a South African slum. Mwepu Ilunga stayed in football and died in 2015, still complaining about the World Cup money owed him. Mobutu Sese Seko himself died in 1997, months after fleeing into exile. His regime had outlived the Cold War, leaving a country in ruins.[44]

9 'A CRAZY DAY, A SHOW OF POWER'
Steaua Bucharest vs. Dinamo Bucharest, Bucharest, June 1988

You've never seen a trophy ceremony like this. It's 9 p.m. on 26 June 1988, a warm Monday evening at the 23 August Stadium in Bucharest. Nobody seems to know what's going on. The Romanian Cup final, a contest between the country's most successful teams, Dinamo Bucharest and Steaua Bucharest, has just finished 1–1, after a late Steaua winner was disallowed for offside. Extra time should be next, but it's not happening. Because the Steaua team, possibly on orders from club president Valentin Ceaușescu, eldest son of the country's communist dictator, Nicolae Ceaușescu, has left the pitch in protest at the offside decision.

For a while, the Dinamo players mill around the centre circle (see Figure 9.1). They then head to the side of the pitch, where, on a trellis table on the running track, the Cupa României stands unclaimed. Goalkeeper Dumitru Moraru takes matters, and the prize, into his own hands. He grabs the cup, raises it above his head, kisses it, and brings it back to his team. Moraru's teammates, including centre-half Ioan Andone (more on him in a moment), take turns holding the cup aloft. The players pose for a team photo, before taking the trophy across the field to the Dinamo fans. They cascade down the stadium steps to celebrate with their heroes.

But celebrate what? A Dinamo win technically, because their opponents forfeited the match by leaving the field. But 1–1 was the score when referee Radu Petrescu blew the final whistle. And, sulking in the

Figure 9.1 Dinamo Bucharest players wait on the pitch at the 23 August Stadium in Bucharest after the 1988 Cupa României final. © Gazeta Sporturilor (GSP.RO/ Romania).

dressing rooms, Steaua think that they've won, thanks to Gabriel Balint's wrongly ruled out ninetieth-minute winner. Valentin Ceaușescu, the man supposedly behind his team's exit, professed bemusement at the bizarre turn of events: 'In the end it was so ridiculous that I didn't care who'd won'.[1]

The 1988 Romanian Cup final took a while to decide. The referee abandoned the match after Steaua's walkout, so Dinamo were initially declared the winners. The following day, the decision was reversed. A commission of Romania's National Sports Council awarded Steaua the cup and, for good measure, suspended Petrescu and his linesmen for a year. After communism fell, Steaua renounced their tainted victory. Today, on the Romanian Football Federation (FRF) website, alongside the result from 26 June 1988, a note says: 'trophy not awarded'.[2]

The tug of war over the trophy doesn't tell half the story of a match surrounded by so much intrigue and mythology that even now it's hard to separate fact from fiction. The lewdest tale centred on Andone. In the post-game confusion, Dinamo's stopper allegedly walked to the VIP box, pulled down his shorts, and waved his penis at Valentin Ceaușescu, an obscene gesture that earned him a one-year ban from football. Well, that's one version of events. Version 2 has an unnamed Dinamo player raise his middle finger and angrily point it at Ceaușescu. Version 3 didn't even happen at the 1988 cup final.

According to this version, Andone's crude gesture came on 22 March 1989, after another heated match, this time in the league, which ended 2–1 to Steaua, after a late Balint winner that wasn't disallowed. Well, that's if it even happened then. Because there's no evidence of Andone flashing his penis or giving the dictator's son the bird. The 'true story', claimed one Romanian newspaper in 2012, was that Andone walked towards the VIP box at Steaua's Ghencea Stadium, sarcastically applauded the army big wigs, and dropped to his knees, raising both hands to the skies in supplication, as if to ask Valentin Ceaușescu, or perhaps referee Ion Crăciunescu, 'what do we have to do to get a win here?'[3]

Welcome to the absurdist theatre that was football in Ceaușescu's Romania, a sport shrouded in rumours and political scheming. Welcome to a country in the 80s that was home to austerity, corruption, megalomania, secret police terror – and two of Europe's best football teams. When we think of Cold War sporting rivalries, we think of East versus West, communism versus capitalism. But bitter rivalries festered too in club football, both in the democratic West and the outwardly monolithic regimes behind the Iron Curtain. And no communist sporting rivalry was higher stakes than the one between the army and the secret police. Particularly in the Socialist Republic of Romania, one of Cold War sport's most idiosyncratic outposts.

Steaua versus Dinamo, army versus secret police. 'The eternal derby' offers a smudged window into the fractured world of late communist Romania. It's another example of football's ability to swim against the Cold War tide, for as Romania's economy went into a tailspin in the 1980s, its top football teams reached new heights. Most significantly, the June 1988 game between Dinamo and Steaua, especially when paired with the equally controversial encounter in March 1989, can be seen as a foreshadowing. A shot across the bows that all wasn't well behind the façade of leadership cults, military parades and Securitate surveillance. Eighteen months after the cup final chaos, Nicolae Ceaușescu was dead and so was the Socialist Republic. Football didn't bring down communism, either in Romania, or in other places where it refused to toe the party line. But football served as an early warning system, a rare public space where dissent could flourish alongside conformity and entertainment. In this sense, it contributed, however indirectly, to the collapse of communism and the end of the Cold War. Nowhere was this more apparent than in Ceaușescu's Romania.

Romanian football was a late starter. The game arrived in Transylvania in the early twentieth century, when it was part of the Habsburg Empire. Romania then was a small kingdom, formed from the unification of Moldavia and Wallachia in 1858, and declared independent in 1877. It wasn't until after World War One that Romanian football, like Romania, expanded. Romania joined the conflict in 1916, on what turned out to be the winning side, the Entente Powers. When the dust settled, the 'Greater Romania' that emerged between 1918 and 1920 included Bessarabia, Bukovina and parts of Transylvania. Expansion brought into the national fold large populations of Germans, Jews and Hungarians.

In the inter-war period, Central Europe was home to the world's most vibrant football cultures, centred on the former Habsburg cities of Budapest and Vienna. Romania wasn't part of this conversation. The national team didn't make its debut until 1922. Football only gradually became Romania's most popular, most politicised sport. In 1930, the exiled king, Carol II, returned to Bucharest to reclaim the throne from his infant son Michael and the regency that ruled in Michael's name. Looking to win popularity, he dispatched a team to the inaugural World Cup in Uruguay. One of four European countries to travel to South America, Romania beat Peru 3–1 and then lost 4–0 to the hosts and eventual winners. This set the tone for the 1930s, when the national team earned marks for participation not achievement. Romania entered the 1934 and 1938 World Cups, but lost both times at the first hurdle, to finalists Czechoslovakia in 1934 and, embarrassingly, to Cuba in 1938.

Political interference didn't do much for the Romanian game, but that didn't stop politicians from meddling. In the 1930s, General Gavrilă Marinescu, an ally of Carol II, helped his favourite team, Venus Bucharest, to win five league titles. Success, though, proved elusive in the Romanian Cup, where the popular railway workers' club, Rapid Bucharest, often stood in Venus' way. After Rapid defeated Venus 2–1 in the 1938 cup semi-final, Marinescu, not only Venus' president but also Bucharest's chief of police, ordered the arrest of four Rapid players and a replay, due to refereeing bias in the first game. It didn't work, as Rapid won the rematch. Marinescu consoled himself by becoming honorary president of Rapid, president of the FRF and Minister of the

Interior, all in 1939, by which time Romania's turn to authoritarianism under Prime Minister Ion Antonescu was obvious. In November 1940, the country's football fixer was one of sixty-four politicians executed by the fascist Iron Guard in the Jilava Massacre.

World War Two hugely disrupted Romanian football. The National Legionnaire State, an uneasy alliance between Antonescu and the Iron Guard, lasted five months, from September 1940 to February 1941, before Antonescu used the army to remove the Guard from his government. In this period, Romania joined the Nazi-led Axis alliance, a precursor to its participation in the invasion of the Soviet Union in June 1941 and the murderous violence unleashed on Europe's Jewish population. Football, inevitably, took a back seat. The league was suspended in 1941 and didn't return until 1944. Under anti-Semitic laws introduced in 1940, 400 Jewish players and sixteen Jewish clubs were removed from Romanian football. Between 1941 and 1944, 220,000 Romanian Jews died in the Holocaust.

On 23 August 1944, a coup led by Michael I, Carol II's son, and supported by various parties (including the small but influential Romanian Communist Party, PCR), deposed the Antonescu dictatorship. Romania's switch to the Allied side came too late to save the country's independence. The kingdom fell into Stalin's sphere of influence, as the Red Army liberated, or occupied, Romania in 1944. Between 1944 and 1947, the communists cut down democratic allies and democratic opposition until all that was left was the PCR. In December 1947, Michael I was forced to abdicate. The PCR merged with the silenced Social Democrats to become the Romanian Workers' Party (PMR) – it would reclaim the PCR designation in 1965 – and Romania became a Socialist Republic. Under the leadership of Gheorghe Gheorghiu-Dej, Romania became one of the most slavishly Stalinist of the Soviet Union's satellite states.

The political revolution that swept across Eastern Europe after World War Two sparked a football revolution. From East Germany to Bulgaria, old 'bourgeois' structures were dismantled. Clubs were dissolved, merged or renamed. As East German propaganda trumpeted, 'learning from the Soviet Union means learning to win!' In sport, this meant importing the Soviet model, whereby clubs were affiliated with, or sponsored by, industries and government ministries.

In Romania, a few pre-war clubs, like Rapid Bucharest, survived the cull. But many others were created or recreated under communist control. They include the protagonists of our story. In June 1947, Army Sports Association (ASA) Bucharest was founded as the team of the Royal Romanian Army. The club underwent several name changes – Central Sports Club of the Army (CSCA) Bucharest from 1948 to 1950, Central House of the Army (CCA) Bucharest from 1950 to 1961 – before adopting the name Steaua, after the red star on the club badge. Eleven months after ASA's creation, the Ministry of the Interior established Dinamo Bucharest. The new club was effectively a merger of Unirea Tricolor, the team of Romanian fascism, and Ciocanul (formerly Maccabi), once the team of Bucharest's Jewish community. Two of the most powerful branches of the communist state, the army and the police, now had football clubs, plus a phalanx of satellite teams to keep them supplied with players.

The Gheorghiu-Dej regime, like many communist dictatorships, was ambivalent about football, a sport far too unpredictable for the party's liking. Romanian football in the 1950s and 1960s continued to struggle. The national team either didn't enter or didn't qualify for any of the World Cups between 1950 and 1966, withdrawing from the 1962 tournament in Chile after scheduling conflicts gave Italy a walkover in Group 7 qualification. Nor did it reach the final stages of any of the early European Championships.

Domestically, football was mired in controversy long before Nicolae Ceauşescu came to power in 1965. Party complaints about the game in 1953 included the bribery of referees and fights in the stands between army and interior ministry officials. Benefitting, like Dinamo, from a loophole in the country's transfer ban that allowed players to be recruited via military service, Steaua won the league for three straight seasons (1951–53). Gheorghiu-Dej, a railway worker and Rapid Bucharest fan, didn't like what he saw. The transfer ban was lifted in 1953, and Dinamo and Steaua's satellite clubs were dissolved. Not much changed. Between 1953 and 1965, when Gheorghiu-Dej died of cancer, Dinamo and Steaua won nine of the twelve Divizia A titles. Only the oil workers' team, Petrolul Ploieşti (twice), and UTA Arad, the team of the textile industry, broke the duopoly. Despite Gheorghiu-Dej's patronage, Rapid failed to win a trophy.

21 June 1978: the final day of the season in Romania's third division. Promotion to Divizia B is between leaders Flacara Automatica Moreni and FC Olt Scorniceşti. Level on points, Flacara have the advantage on

goal difference. At half-time in Scorniceşti's match versus Electrodul Slatina, it's 1–0 to the promotion hopefuls. Bad news arrives: Flacara are apparently 9–0 up in their game (in fact, it's only 2–0). Scorniceşti think they need a miracle, or seventeen second-half goals. The final score? FC Olt Scorniceşti 18 Electrodul Slatina 0. Scorniceşti get promoted.

One year later. The final weeks of the 1978/79 Divizia B season. Scorniceşti are again locked in a battle for promotion, this time with Metalul Bucureşti. It's 1–1 at the final whistle, but no matter. Scorniceşti score just after the ref brings his whistle to his lips, claiming a 2–1 win that helps them pip Metalul to promotion to Divizia A by two points. A few days later, Petrica Nicolae, a Metalul official, asked the referee what happened. He replied: 'Don't you know to whom the team belongs?'[4]

How did a small club from a village in Olt County get to the top so quickly – and so controversially? The answer, in one word, is Ceauşescu. Scorniceşti was the birthplace in 1918 of Nicolae Ceauşescu, the place where he lived until the age of eleven, when the future dictator moved to Bucharest to become a shoemaker. Its population in 1972, the year Viitorul (later FC Olt) Scorniceşti was founded, was 15,000. The village's football stadium, opened in 1975, had a capacity of 30,000, plus press facilities, a sauna and a swimming pool. Scorniceşti's rise from obscurity was a political project, driven by the Ceauşescu clan. Its patron was Lica Barbulescu, Ceauşescu's brother-in-law. And you didn't oppose the Ceauşescus. As Petrica Nicolae recalled in 1990: 'Because it was Barbulescu, everyone shut up … It wasn't cowardice, it was realism.'[5]

The FC Olt Scorniceşti story is emblematic of the venality the Ceauşescu regime brought to the country's favourite sport. Nicolae Ceauşescu might have been more of a chess and gymnastics guy, but he'd been a prominent backer of Steaua in the 1950s. He was happy, once in power, to give Barbulescu free rein at his hometown club, and to allow his wayward youngest son Nicu, First Secretary for Sibiu County, to put his weight behind Inter Sibiu, who won promotion to Divizia A in 1988.

Football as the plaything of dictators: it's a familiar tale. The twist in the plot in Romania came from Nicolae Ceauşescu's eldest son, Valentin. Valentin Ceauşescu wasn't what you'd expect in the offspring of a feared ruler. He showed no desire to follow in his father's footsteps.

Instead, he studied physics at the University of Bucharest, then went to Imperial College in London, where he played in goal for the college team. Valentin's younger brother, Nicu, loved fast cars and drank heavily. He allegedly had a relationship with Romania's most famous athlete, gymnast Nadia Comăneci.[6] Valentin, in contrast, was quiet and modest, with no obvious political ambitions or interest in communism. He drove a Dacia, Romania's ubiquitous version of the Renault 12. His parents despaired of him.

In 1983, Steaua Bucharest, Romania's most successful club, were struggling. The army team hadn't won the league since 1978. They'd been overtaken not only by arch-rivals Dinamo, but by upstarts like FC Argeş Piteşti (champions in 1978/79) and Universitatea Craiova, league winners in 1979/80 and 1980/81 and UEFA Cup semi-finalists in 1983. Minister of National Defence Constantin Olteanu felt a shake-up was required. And a helping hand from the ruling family. So, he appointed Valentin Ceauşescu, a huge football fan, as club president.

Nicolae and Elena Ceauşescu were unimpressed. They felt Valentin was wasting his life. 'They didn't think being head of a football team was good enough for a president's son', he later explained. But Valentin had found his calling. Ceauşescu Jr. worked long hours, developing close relations with the players. Midfielder László Bölöni called him 'the best manager I ever worked for' and forward Marius Lăcătuş, who joined Steaua in 1983, 'our friend'.[7] As Romania strengthened economic ties to the West, Valentin sought commercial opportunities for Steaua, securing a shirt deal with Ford for the 1988/89 season. He organised annual winter training camps in the Transylvanian mountain resort of Predeal, where the players did long runs in the snow and built team spirit. The culture shift paid quick dividends. In 1984/85, Steaua were champions for the first time in seven seasons, breaking Dinamo's three-year run at the top, and won the Cupa României, defeating Universitatea Craiova 2–1 in the final. Valentin Ceauşescu was assembling a high-quality team, whose spine featured maverick goalkeeper Helmut Duckadam, elegant sweeper Miodrag Belodedici, midfielder and captain Tudorel Stoica and striker Victor Piţurcă. It would soon send shockwaves through European football.

For most of the history of the Socialist Republic of Romania, football was a disappointment. The national team muddled along in the middle ranks of European football. Officials complained constantly about under-performance. Here's a typical comment, from General Dumitru Petrescu in 1953: 'By losing international games, we also lose politically. It might be asserted that football ... does not rise to the height of the international prestige of our Republic'.[8]

Many communist countries had success in Cold War football. We know all about Hungary's golden squad from Chapter 2. The Soviet Union, as we saw in Chapter 4, won the inaugural European Championship in 1960 and were runners-up in the same tournament three times. Czechoslovakia lost the 1962 World Cup final and won the 1976 Euros. Both Poland, at the 1974 and 1978 World Cups, and Yugoslavia (twice runners-up in the Euros, in 1960 and 1968) had moments in the sun. Romania's record, until the late Ceaușescu era, was comparatively modest. The national team made one appearance at the World Cup (1970) and one at the Euros (1984). The country's top clubs struggled. Dinamo Bucharest didn't get beyond the second round of any UEFA competition until 1981/82. Between 1958 and 1979, Steaua only once cleared this hurdle, reaching the quarter-finals of the 1971/72 European Cup Winners' Cup.

Then, suddenly, the narrative changed, at least in club football. From the early 1980s to 1989, in a reverse of Petrescu's 1953 lament, it was the socialist republic that couldn't rise to the height of socialist football. As Ceaușescu's megalomania brought the country to its knees – with villages forced into agro-industrial communes, Bucharest razed to the ground, and crippling austerity imposed to pay back IMF loans – its football teams thrived. The Securitate were everywhere, there was scarcely any meat, and power cuts were part of daily life. Petrol was so scarce that people returned to the horse and cart, heating so costly that you wore coats to the opera. Anyone who tried to escape risked being shot at the border.

Elite footballers were among the few citizens cushioned from these appalling conditions. They got plenty of food, owned cars and could sell goods bought abroad on the black market. With gifted players and settled squads, the top Romanian teams cut a swathe through Europe. It began with Universitatea Craiova, an unfavoured club capable of upsetting the big two in Bucharest. In 1981/82, Craiova became the first Romanian club to reach the European Cup quarter-finals. The following season, 'the Lions of Bănie' made the UEFA Cup semis, losing on away goals to Benfica. Dinamo Bucharest then got in on the act, reaching the semi-finals of the European Cup, where they narrowly lost to Liverpool. Then Steaua took over. After decades of unremarkable results, the army team's record in the European Cup from 1985/86 to 1988/89 read: winner; second round; semi-finalist; finalist. Valentin Ceaușescu's protégés became the first Eastern bloc team to win Europe's most prestigious club competition. For that four-year period, they were arguably the continent's best football team.

What changed? It wasn't as if Ceaușescu Sr. suddenly fell in love with football. Many of Steaua's games during its long golden run weren't broadcast on state television (TVR), a situation that sent desperate supporters to illicit meeting places on higher ground where Hungarian television could be received.[9] But the sport that brought Romania global attention in the previous decade, gymnastics, had lost its sparkle. Nadia Comăneci, star of the 1976 Montreal Olympics, inched towards retirement after the 1980 Moscow Games. Her controversial coaches, Béla and Márta Károlyi, defected to the United States in 1981. Romania remained dominant: five of the country's twenty gold medals at the 1984 Olympics in Los Angeles, a competition boycotted by the Soviet Union and its allies, came in women's gymnastics. But nobody could match Comăneci's celebrity. Nor replicate her role in giving the Ceaușescu regime international legitimacy and hard currency, earned from tours of the non-communist world.

Perhaps football stepped in, then, as Comăneci's sportswashing replacement? It helped that, by the early 1980s, a talented generation of players was emerging, most of whom ended up at Dinamo or Steaua. The pick of the bunch, Gheorghe Hagi, was nineteen when he was 'loaned' by his club, Sportul Studențesc, to Steaua for one game, the European Super Cup final against Dynamo Kyiv in February 1987. Hagi scored the winner and never went back (see Figure 9.2). 'Hagi was taken from us and they gave us nothing', complained Sportul president Mac Popescu.[10] That was how the system worked.

It helped too that football in Romania was popular, one of the few reliable distractions from the misery of national communism. Attendances remained strong in the 70s and 80s, as they fell elsewhere in Europe. When TVR, as it often did, cancelled transmission of a Divizia A double-header (Rapid vs. Steaua, Dinamo vs. Sportul) in 1985, angry citizens broke through police lines to watch the games live in the 23 August Stadium. For all the security might at its disposal, the Ceaușescu regime understood football's importance, not just as bread

Figure 9.2 'The Maradona of the Carpathians' Gheorghe Hagi (Steaua Bucharest) in action during the 1988 Cupa României final. © Gazeta Sporturilor (GSP.RO/Romania).

and circuses entertainment but as a potential flashpoint, a rare place where people could poke the neo-Stalinist bear.

And, of course, it helped that, from 1983, the president's eldest son ran the country's army team. That made it easier to get players like Hagi. To ensure referees were in your pocket and results could be manipulated (hardly practices confined to Romania or communism in this period, as any history of Italy's Serie A could attest). To have the money to provide your players with luxuries (nice apartments, cars, foreign travel) denied to ordinary Romanians. The results were clear. Between 1985 and 1989, Steaua Bucharest went unbeaten for 104 league matches. They won the title in 1986/87, 1987/88 and 1988/89 without losing a game.

But the Ceaușescu factor was confined to domestic football. Like Nadia Comăneci and her teammates, who often faced unfriendly East German and Soviet judges in international arenas, Valentin and his charges were on their own in UEFA competitions. In the European Cup, no fatherly intervention could bend the narrative Steaua's way. Which makes the club's achievement in winning the European Cup even more remarkable.

Steaua Bucharest entered the 1985/86 European Cup as an outsider. In six previous appearances in the competition, they'd failed to win a single tie, losing to the likes of Czechoslovakian duo FC Hradec Králové and Spartak Trnava. But the (red) stars aligned when Steaua kicked off against Denmark's FC Vejle in September 1985. There were no English teams to worry about, following UEFA's decision to ban them after the Heysel disaster in May. Among the European heavy-weights entered in 1985/86 – Barcelona, Bayern Munich and holders Juventus – it wasn't a vintage crop. And Steaua's draw was kind. After beating Vejle 5–2 on aggregate, Steaua's path to the final went through a Honvéd side far removed from its 1950s pomp, Finnish champions FC Kuusysi and, in the semi-final, a storied but second-tier outfit in Anderlecht.

Before the quarter-final against Kuusysi, Valentin Ceauşescu told the Steaua team: you can win the European Cup. The players waited until he left the room, then burst into laughter. Perhaps they gained confidence from wins over Kuusysi and Anderlecht, whose coach, Arie Haan, said after a 3–0 defeat in Bucharest that he'd never seen a team play with Steaua's rhythm. Still, few gave Emerich Jenei's side a chance in the final against Barcelona on 7 May 1986. Not least because it was effectively an away game, to be played in front of 65,000 Spaniards in Seville's Ramón Sánchez Pizjuán Stadium. The Romanian champions didn't travel well. The team also struggled under floodlights, which meant training for the final at the 23 August Stadium, Romania's only floodlit ground, not the Ghencea. Steaua officials tried to make the squad feel at home in Spain, packing Romanian food (chicken, beef and potatoes) and bottles of Jidvei, a Romanian wine, and Romanian cham-pagne. Just in case.

Stephen Bierley's preview reflected the consensus: 'there is an overwhelming feeling that nothing can stop Barcelona'. Forty thousand Catalans had come to Seville by train, he reported in *The Guardian*. 'At the last count, there were nine from Bucharest. People that is'.[11] The Steaua entourage had trouble finding a hotel. The team tried to do a night session at Real Betis' stadium, but the floodlights didn't work. They had to change their red kit for a white one with red trim, to avoid clashing with Barcelona's red and blue shirts – as if to reinforce the point that Barcelona were, in every sense, the 'home' team. Around 1,000

Romanians watched the final in Seville, but they weren't Steaua fanatics. Two hundred were club officials, the other 800 PCR members, forty of whom used the trip to Spain to defect. Everyone, it seemed, awaited Barcelona's coronation, perhaps forgetting that the Spanish club, like their Romanian opponent, had never won the European Cup.

The final wasn't a great game, but it was a great occasion, as a partisan crowd willed Barcelona to victory. The noise seemed to inhibit Terry Venables' team, who looked less convincing the longer the game lasted. West German playmaker Bernd Schuster and Steve Archibald, the barely fit Scottish striker, missed their best chances. Led by Ştefan Iovan and Adrian Bumbescu, Steaua defended, in Bierley's words, with 'a mean resolution', producing a backs-to-the-wall performance reminiscent of Red Star Belgrade's in the 1991 European Cup final vs. Marseille. In both cases, an Eastern European team known for attractive football battened down the hatches against star-studded opponents. Steaua in 1986, like Red Star in Bari, played for penalties. The army team had two shots in 120 goalless minutes. 'Once they reached the 18-yard line', lamented the *Daily Telegraph*, 'the Steaua team fell apart'.[12]

It was a different story from twelve yards. For the second time, following Liverpool's win over Roma two years earlier, the European Cup final went to penalties. Steaua missed their first two (from Mihail Majearu and László Bölöni), but no matter. Because Barca failed to convert any of their spot kicks. All four were saved by Steaua keeper Helmut Duckadam, three low to his right, with the pick of the bunch a brilliant stop from Ángel Pedraza in round two. Penalties from Marius Lăcătuş and Gabi Balint, and Duckadam's final save from Marcos Alonso (a woeful effort, more back pass than shot), meant Steaua had done the unthinkable, becoming the first communist team to claim the European Cup (see Figure 9.3). After the game, Duckadam remembered, 'we had absolutely no idea how to celebrate. It was a total shock'. A glass or two of champagne at the hotel 'and that was pretty much it'. A celebration 'with discipline and moderation', as Emerich Jenei put it.[13]

Nicolae Ceauşescu wasn't that impressed by Steaua's monumental achievement. 'It would have been better if you had won it during the 90 minutes', he chided the players at a reception in Bucharest.[14] Even at this moment of triumph, there remained a sense that the regime didn't trust football. Half of Steaua's matches in the 1985/86 European

Figure 9.3 Helmut Duckadam saves Barcelona's final penalty and celebrates Steaua Bucharest winning the European Cup, Seville, 7 May 1986. © Bob Thomas Sports Photography via Getty Images.

Cup weren't shown live on television. Only 'intense pressure' from football officials ensured that TVR showed the final, which coincided with the eve of the 'Day of the Party'. The lead article on the front page of sports daily *Sportul* on 8 May 1986? A festive poem for Ceauşescu, alongside a portrait of the dictator. Only at the bottom of page one could you read, 'Steaua won the European Champions' Cup!'[15]

Every Steaua player received the Star of the Romanian Socialist Republic First Class, the country's highest state honour, for their heroics in Seville. But many perks didn't materialise. Instead of fancy cars, the players got second-hand ARO 4 × 4s, previously used by the army. Captain Ştefan Iovan's vehicle was apparently made from spare parts. Iovan got off lightly compared to the shootout hero. Duckadam, an ethnic German, was quickly dropped from the team, kicked out of the army, and forced to retire from football, ostensibly because of a blood clot in his arm. But his disappearance coincided with rumours that he'd been beaten up, shot, or had an arm cut off, by one of Ceauşescu's henchmen (or possibly by Nicu Ceauşescu), after complaining within the dictator's earshot about the meagre rewards offered to European Cup winners. Duckadam's fate symbolised the cruelty of Romanian football, and Romanian society, in the 1980s. 'I couldn't believe it – I'd gone from this amazing high to a terrible low so fast'.[16]

Ordinary Romanians saw football differently to the regime. Thirty thousand people packed the streets of Bucharest to welcome home the European champions, the biggest spontaneous gathering since World War Two. Or, in László Péter's phrase, 'an unexpected football happiness riot'. The Securitate were spooked but left well enough alone. The media ignored what was in front of their eyes. Newspaper photos only showed the players returning home; television reports edited the sound to remove the noise made by the 'rooters', the football lovers, or 'social bandits' (depending on your viewpoint), who saw the game as the highest form of socialist escape.[17] Four-and-a-half years later, the regime wouldn't be able to ignore larger, angrier incursions into heavily policed public spaces, incursions that would bring down Romanian communism and cost Nicolae Ceauşescu his life.

Steaua's 1986 win was no flash in the pan. Anghel Iordănescu, the Steaua legend who came out of retirement for a vital cameo from the bench against Barcelona, succeeded Emerich Jenei as manager in the summer of 1986. The team won the European Super Cup in 1987, reached the European Cup semi-finals in 1988, and, a year later, reached another European Cup final, this time against AC Milan. If Barcelona in 1986 lacked flair, AC Milan in 1989 were one of the great European sides, built around a superb defence, three brilliant Dutchmen (Frank Rijkaard, Ruud Gullit and Marco Van Basten), and the revolutionary coaching of Arrigo Sacchi. It was too much even for Hagi's genius. There'd be no repeat of Seville in, ironically enough, Barcelona's Camp Nou on 24 May 1989. Milan thrashed Steaua 4–0. A half-fit Gullit and Van Basten scored two goals apiece. 'The only regret', reported *The Guardian*, 'was that the Romanians totally failed to live up to their billing as an organised, disciplined team who could counter Milan's flair'.[18] Steaua lost their grip on Europe – the club would never again scale the dizzy heights of 1985–1989 – as Nicolae Ceauşescu lost his grip on Romania. The army's football party was over. The Communist Party wouldn't be far behind.

Romanian football's success in the 1980s was built on what Robert Adam called 'a very corrupt and authoritarian system'. Domestic arrangements benefitted two clubs, Steaua and Dinamo, at the cost of everyone else. They got the best players, the friendly refs and, unsurprisingly, the results. Dinamo might have been overshadowed by their rivals, but they played plenty of dirty tricks, using the Securitate to intimidate coaches, players and officials. In 1986/87, with Steaua again running away with the league, Dinamo officials sought prestige elsewhere. Striker Rodion Cămătaru was in a race with Austrian Toni Polster for the European Golden Boot, the prize for the continent's top goalscorer. In the final six games of the season, Cămătaru scored an implausible twenty-one goals to claim the award. UEFA found the pattern suspicious enough to strip Cămătaru of the Golden Boot and give it to Polster instead. Supporters of Rapid Bucharest, a team regularly disadvantaged by Dinamo and Steaua, would've been delighted. In the final game of the 1986/87 season, Rapid beat Dinamo 4–3 at the Giuleşti Stadium, with Cămătaru (naturally) scoring all three of the visitors' goals. Rapid fans threw old shoes on the pitch, in mockery of Cămătaru's Golden Boot efforts, and asked Austria Vienna's finest, 'Toni Polster, where are you, to see the circus in Giuleşti?'[19]

The Steaua–Dinamo duopoly meant that every 'eternal derby' in the mid–late 1980s mattered. Given how far ahead the two Bucharest clubs were, their matches were invariably cup finals or de facto title deciders. The peak, or nadir, of these encounters was the 1988 Cupa României final. The match was a Who's Who of Romanian football legends. In Anghel Iordănescu's Steaua side, there were four starters from the 1986 European Cup final (Ştefan Iovan, Adrian Bumbescu, Miodrag Belodedici and Marius Lăcătuş), as well as Gheorghe Haji, Romania's greatest footballer; prolific striker (and Hagi rival) Victor Piţurcă; and – on loan from Universitatea Craiova – the stylish sweeper (and future Spurs and Barcelona star) Gheorghe Popescu. Dinamo's team, coached by Mircea Lucescu, included several key players from the run to the 1984 European Cup semi-finals (goalie Dumitru Moraru, defenders Mircea Rednic and Ioan Andone, and midfielder Costel Orac), plus the striking talents of Toni Polster's nemesis, Rodion Cămătaru.

The 1988 cup final makes for fascinating viewing, long before we get to the controversial denouement. The pre-game sights and sounds at the 23 August Stadium – the flickering electronic scoreboard, the unevenly populated terraces, the marching band music – offer a time capsule of late communist Romania, a place where, at least to outsiders, a familiar activity seems strangely de-familiarised. When the game kicks off, the viewer is struck by the noise from the stands (boos and whistles, chants of 'Dinamo') and the testy atmosphere on the confetti-flecked pitch. These teams clearly don't like each other. Lăcătuş takes exception to an early nibble from Ioan Varga and the pair square up after another clash on the touchline. Steaua dominate the first half and take the lead in the twenty-seventh minute courtesy of a Lăcătuş header.

In the second half, amid the tetchiness and scything tackles, Dinamo attack with greater urgency. Midfielder Dănuţ Lupu hits the post. Cămătaru heads over the bar from six yards out. Other chances go begging. Meanwhile, referee Radu Petrescu is struggling to keep a lid on tempers. Rattled perhaps by losing the upper hand, Steaua players surround Petrescu after various off-the-ball incidents. But the white tide keeps coming. In the eighty-seventh minute, with darkness falling, substitute Florin Răducioiu blasts home the equaliser. A jubilant Dinamo ballboy joins the celebrations. The electronic scoreboard, in full working order, reads 'GOL'.

Dinamo's joy is short-lived. Whether by accident or design, footage of Gabi Balint's 'winning' goal is patchy.[20] One minute, Steaua are attacking down the left, then Muraru appears to spill a cross, and the Steaua sub sweeps the ball home. At which point, things fall apart. The linesman, off camera, flags for offside. Furious Steaua players surround him and the referee. The game never resumes. Steaua are in the dressing room when, half an hour after Balint's goal, Dinamo lift the Romanian Cup in front of their delighted supporters.

'A crazy day, a show of power' was Mircea Lucescu's verdict on the 1988 cup final.[21] The craziness isn't in dispute, but whose power was on show? For Lucescu, it was the power of Valentin Ceauşescu and his family. But Ceauşescu denied sending his players to the dressing room, claiming the decision was Iordănescu's. Either way, Steaua left the field because they felt that another state organ, Dinamo's Securitate backers, had robbed them of victory. Whatever happened at the 1988 cup final, it tells us something about the murkiness of Romanian football in its imperial phase – and about competing lines of state power in the final days of Nicolae Ceauşescu's rule.

The 1988 cup final was the first half of a play in two acts: the first of two Steaua–Dinamo matches that serve as cautionary tales about football at the end of communism. The second, a league match, took place at Steaua's Ghencea Stadium on 22 March 1989. As we saw at the start of this chapter, what happened at these matches has often been confused in the history books. Leaving aside the competing stories about Ioan Andone's anti-Steaua (and so anti-Ceauşescu?) gesture, the blurring of the two games might also relate to the fact that they followed a similar pattern. An early lead for Steaua (thanks to a brilliant Hagi free kick), a late Dinamo equaliser (Andone's bullet header), and then, in the eighty-seventh minute this time, a superbly worked winner from Gabi Balint, the ghost goal scorer the previous June. Balint vaults a security fence to celebrate with ecstatic Steaua supporters. At the final whistle, he walks off the field arm in arm with Hagi. Andone's fury, meanwhile, whether directed at the Ceauşescus or at referee Ion Crăciunescu ('we were outraged by the way he led the game'), reflected the fact that another title was slipping from Dinamo's grasp.[22] Steaua officials wanted Andone banned for life for ironically clapping the VIP box and falling to his knees in mock prayer; the FRF imposed a three-month suspension. He returned in time for the 1989 cup final against – who else? – Steaua. Dinamo lost 1–0, thanks to another screamer from Hagi. Nobody in the 23 August Stadium knew it then, but they were watching the final showpiece match of the Ceauşescu era.

March 1989. The week Steaua beat Dinamo 2–1. The future wife of one of the authors was in Romania. She was a member of an Ottawa gymnastics club invited to train in the world capital of gymnastics, a rare behind-the-scenes look at Romania's sports system. The Gloucester Garnets went to Dracula's castle in Transylvania, spent an afternoon at the Canadian embassy, ate mountains of iceberg lettuce dressed in white vinegar (no oil) and took part in a competition with a gymnastics club in Bucharest, where they met Nadia Comăneci. Wearing blue eye shadow, smiling, and holding a Canadian flag, she's there, multiple times, in the photo album of the trip.

But the Comăneci photos aren't the ones that grab your attention. Instead, you're drawn to shots betraying the bleakness of Ceauşescu's Romania: the kid with the sole flapping off his shoe; the peasant in a low, horse-drawn cart; the lone West German Porsche in a sea of Dacias; the drab emptiness of the capital; and what one Ottawa newspaper called the 'outdated or makeshift' equipment at Clubul Sportiv Scolar Nr. 2 ('old and dimly lit').[23] These photos match the words of Liverpool fans who'd visited Romania five years earlier for the semi-final versus Dinamo Bucharest. 'A place of brutally grey Stalinist buildings', said one. Another remembered how 'we decided to have a look around the city and were surprised at some of the primitive sights – horse-drawn carts, women cleaning the streets and plenty of empty shops'.[24]

Six months after posing for photos with young Canadian gymnasts, on the night of 27–28 November 1989, Nadia Comăneci illegally crossed the border between Romania and Hungary. The world's most famous gymnast became the world's most famous defector. Within days, she was in the United States. At a press conference on 1 December, she told reporters why she left: 'I wanted to live a free life ... It was a personal decision'.[25] Comăneci was one of the last in a long line of Romanian athletes to escape the communist regime, including 185 in the final decade of Ceauşescu's rule, of whom ninety-four left between 1987 and 1989.[26] One was Steaua Bucharest defender Miodrag Belodedici, an ethnic Serb, who failed to return from a holiday to Yugoslavia in December 1988. He signed for his boyhood team, Red Star Belgrade, and in 1991 became the only footballer to win the European Cup with two communist teams.

Sporting defections were an embarrassment to the Ceauşescu government. Belodedici, one of the heroes of Seville, was declared a traitor and sentenced *in absentia* to ten years in prison. The Securitate launched an investigation into Comăneci's border crossing at Cenad, putting the squeeze on friends and family left behind, including her mother and brother. Political events, however, soon rendered her defection irrelevant. Unrest bubbling close to the surface for years burst into nationwide view. On 16 December 1989, an uprising in Timişoara triggered the collapse of communist rule. Five days later, in one of the most astonishing moments of the 1989 revolutions, Nicolae Ceauşescu attempted to reassert his authority during a televised rally in Bucharest, only to be met with boos and missiles. Unrest spread rapidly across the country. Within four days Nicolae and Elena Ceauşescu were dead, executed by firing squad on Christmas Day after a military tribunal convicted them of mass murder. The Socialist Republic of Romania, like the PCR, disappeared almost overnight.

Romanian football didn't go so quietly. In fact, the collapse of communism, and the political and economic uncertainty that followed, coincided with the national team's greatest period. Under Emerich Jenei, Romania qualified for Italia '90, beat the Soviet Union 2–0, and made it through a tough Group B (also featuring Cameroon and Argentina) to the knock-out stages. There, the Romanians lost to Ireland on penalties, not for the last time in the 1990s failing to beat an inferior opponent when opportunity knocked. The same thing happened at the 1998 World Cup, where Romania topped Group G (ahead of England), but lost in the round of sixteen to Croatia, coincidentally or not after the squad decided to bleach their hair. 'They butchered us. It was so painful', remembered striker Gheorghe Craioveanu. Coach Anghel Iordănescu suspected divine retribution: 'We've angered God'.[27]

In politics, as in football, Romania remained reliant on personnel from the Ceaușescu era. The country's president from 1990 to 1996 (and from 2000 to 2004) was Ion Iliescu, formerly a PCR functionary and the epitome of Eastern Europe's neo-communist transition to post-communist democracy. It was during Iliescu's first presidency that Romania's national team – led by key figures from the 80s, Iordănescu and Hagi – achieved its best result, reaching the quarter-finals of the 1994 World Cup in the USA. Romania's performances in the tournament, particularly the 3–2 round of sixteen win over Argentina, marked a culminating moment for a 'national' style of play: what football theorist Virgil Economu envisaged as a combination of 'traditional' Romanian virtues (the physicality of the 'Latin fury') and cutting-edge tactics, built around 'the loveliest arabesques' of the midfield playmaker.[28] This was technically skilled attacking football, led in 1994 by 'the Maradona of the Carpathians' (Hagi), but it remained vulnerable. In the quarter-final in Stanford on 10 July, Romania lost on penalties to a workmanlike Swedish team. Miodrag Belodedici, long since pardoned for his defection in 1988, missed the vital spot kick. Things were never as good again.

In the 1990s, football was a distraction from the difficulties of life after communism. The Italian summer of 1990, the 'American nights' of 1994, the street parties after Romania's successes in 1994, 1998 and 2000 (when the team reached the quarter-finals of the Euros) all helped to conceal less pleasant socio-economic realities: steadily rising inflation and 10 per cent unemployment rates – lower than the figure for many post-communist states in this period (for example, Poland), but a far cry from the guaranteed jobs of the Ceaușescu era.[29] In the twenty-first century, football provided no such escape. The Romanian game went into seemingly terminal decline. The post-Hagi national team (he retired in 2000) was a pale shadow of its predecessors, failing to qualify for any World Cup between 2002 and 2022. The same applied in club football, where the giants of the communist era, Dinamo and Steaua (renamed FCSB in 2017), floundered in lucrative but stratified competitions like the Champions League. The 1986 European Cup winners became embroiled in a bitter and ongoing legal dispute over the Steaua name, claimed by both the Ministry of Defence (Steaua's original patrons) and property tycoon George Becali, who took ownership of the club in 2003. The 2017 name change followed a court ruling that Becali's club had 'no ownership of the Steaua brand', and thus no rights to Steaua's glittering history.[30]

Whether as Steaua or FCSB, the army club has remained a leading force at home, winning eight league titles in the first quarter of the twenty-first century, a haul matched only by CFR Cluj. But domestic competitions, like Romania's international results, have suffered in the post-communist era. Professionalism has often been a fig leaf for corruption, greed and failure: dubious or controversial investors (such as Becali), match-fixing and an exodus of players. Not so different from the late Ceaușescu and early Iliescu eras then? There was one difference. Romanian football might have always been corrupt, but it enjoyed success in the 1980s and 1990s. There was no such consolation after 2000. Hence, contemporary nostalgia for the 'good old football times' under Ceaușescu, when Romanian teams made Europe sit up and take notice.[31]

That nostalgia seems ironic, because football helped to defeat communism. Wherever you looked behind the Iron Curtain in the 1980s, football was a quietly destabilising force, the biggest slash of graffiti on the walls of the Potemkin villages built by Brezhnev, Ceaușescu, Honecker and Zhivkov. Look at the 1985 Bulgarian cup final between Levski Sofia and CSKA Sofia, a match so violent, such a 'breach of socialistic morals', that both clubs were disbanded.[32] Look at the hostility to Dynamo Berlin's corrosive dominance in East Germany, a range of protests (from chants to petitions) that first created 'a climate in which unaccountable authority was challenged and made accountable'.[33] Look at the *samizdat* terrace cultures in Czechoslovakia, the Soviet Union or Yugoslavia, where foreign fan models (the English hooligan, the Italian ultra) combined with fierce club loyalties to create autonomous spaces for young men.

Journalist Traian Ungureanu wasn't alone in seeing football in Romania in the 1980s as a form of political castration, a distraction from the brutal whims of a hated dictatorship.[34] Certainly, it doesn't pay to exaggerate the sport's political role. Communism's collapse had more to do with Gorbachev and *perestroika*, or Ceaușescu, austerity and 'systematisation' (an urban planning programme so destructive it was called 'Ceauşima', Ceauşescu's Hiroshima), than with anything that happened on, or around, the football pitch.

Yet, football in Romania, that source of national communist pride, was always capable of slipping its moorings, of moving beyond state control, of galvanising opposition, however coded or indirect, to the authorities. If there was sickness in communist society, it often came to public attention through football. That's what happened in Romania's golden era, a period tainted by the machinations of the Ceauşescus and the teams they patronised. The 1988 cup final between Dinamo and Steaua showed the chaos that could follow when the authorities lost control and started arguing among themselves. When the authoritarian mask slipped, allowing a glimpse at the freedom and uncertainties of a post-communist world. That world, seemingly so far away in the summer of 1988, would come into being little more than a year later, as communism collapsed, violently in Romania and peacefully elsewhere in Eastern Europe. The Cold War didn't end because of football, but football, indisputably, was the canary in the mine, helping to light the way to the revolutions of 1989.

10 A NEW ERA
China vs. Norway, Guangzhou, November 1991

Sixty-five thousand people turn their eyes to the centre of the Tianhe Stadium. At either end of the pitch, two flags: one for the People's Republic of China (PRC), one for FIFA. At 7.10 p.m. on 16 November 1991, motorcyclists ride into the stadium, each carrying one of twelve national flags. Music starts up from the loudspeakers and a vast golden phoenix rises into the sky. Hundreds of girls emerge from the stands to join the phoenix on the field. Singing and dancing, they shake threads from the bird, creating a red sun set against the evening sky. The crowd cheers 'the heroic women' about to enter 'the new world of … women's football'.[1]

At 8.45 p.m., Tone Haugen glances at Chilean referee Salvador Imperatore. He blows his whistle, Haugen passes to teammate Linda Medalen, and we're off into that new world. Norway against China. The first match of the first FIFA Women's World Cup. Onlookers in Guangzhou, the capital of Guandong province in south-east China, include the greatest male footballer of all time, Pelé, plus FIFA president João Havelange and his Swiss sidekick, Sepp Blatter. Also in attendance are heavy hitters from China's ruling elite: the governor of Guandong, Ye Xuanping; 'red capitalist' Rong Yiren; and Communist Party veterans Li Tieying, chairman of the State Education Commission, and Wan Li, head of the National People's Congress. These men had survived, sometimes narrowly, the political crisis of 1989, when a pro-democracy student movement challenged communist rule. Martial law was declared, and hundreds of peaceful demonstrators were massacred in Beijing's Tiananmen Square on the night of 3–4 June. Rong Yiren and

Wan Li had cautiously supported the students before backtracking. Now, they're in VIP seats at Tianhe Stadium, watching an event designed to restore China's international reputation. To show that, despite the bloodshed, the communist dictatorship was open for business.

Our final chapter examines a match from the edge of the Cold War, both in terms of chronology (the Soviet Union would be dissolved on 26 December 1991) and focus. For forty-plus years of East–West conflict, men's football mattered more than women's football, to which most powerful men – dictators, democrats and sports administrators – paid little attention. China vs. Norway in 1991 didn't carry the political weight of, say, Spain vs. the Soviet Union in 1964. But this was a match, and tournament, that helped mark the end of the Cold War era, and the start of several new ones, in women's sport and in sports diplomacy.

The first Women's World Cup was about a changing of the guard. China's hosting of the tournament, its close relationship with FIFA and its surprise thrashing of Norway spoke of a new Asian sporting superpower. The last major communist rival to the United States, the last defence in a crumbling red wall against the West, which was cock-a-hoop in 1991 at the Soviet Union's collapse and the 'end of history'. Cold War binaries, whether political, economic or sporting, were breaking down, or breaking into something new.

Communist China won the football battle on 16 November, beating Norway 4–0, but the West won the war, as the USA defeated Norway 2–1 to claim the inaugural World Cup in Guangzhou on 30 November. These three countries, so politically different, dominated women's football in the 1990s, a vital decade in the game's development, starting in Guandong in 1991 and ending in California eight years later, when the USA beat China to win the third World Cup. Women's football in China, Norway and the United States succeeded because the game there wasn't 'completely occupied by men', wasn't embedded in a 'hegemonic sports culture' that encouraged exclusion based on typecasts, whether about 'worker-mothers' in the East or slim, attractive housewives in the West.[2] With notable exceptions, such as East German swimming or Romanian gymnastics, elite sport was a male-focused story during the Cold War. And even the exceptions – the child gymnasts controlled by male coaches, the over-muscled swimmers – seemed to somehow confirm the rule. 'Sports shouldn't come to having a woman looking like a man', said American swimmer Wendy Boglioli about her East German rival Kornelia Ender after the 1976 Montreal

Olympics, where 'king-sized Kornelia' won four gold medals, as part of what the *Los Angeles Times* called 'the world's first bionic swim team'.[3] Sport as a man's world certainly applied to Cold War football, as did crass portrayals of women as either too fragile or too threatening to participate. The 1991 World Cup didn't overturn either male domination of the world's biggest sport or Cold War gender stereotypes. But it suggested other directions, 'a colorful world and a bright future', where women footballers were in the vanguard of 'a new femininity' that was anathema to Cold Warriors on both sides of the now torn Iron Curtain.[4]

The journey to the 1991 World Cup was long. FIFA had spent most of its almost ninety-year existence as a boy's club, an international governing body dominated by white male Europeans. People like our old acquaintance Sir Stanley Rous, FIFA president from 1961 to 1974. Under Rous' leadership, FIFA commissioned a 1970 survey of its 139 affiliated national associations about women's football. Only twelve of the ninety respondents showed interest in the women's game. FIFA wasn't involved in early tournaments. Both the 1970 Coppa del Mondo in Italy (officially the Martini & Rossi Cup) and the Campeonato de Fútbol Femenil in Mexico a year later were organised by the Federation of Independent European Female Football, a governing body that UEFA, the most powerful of FIFA's continental confederations, distrusted. Under pressure from FIFA, the Mexican Football Federation refused to allow its grounds to be used in 1971.

But the world was changing in the 1970s and FIFA, however reluctantly, changed with it. The rise of second-wave feminism. Title IX in the United States in 1972. The re-legalisation of women's football in places where it had long been banned, like England (1971) and Brazil (1979). FIFA leaders could hardly have missed the popularity of the unofficial World Cups in the early 1970s. One hundred and ten thousand people watched the 1971 final between Denmark and Italy at Mexico City's Azteca Stadium. The 2023 documentary *Copa 71* dazzlingly reveals another universe, where women footballers are mobbed on buses, pursued as celebrities and perform to vast audiences in the world's biggest stadiums.

Rous' replacement as FIFA president in 1974, João Havelange, was no feminist. If FIFA started showing an interest in the women's game, it was to control it. Order 142, FIFA's 1970 survey of women's football, was about finding out what was being played and, where possible, taking it over. Incorporation not liberation. Havelange wanted to make football (or, rather, FIFA-controlled football) a truly global force. Commercialisation (partners like Adidas and Coca Cola) and globalisation – new markets in Africa and Asia – went hand in hand in Havelange's vision. This vision prioritised the men's game. But the Brazilian was savvy enough to know that women's football could be part of this legacy-boosting narrative of growth.

Progress, though, wasn't driven from FIFA headquarters in Switzerland but from inside the women's game. In 1986, at FIFA's annual congress in Mexico City, Norwegian Ellen Wille took to the congress floor – the first woman to do so in FIFA's eighty-two-year existence – to highlight women's football's absence from FIFA's annual report. 'I got very angry', Wille told the BBC in 2024, 'and I said we have to do something about it'. She made two proposals: to include women's football in the Olympics and to create a women's World Cup. FIFA General Secretary Sepp Blatter was struck by Wille's size – at four feet ten inches, she struggled to reach the podium microphone – but also by her message. So was Blatter's boss. 'Havelange told me, "From now, you must remember the women's football"'.[5] For a women's world championship, Havelange turned to the hosts of the inaugural FIFA U-16 World Championship in 1985. A country that could organise sports events efficiently and on budget. A country seeking greater influence in FIFA's football family. A country with the biggest potential football markets of all. The People's Republic of China.

Women's football arrived in China around the same time as communism. The Communist Party of China (CCP) was founded in Shanghai in 1921. Three years later, in the same city, Sheng Kunnan, a teacher at the Lianjiang Women's Physical Education Institute, translated football's rules into Chinese and taught students how to play. With support from the Institute's principal, the feminist Lu Lihua, Lianjiang started competing against local men's teams. While there were no other women's teams in Shanghai, women played football in other coastal cities in the 1920s.

China's war with Japan (1937–45), and the subsequent civil war between the CCP and the nationalist Kuomintang (1945–49), halted early developments. A male-dominated society built around the doctrine of Confucianism, whose strictly defined gender roles confined women to submissive, domestic lives, hardly helped either. A few women played football at Xibei University in Nanzhou in 1939, but that was about it. War and conservatism kept the game at the margins of society.

Things didn't improve in the People's Republic of China, the communist state founded on 1 October 1949. There were mixed matches in schools in Guandong, close to the British colony of Hong Kong, but football under Mao was understood as a male game. Maoism promoted the cult of swimming (the Great Helmsman's preferred activity), sport for military purposes, and sport for geopolitical advancement, notably the 'ping pong diplomacy' that sparked rapprochement between China and the USA in the early 1970s. As a foreign sport and a global sport not centred on the Olympics, football didn't get a look in. The women's game disappeared amid the chaos of Mao's Cultural Revolution (1966–76).

Mao's death in 1976 paved the way for a rebirth, this time on surer footing than in the 1920s. Most of women's football's foundational dates come from the decade after the Cultural Revolution, a period marked by the ascension to power of Mao's rival, Deng Xiaoping, and Deng's 'open door' policy. Announced in December 1978, this major shift in economic strategy opened China's quasi-autarkic command economy to foreign businesses, with the goal of making China 'the world's factory'. Keen for Western investment, Deng dialled back China's Cold War partisanship, cutting support to Global South revolutionaries and promoting an 'independent foreign policy' that kept a foot in both superpower camps. Opening doors applied to sport as well as economics. After a twenty-one-year absence, China rejoined the IOC in 1979 and sent teams to the 1980 Olympics.

Women's football began to thrive. The first teams at the Xi'an Dongfang Machinery Factory and Xi'an Railway No. 1 Middle School in 1977. The first match, a 2–2 draw between the same teams, the following year. The first nationwide tournament in Chuxiong City in 1981. The first international tournament in Guangzhou, against teams from Japan and Singapore, in 1983. Women's football's debut in 1987 at the National Games, the country's largest multi-sport event. By 1985, thirty-seven teams were competing for the national championship. Women's teams could be found in the provinces of Yunnan, Liaoning, Yanbian, Guandong and Shaanxi. They played in such cities as Beijing, Tianjin, Datong, Guangzhou, Shanghai and Changchun.

In Jesolo in northern Italy on 21 July 1986, China's national team played its first competitive match. Fittingly, given the rivalry that would develop between the nations, it was against the USA, in the fourth edition of the Mundialito ('little World Cup'), the closest thing at the time to a world championship. China lost 2–1 to the improving Americans but recovered to finish third. A few months later in Hong Kong, Cong Zheyu's side entered the Asian Cup for the first time – and won, going unbeaten through the tournament, scoring twenty-three goals, and conceding none. This was the first of seven straight Asian Cups, a run of success (1986–1999) that bookended a golden age. In this period, China also won an Olympic silver medal (1996) and reached the 1999 World Cup final. Along with the United States, the Steel Roses, said star player Sun Wen, became 'the pre-eminent powers in women's soccer'.[6]

Success came against the odds. In 1989, China had eight professional women's teams, down from thirty-seven four years earlier. In 1986, there were only 300 professional players. State support was patchy and easily withdrawn. Partly because the IOC excluded women's football from the Olympics, China's National Sports Commission decided in September 1987 to omit the sport from the 7th National Games in Beijing in 1993. Exclusion from China's biggest sports competition, after featuring in it for the first time, was a blow. It meant reduced funding and media coverage, and a decline in the number of teams and players. Despite the national team's success, women's football in China was on a downward curve by 1991.

The story of China's women footballers is part of a global narrative: a constant struggle against the indifference or hostility of male-dominated institutions, like the CCP and the Chinese Football Association (CFA), and the chauvinism of patriarchal societies. Sun Qingmei, one of China's best players at the 1991 World Cup, recalled how her parents locked her in her bedroom to stop her playing football. Teammate Liu Ailing remembered her parents' lament that 'such a lovely girl' wanted to play 'a boy's sport'.[7] The national team's first training centre, in Yingde in Guandong province, was a former warehouse. There was no hot water for showers, not enough tables to seat everyone for dinner and no electric fans to drive away mosquitoes in the summer. Players in the mid–late 80s never forgot the 'terrible' training pitch: 'On wet days the ground became a muddy puddle and we played in it. Tears and rain ran down our faces'.[8] Women footballers around the world encountered such conditions throughout the twentieth century, cut off from government purse strings and outside the public eye.

But the story in China had a twist. A twist that had more to do with the geopolitical ambitions of Deng's CCP and Havelange's FIFA than with concern for women's football, but a twist, nonetheless. China's government was reluctant to support the women's game, but it was happy to seek private capital for sports events that might showcase a 'new' China to the world. FIFA's ambitions – this was an organisation with the chutzpah to nominate its president for a Nobel Peace Prize in 1988! – dovetailed nicely with Beijing's. Havelange and co. wanted a reliable Asian partner to tap into football's vast markets there. Deng and co. wanted to use sport to normalise China's presence in international affairs. The end goal was hosting the Olympics. In 1985, Deng gave the green light to Beijing's bid for the 2000 Summer Games. The following year, Havelange suggested China bid for the 2002 World Cup, which FIFA was awarding to Asia for the first time.

The Olympic goal was a distant dream in 1985, when China hosted its first major football tournament, the U-16 World Championship. Before the country could host an Olympics (or indeed a World Cup), further proof was needed that it could run big competitions. Neither Havelange nor Blatter forgot Ellen Wille's demand at the FIFA Congress in 1986. So, FIFA suggested that China host a Women's Invitation Tournament in 1988, a dry run for a FIFA-sponsored World Cup. China agreed, and the 12-team tournament was scheduled for Guandong from 1–12 June.

The location was no accident. Guandong was among China's fastest-growing provinces, an export-driven poster child for Deng's economic reforms. Close to Hong Kong, it was also one of China's football centres. The capital, Guangzhou, hosted the first international women's tournament in 1983. Guandong hosted the 6th National Games in 1987, where women's football made its debut. The province knew how to host sports events without imposing on Beijing. In 1988 as in 1991, private capital – some from FIFA sponsors, some from Hong Kong businessmen – bankrolled women's football's arrival in China. Presented by International Sport and Leisure, the Swiss marketing company yoked to FIFA, the 1988 tournament got support from Huo Yingdong, a.k.a. Henry Fok, one of Hong Kong's richest men, president of the Hong Kong FA, and vice-chairman of FIFA's Women's Football Committee. Corporate sponsorship, meanwhile, kept the hosts afloat. A 1988 deal with Guangzhou Qixing Pharmaceutical Company gave an annual total of $15,000 to the women's team. The Steel Roses would no longer cost the CFA a penny.

Forty-five thousand people came to Tianhe Stadium for China's opening game in the Invitation Tournament, a 2–0 win over Canada, part of an aggregate crowd of 375,780 for twenty-six games in four cities, Guangzhou, Foshan, Jiangmen and Panyu. China's run ended with a narrow defeat in the semi-finals to Sweden, who lost 1–0 in the final to Norway in Guangzhou on 12 June. A crowd of 35,000 watched an exciting game, settled in the fifty-eighth minute by Linda Medalen's individual goal.

FIFA liked what they saw in 1988. Havelange praised China's 'excellent' work. With improvements to transport and telecommunications, he suggested, the country could run the inaugural World Cup.[9] In July 1989, a month after government forces crushed student unrest in Tiananmen Square, with the loss of between 300 and 1,000 lives, the authorities selected Guandong as the host province.[10] Some FIFA officials argued China was unfit to host a major tournament. Havelange held firm, wheeling out the adage beloved of sports administrators (when it suited them), that sport and politics shouldn't mix. Nonsense, of course. As Hong Kong's *South China Morning Post* observed, Guandong's hosting efforts in 1991 weren't about a love for football. 'China has grabbed this opportunity to further its post-Tiananmen rehabilitation ... to show off the better points of its brand of communism'.[11] That won't be the last time we hear the word 'brand' in relation to the first World Cup. The twelve-team tournament, featuring representatives of all six FIFA confederations, went ahead, despite the blood on the regime's hands.

When Sun Wen claimed in 2000 that China and the United States were the 'pre-eminent powers' in women's football, she omitted one name. In the 1980s and 1990s, Norway (1991 population: 4.26 million) matched the achievements of its superpower rivals. Olympic bronze in 1996, Olympic gold four years later. European champions in 1987 and 1993. World Cup finalists in 1991, World Cup winners four years later. 'Small country – big results'.[12]

Women's football began in Norway as a 'curiosity', a game played on Constitution Day and other national holidays in the capital, Oslo, and in regions like Østfold, on Norway's eastern border with

Sweden. Early matches against men's teams were reported as freak shows, like this encounter in Brumundal in 1931: 'Humorous football match. Women's team against old men'. The attitude of the Norwegian Football Federation (NFF), founded in 1902, echoed that of associations from Brazil to England. Football, said board member Per Christian Andersen in 1922, was 'a game for strong men and powerful boys'. When Fløya Ladies requested support for a fund-raising match in 1931, the NFF replied: 'Ladies should not play football!'[13] For the next forty years, women's football had close to zero institutional support or media coverage.

In the 1970s and early 1980s, the women's game emerged in the public sphere, benefitting from moves towards gender equality at home and abroad. With the Norwegian Olympic Committee promoting 'sport for all', the creation of a Gender Equality Council in 1972, and challenges to the idea that women were too fragile for competitive team sports, football became, in Eivind Skille's words, 'a symbol of women's liberation'.[14]

The transformation happened from below, with federations trailing, often reluctantly, in the wake of pioneers. People like Ellen Wille, from Oslo club Frigg, who organised the first national championship in 1971. Or Målfrid Kuvås, captain of BUL-Oslo's women's team, who helped organise the first all-women's match (Amazon Grimstad vs. BUL, 12 July 1970), arranged tours of Europe and Asia, and played a key role in early editions of the Norway Cup (established in 1973), the world's largest youth tournament for boys and girls.

The usual chauvinist claptrap floated around the NFF. Women's football encouraged lesbianism, made football 'a game for wimps' (*frøkensport*) and meant too few changing rooms and toilets for male players. But influential figures, like ex-national team player Per Pettersen, NFF general secretary Nikolai Johansen and former NFF president Per Ravn Omdal, backed the pioneers. 'Men and women can use the same toilets and dressing rooms, but at different times', Omdal wryly noted.[15] In 1976, the NFF officially recognised women's football. Two years later, the national team, coached by Pettersen, made its debut, losing 2–1 to Sweden at the Nordic Championships in Denmark.

Norway's golden age ran concurrently with China's, from a first European Championship in 1987 to Olympic gold in Sydney in 2000. This was a period in which diplomatic and economic ties between the countries intensified, as Norway – which had recognised the PRC in

1950 – sought to balance 'small state idealism' (condemnation of the Tiananmen Square massacre, support for the Dalai Lama) with 'small state realism' (ongoing economic and political 'normalisation') in its dealings with Beijing.[16] The football models were different. While the CFA never had more than 2,000 registered players before 1992, the NFF had almost 20,000 registered footballers in 1985, plus another 30,000 U-17 girls. Grassroots activism, the NFF's post-1976 support and football's rise as Norway's number one sport for females all helped shape Norway's success. As did the emergence of players like Hege Riise and Linda Medalen, one of three Norwegians in FIFA's all-star team at the 1988 Invitation. Norway won the tournament, as they won the 1987 Euros. They returned to China in November 1991 among the favourites for the World Cup.

Let's start with the scale of the occasion. China's players entered the Tianhe Stadium on 16 November 1991 to the sound of 65,000 cheering people. Not something they'd heard before. Sun Wen – later co-voted (along with Michelle Akers-Stahl) FIFA's player of the twentieth century – was then just eighteen. As she walked on to the pitch, she remembered, 'I was so nervous that the rhythm of my breathing changed; "is the next breath in or out?", I asked myself – it was so funny!'[17]

The opening fifteen minutes are a mess. A bubbly pitch doesn't help. Passes are miscontrolled or overhit, possession cheaply surrendered. Norway look marginally the more composed of two nervous teams and get a chance to take the lead in the third minute, when Yang Zhou cleans out Hege Riise in the box. A clear penalty. Up steps midfielder Tone Haugen, but goalie Honglian Zhong dives to her left to make a good save.

An early let off for the hosts. And the game's decisive moment. After the penalty, admitted Norway coach Even Pellerud, 'we didn't have the ball, China totally outplayed us'. The hosts cut out the 'chaotic passing' and mistakes. They moved the ball well and pressured Norway's backline, never allowing the European side to 'show its true level'.[18] Watching the game, you're struck by the fluidity of China's play, a contrast with Norway's agricultural approach. Perhaps China's quality surprised the visitors. Having avoided each other at the 1988 Invitation, this was the first competitive meeting between the sides (see Figure 10.1). 'We hadn't seen the Asian countries', recalled Pellerud,

Figure 10.1 China vs. Norway, Tianhe Stadium, Guangzhou, 16 November 1991. © TOMMY CHENG/AFP via Getty Images.

who became coach in 1989. '[The tournament] was so big, you kind of lose yourself a little bit.'[19]

The twenty-second minute. Wu Wieying is fouled outside the Norwegian box. Her free kick is headed home by unmarked defender Ma Li. The first goal in a FIFA Women's World Cup. Others follow in the second half, as the ragged Norwegians are pulled apart by the hosts. Six minutes after the break, Liu Ailing receives a cute pass in the penalty area and slots the ball past goalkeeper Reidun Seth. Liu then scores the goal of the game five minutes later, a thirty-yard screamer that crashes in off the underside of the bar. Two minutes from time, Qingmei Sun's clever chip seals the rout. 'A team that was not used to losing, and to lose 4–0, that was tough', grimaced Pellerud.[20]

For China, it was a dream start. Tournament openers, reckoned the *People's Daily*, are always difficult, 'but tonight the Chinese women's football team played very beautifully'. Coach Shang Ruihua noted how his players had learned from European teams they'd encountered in the 1988 Invitation and the 1987 Mundialito, especially in terms of defensive and midfield shape.[21] And don't forget the crowd. Even if the organisers handed out free tickets, or pressured local workers to attend, the numbers and the atmosphere were impressive. An abiding memory of the tournament for Sweden's Anneli Andelén was 'a lot of screaming Chinese people in the crowd!'[22] That was certainly the case in Tianhe Stadium on 16 November.

Football was popular in China, but the men's team was a constant disappointment. Following an embarrassing loss to Hong Kong in a 1985 World Cup qualifier, fans in Beijing had rioted, attacking foreigners and journalists, burning buses and smashing up underground stations. One hundred and twenty-seven people were arrested; five got jail sentences. The Steel Roses, in contrast, brought joy. They had an excellent, likeable team. A team, moreover, that previewed a better China. Football was a rare happy public space in the aftermath of the Tiananmen massacre, and one of the few places where gender equality, as per Mao's injunction that 'women hold up half the sky', looked like more than CCP rhetoric. 'We have left the image of the demure Oriental woman far behind', said midfielder Li Xiufu during the tournament.[23] This 'new China' was easier to get behind than Deng's authoritarian regime. Perhaps that helps explain the excitement in the stadium for the Norway match. If FIFA hadn't expected much from the tournament, 'someone had forgotten to tell ... the fans'.[24] And the players. On and off the pitch, China's first World Cup experience could hardly have gone better.

FIFA hedged its bets in 1991. Just look at the tournament name. The competition in Guandong was a World Cup that wasn't a World Cup. The women's game wasn't yet entrusted with FIFA's gold standard branding. Instead, Havelange and Blatter presented the Women's World Championship for the M&Ms Cup (see Figure 10.2). It was a 'privilege', said Theo Leenders, M&Ms' Managing Director, 'to be so deeply involved in an event which helps to cast away old prejudices'.[25] While FIFA's name was placed almost apologetically, in small type, on the front of match tickets, the yellow and brown M&M branding took up the entire reverse side.

The prominence of an American confectionery product reflected not only FIFA's financial caution, but also the spirit of the times. At the end of the Cold War, as post-communist economies elsewhere became blank canvasses for ruinous neo-liberal 'restructuring', China was ahead of the game. The Deng regime, like FIFA, sought private funding for an event that might bring political benefits. Hence the title sponsorship given to M&Ms (no FIFA men's tournament was

Figure 10.2 A policeman on guard at the Tianhe Stadium, Guangzhou, 15 November 1991. © TOMMY CHENG/AFP via Getty Images.

sullied by such blatant advertising) and the grateful receipt of Henry Fok's patronage. The tycoon built the 15,000-capacity Ying Tung (later Henry Fok) Stadium in Guangzhou, which hosted five matches, and paid for much else too. Eager to prove its business credentials, the Guandong government wooed investors and poured energy into its hosting duties. Locals, perhaps under 'voluntold' orders, chipped in, raising funds by purchasing raffle tickets and sports memorabilia. You might think, reading this, that everyone paid for the 1991 World Cup bar Beijing and Zurich. In its small way, the tournament anticipated the Sports Mega-Event of the twenty-first century: multinational corporate sponsorship, an authoritarian host government and an 'apolitical' governing body with its eyes on the bottom line.

FIFA's ambivalence came across in the tournament regulations. The governing body considered playing with a smaller ball in 1991, before rejecting the idea. But it confirmed a widespread practice at the time, reduced match duration. Just as the IOC felt that women should run 3,000 not 5,000 metres at the Olympics, so FIFA decreed that women's games should last 80 minutes. As if, joked American captain April Heinrichs, Havelange and his colleagues were 'afraid our ovaries were going to fall out if we played 90'.[26]

FIFA undercut this concession to the 'fragility' of women footballers by cramming a twenty-six-match tournament into two weeks. When the USA met Norway in the final on 30 November, both were playing their sixth game in a fortnight, a game every two days, often in warm conditions. Why the compressed schedule, when teams at men's World Cups typically had four days' recovery between games? To save money. The shorter the tournament, the less it would cost FIFA and its corporate and government partners.

The commitment to thrift was reflected in the finalists' accommodation. Opened in 1983, the White Swan Hotel was a five-star venue on the banks of the Pearl River in Guangzhou. Accommodation quality wasn't the issue; the issue was that both teams were staying there, a cost-reduction exercise not implemented at men's tournaments. The Americans didn't like it, even if a lavish pre-match Thanksgiving dinner – after weeks of eating Snickers bars on a $10 per diem – helped soften the blow. 'Can you imagine Van Basten and Baresi meeting in a lift the morning of the 1994 World Cup final?', Heinrichs asked. 'It's a bit of an insult to the two teams here in China'.[27] Perhaps not coincidentally, the White Swan was a Henry Fok property, a luxury hotel for foreign businessmen and tourists built in partnership with the provincial government.

FIFA's approach in 1991 was clear. Let's see how this turns out, before we decide whether to support it. It turned out, most agreed, better than anticipated. FIFA's Technical Report on the 1991 World Cup praised playing standards, much improved from the 1988 Invitation and the 1989 Euros. 'Switching from defence to attack was faster', noted China, 'and great technical progress was evident'. Brazil, third in 1988 but eliminated in the group stages in 1991, were surprised by the quality of 'their European and American counterparts', New Zealand by 'the pace at which other teams played'. Havelange praised China for hosting 'an excellent party'.[28] The 1991 World Cup served as a launch pad, as Uruguay did in 1930 for the men's tournament, for FIFA to do the whole thing again in four years' time.

Like Copa 71, the 1991 World Cup proved that women's football could attract large audiences. Some supporters got free tickets, yes. And there were stage-managed elements in the public's enthusiasm, as at any big sports event. Guandong TV provided saturation coverage, with all matches shown live and extensive highlights programmes. Billboards advertising the tournament ('Hail the first FIFA Women's

World Championship'; 'Welcome to our visitors from five continents') were inescapable in Guangzhou. A fish restaurant in the city offered a 'World Cup discount'.[29]

Local passion for the tournament, though, astonished the players. New Zealand striker Wendi Henderson remembered the media circus around the Ferns, the sense that China 'didn't want to fail at hosting this': 'The experience was mind-blowing.' Germany's Doris Fitschen recalled 3,000 fans at one training session ('amazing') and lots more Chinese support in the stadiums, which was just as well, as only eight German supporters made the trip to Asia. All this reinforced Sun Wen's observation that 'hosting the 1991 Women's World Cup was so natural for us ... the fans were always very enthusiastic'.[30]

The form of the Steel Roses only fed the excitement. Riding momentum from their demolition of Norway, China cruised through Group A, drawing 2–2 with Denmark and beating New Zealand 4–1 in Foshan, Liu Ailing again scoring twice. The atmosphere in Guandong Provincial Stadium for the Denmark game was 'electrifying', as chants of *ga jau, ga jau* ('pump more gas') spurred the hosts to come from behind twice.[31]

China's reward for topping Group A was a quarter-final against Sweden. The *Daily Telegraph* called it 'the best match of the tournament', played in front of another large, noisy crowd in Tianhe Stadium: 'every time their team crossed the halfway line [the fans] were on their feet'. Pia Sundhage's header put the Swedes in front after three minutes. China attacked incessantly, but the team had left its shooting boots at home. Chance after chance went begging, while Liu Ailing hit the post with a superb long-range effort. Honglian Zhong kept out everything at the other end, including a Sundhage penalty, but it wasn't enough. China exited the tournament with pride. 'Never have women [in China] been the focus of such national attention and respect', commented the *South China Morning Post*. It was just a shame more women weren't in the stands. About three-quarters of the crowd at Tianhe Stadium on 24 November were male. Where were all the women? Li Xiufu knew: 'Putting the children to bed.'[32]

Norway, meanwhile, recovered superbly from their humbling to the hosts. After finishing second in Group A, Even Pellerud's side beat Italy 3–2 in extra time in Jiangmen to set up a semi-final against Sweden. There they produced the performance of the tournament, trouncing Pia Sundhage and teammates 4–1. After Lena Videkull's sixth-minute opener for the Swedes, Norway took over. They hit the bar and post in one move before Tina Svensson equalised from the spot just before half time. The second half was one-way traffic, as two goals from Linda Medalen and a solo effort from Agnete Carlsen secured a dominant win. Opening night seemed like a lifetime ago.

Sunday 30 November 1991, Tianhe Stadium, Guangzhou. The first Women's World Cup final. The USA vs. Norway. The coming force – an aggressive, high-scoring team that had 'captured the attention of even the old stodgies here'[33] – against what American striker Michelle Akers-Stahl called 'one of the best teams in the world', 'so good and tough and dirty'.[34] Pellerud knew the scale of the American challenge, led by the triple attacking threat of Akers-Stahl, April Heinrichs and Carin Jennings. Norway had beaten the USA in the quarter-final of the 1988 Invitation, but the Americans won their most recent meeting 4–0 in Winnipeg in 1990, 'a big eye-opener', said Pellerud, 'the USA played us off the field'.[35] Despite China's absence, a crowd of 63,000 watched the 1991 final, including the ubiquitous Pelé, called off the bench as a late substitute for Franz Beckenbauer as FIFA's ambassador at large.

Like many finals, USA vs. Norway didn't live up to expectations. The compressed schedule left both teams exhausted. Especially in the second half, they seemed to be running on fumes. Akers-Stahl had opened the scoring in the twentieth minute with a great header from Shannon Higgins' cross; Linda Medalen equalised nine minutes later, another header after US keeper Mary Harvey came for a cross and got nowhere near it. The game looked set for extra time when, in the seventy-eighth minute, Tina Svensson intercepted Higgins' punt forward. But Svensson underhit her back pass, allowing Akers-Stahl to take the ball around Reidun Seth and roll it into the empty net, her tenth goal of the tournament. Svensson collapsed in despair. Akers-Stahl looked too knackered to celebrate. Two minutes later, Belarusian referee Vadim Zhuk blew the final whistle. The USA were world champions (see Figure 10.3).

After 1991, the Women's World Cup was on its way. As were the two finalists. China '91 was successful enough, FIFA concluded, to retroactively call it the first Women's World Cup, and to take a more hands-on approach to future editions of the tournament. Sweden in 1995 was a backwards step. Average attendance across five cities was 4,315, compared to 19,615 in Guandong four years earlier. Only 17,158

Figure 10.3   Michelle Akers-Stahl (centre) celebrates with teammates Julie Foudy (left) and Carin Jennings after the USA beat Norway to win the first Women's World Cup, 30 November 1991. © TOMMY CHENG/AFP via Getty Images.

watched the final, played in torrential rain at Stockholm's Råsunda Stadium on 18 June. Norway, led by player of the tournament Hege Riise, beat Germany 2–0 to become world champions. This was a huge deal for the second smallest country (after Uruguay in 1930 and 1950) to win a World Cup. One in four Norwegians watched the final on TV.

The breakthrough came four years later at the third World Cup in America. Average tournament attendance was 37,944, rising to 69,000 for the USA's six matches. Ninety thousand people watched 'the dream final', a rematch of the 1996 Olympic final between the USA and China, at the Rose Bowl in California. It's perhaps the most iconic game in women's football history, occurring just two months after NATO's bombing of the Chinese embassy in Belgrade inflamed Sino-American relations. Here was China's chance to strike back against 'American hegemony' on and off the pitch: 'China has to win', implored one Beijing security guard. 'We have to beat America'.[36] He was out of luck. After a gripping but goalless 120 minutes in sweltering heat, the final went to penalties. Briana Scurry, miles off her line, saved from Liu Ying in round three (see Figure 10.4). And then Brandi Chastain converted the winning kick, to give the USA a second world title.

Figure 10.4 USA goalkeeper Briana Scurry saves Liu Ying's penalty in the World Cup final, Pasadena, California, 10 July 1999. © HECTOR MATA/AFP via Getty Images.

The American team arrived home from China in 1991 to zero fanfare. 'There were no TV crews or fans waiting for us', remembered Mia Hamm, just a few friends and US Soccer officials. In 1999, there was fanfare to spare for the 'girls of summer'. President Bill Clinton received the team at the White House: 'The whole country is caught up . . . It's going to have a bigger impact than people ever realised'.[37] The players appeared on David Letterman's Late Show and made the cover of *Time* and *Sports Illustrated*. For the first time, American boys wore the jerseys of a female team in large numbers. The popular explosion of 1999 wouldn't have happened without the groundwork laid eight years earlier, often (Akers, Hamm, Julie Foudy, Carla Werden, Kristine Lilly) by the same players. The 1991 World Cup, in April Heinrich's words, was 'a silent trigger' for the revolution that followed.[38]

Momentum proved difficult to sustain domestically, as professional leagues struggled to get off the ground in the early twenty-first century. Internationally, though, the US Women's National Team (USWNT) became dominant just as women's football emerged as a commercial, sporting and political force – and just as the United States drew some final benefits from what journalist Charles Krauthammer termed the 'unipolar moment', the brief window between the early

1990s and early 2000s when it was the world's sole superpower. Old rivals like China and Norway were seen off, as, more often than not, were new ones, like Germany and Japan. It wasn't all smooth sailing: the Americans didn't win their third World Cup until 2015. But they won it again in 2019, were runners-up to Japan in 2011, and racked up four Olympic gold medals (2004, 2008, 2012, 2024). No women's team came close to matching this level of success.

It wasn't just the football. From Mia Hamm to Megan Rapinoe, the best American players were global stars, in ways that the best Norwegian or Chinese women footballers rarely were. This reflected an American supremacy that encompassed not only politics, economics and the military, but popular culture too. Some resented the hype around America's 'golden girls', especially after the 1999 World Cup. More recently, some on the right have resented the activism: Rapinoe's support for Black Lives Matter and criticisms of US president Donald Trump, or the gender discrimination lawsuit the USWNT brought against its employer, US Soccer, in 2019, resulting (in 2022) in a settlement guaranteeing pay equity for the men's and women's teams. A quarter of the way through the twenty-first century, not much is left of post-Cold War America's global reputation. Women's football is an honourable exception: an enduring, progressive American legacy from the 1990s that continues to set international standards.

Norway, like the USA, had many memorable moments after the 1991 World Cup, winning the tournament in 1995 and claiming Olympic gold in Sydney in 2000, beating the USA 3–2 after extra time. 'It is good for the sport that someone beat America', said one of Norway's goal scorers, Gro Espeseth. After 2000, Norway, like China, wasn't often that someone, as other countries emerged to challenge American hegemony. In China's case, the decline was about vast resources allocated elsewhere; in Norway's, it was about finite resources catching up with you in a competitive global game. Hege Riise reflected in 2023 that 'with all the big nations really putting money into their women's programmes now, little Norway … will struggle to get to finals like we did when I played'.[39]

Decline is relative. Norway's recent teams haven't replicated the heroics of Riise and co. in 1995 and 2000, but they've hardly been terrible. Runners-up in the 2005 and 2013 Euros, World Cup quarter-finalists in 2003 and 2019, and fifteenth in FIFA's world rankings as of March 2025. Results Norway's men's team, who didn't make a single

World Cup between 1998 and 2026 and have never been higher than thirty-eighth in the FIFA rankings, would kill for. Add to that the fact that football is Norway's biggest women's sport (113,036 players and 8,416 teams in 2019), and that this system produces superstars like OL Lyonnes striker Ada Hegerberg and Barcelona winger Caroline Graham Hansen. Not bad for a country of 5.52 million.

By 1991, it was clear that China's football success was built on shaky foundations. Poor facilities. A small player pool. Football's exclusion from the National Games. The government's focus on individual sports as the most cost-effective means of winning Olympic medals. The 1991 side was a product of an under-funded system that was already malfunctioning. The 1999 team, which pushed the USA all the way in the World Cup final ('In my mind, there's two champions here', said American coach Tony DeCicco), 'was a product of an environment that no longer existed'.[40] China's excellence proved unsustainable.

Neglect in China coincided with the development of women's programmes elsewhere. Japan, North Korea and Australia won six of the seven Asian Cups between 2001 and 2018. A raft of strong nations – the likes of England, Spain, Canada, Brazil, France and the Netherlands – made Olympic and World Cup success harder to attain. 'In the past, we'd feel that the strong women's soccer teams were the same few sides, but now it's completely different', lamented midfielder Zhang Linyan in 2023.[41] From 2003 to 2023, China got no further than the World Cup quarter-finals and failed to qualify for the 2011 tournament. The biggest humiliation came seven years earlier, when the Steel Roses lost 8–0 to Germany at the Olympics. Fans left. Funding was cut. Women's football, wrote Wang Yong, 'lost its previous exulted status in Chinese society'.[42] A year later, the China Women's Super League was suspended because teams could no longer afford travel and accommodation costs. By 2011–12, China had sixteen professional teams and 10,000 registered footballers in a country of 1.3 billion people.

Mao enjoyed a dip in the Yangtze River and made table tennis China's national sport. Deng Xiaoping played bridge and billiards. Xi Jinping, who became president in 2012, was the first Chinese leader who loved football. His 'three wishes' on coming to power were all football-related, or rather, all related to the *bête noire* of Chinese sport, men's football: to qualify for a World Cup, to host a World Cup and to win a World Cup. None of these wishes have yet come true, at least for the men, whose only finals appearance came in 2002, when Jiang Zemin was president. There are many theories for the wretchedness of Chinese men's football: poor infrastructure; players' lack of creativity; CCP interference; corruption in the professional game; passivity encouraged by China's Confucian and Taoist traditions; Covid's impact on the briefly insurgent Chinese Super League. The list goes on, as do China's woes. After China lost 7–0 at home to Japan in a World Cup qualifier in March 2025, fans and the media rounded on a team ninety-fourth in FIFA's world rankings. 'It seems like the national team's performance is as consistent as ever', joked one supporter. China's main sports newspaper, the *Oriental Sports Daily*, couldn't see the funny side: 'When the taste of bitterness reaches its extreme, all that is left is numbness'.[43]

Compared to this national disaster, the post-90s decline of the Steel Roses looks gentle – the women's team won the Asian Cup in 2006 and 2022 – and easier to explain: decades of chronic underfunding. Perhaps there's an argument that CCP disinterest gave women's football breathing space, making it less reliant on the whims of an authoritarian state, less vulnerable to media scrutiny and corruption. But it's not convincing. Imagine what China's women might have achieved with a fraction of the backing the men get. It's possible that Xi Jinping and the CFA are finally asking the same question. In 2022, the authorities pivoted towards the women's game, announcing a thirteen-year plan, with the aim of winning the 2035 World Cup. 'Women's soccer', said Tom Byer, a consultant on the plan, 'is where they can build hopes and dreams'.[44]

Time will tell whether greater state support will bear fruit for what many people call China's real *guozo* ('national team'). At the end of the golden era, President Jiang Zemin praised the Steel Roses for their tenacity in winning glory for the socialist motherland. But, to borrow from something written during the 1991 World Cup, 'it is the Chinese woman, not the Chinese state' who is 'the greatest winner' in the story of Chinese football.[45] As the Cold War ended, a new sporting superpower emerged. And it did so first in women's sport. In swimming, in athletics, in gymnastics, and – despite many obstacles – in football. The Steel Roses became the most visible representatives of a new Chinese femininity, leading proof that, in Li Xiufu's words, 'women really can really do anything men can do'.[46] And can do it, in fact, better.

Xi Jinping's football ambitions for China have hitherto been stymied. The same can't be said for China's sports diplomacy. Since

1991, China has hosted countless international events. No men's World Cup, but a second Women's World Cup in 2007 (delayed from 2003 due to SARS), numerous Asian Games, and, crucially, two Olympics. Ignoring international criticism, whether about migrant workers, Tibet or the Uyghurs, Beijing hosted the 2008 Summer Games and the 2022 Winter Games, showcasing to the world what Norwegian sociologist Stein Ringen called 'the perfect dictatorship'. The Cold War ended in 1991, but the idea of using spectacles like the Olympics or the World Cup to polish a country's image went nowhere. Alongside Saudi Arabia, China has become the twenty-first century's most ruthless exponent of what's now called sportswashing. That process began in Guandong in November 1991, when the PRC, barely two years after Tiananmen Square, embraced a new world. A new world of women's football and, more importantly for the CCP, a new world of sports geopolitics, where China called the shots.

EPILOGUE

It looks more like a medieval castle than a football stadium, with copper turrets, mahogany beams and a swooping, black-shingled roof. Or perhaps 'an art nouveau church or a great country mansion'.[1] This is the Pancho Arena (capacity 3,500), in the village of Felcsút (population 1,860), twenty-five miles west of the Hungarian capital, Budapest. Opened in 2014, it was designed by Imre Makovecz and built by Tamás Dobrosi's Doparum Architects, after Makovecz's death in 2011. Makovecz hated communist buildings, and it shows. The Pancho Arena, an example of organic architecture, is the antithesis of the Népstadion, the vast bowl opened in Budapest in 1953, Hungarian football's greatest year.

The Pancho Arena, like much else in twenty-first-century Hungarian football, is named for the brightest star of 1953, Ferenc Puskás. 'Pancho' was the name Real Madrid supporters gave Puskás after he left Hungary in 1956 and built a second brilliant career on the other side of the Iron Curtain. The team that plays in the Pancho Arena is Puskás Akadémia FC. Founded in 2005, Puskás Akadémia have played in Hungary's first division since 2013, finishing runners-up in 2020–21 and 2024–25.

Why has a village outside Budapest become the cathedral of Hungarian football? The answer, echoing Scornicești in 70s Romania, is simple: Viktor Orbán. Felcsút is the home turf of the most powerful politician in post-Cold War Hungary, and one of Europe's most influential populists. The Pancho Arena is a stone's throw from Orbán's dacha, in the village where the four-term Prime Minister spent his childhood and played semi-professional football. Orbán was knocking around on fourth-division pitches in Felcsút during his first stint as national leader (1998–2002). The ex-law student, the man who founded Fidesz (Alliance of Young Democrats) in 1988, is football crazy (see Figure E.1). A decent player and an avid spectator (watching up to six games per day), Orbán has placed football at the heart of his conservative reinvention of post-communist Hungary. To make Hungary great again means, in the Trump-esque words of journalist György Szöllősi, 'to make Hungarian football great again'.[2] So, the Pancho Arena serves as the court of King Viktor, a place where Hungary's elites gather like courtiers around their monarch to cut deals and talk politics. 'Even if you hate football, you have to go to these matches', says Gyula Mucsi of Transparency International.[3] It's in the VIP skybox at Felcsút's monument to populism that Hungary's future is decided.

For Orbán, Hungary's proud footballing past under communism is something to both reject and exploit. But Hungary's greatest footballer remains 'the eternal role model': 'The communist leaders

Figure E.1 Hungarian Prime Minister Viktor Orbán in action, Woodbridge, New Jersey, October 1998. © STAN HONDA/AFP via Getty Images.

once shamefully disowned Ferenc Puskás, declaring him a traitor. Yet he was arguably the most famous Hungarian of the 20th century, who brought pride to Hungary even during its darkest times'.[4] Orbán gave this paean at the 2024 opening of the Puskás Museum, located at the (yes, that's right) Puskás Arena in Budapest. Opened in 2019, the Puskás Arena was the successor and antidote to the former national stadium, the Nép, demolished (as the Ferenc Puskás Stadium) in 2016. The Puskás Arena is part of a generous, possibly corrupt programme of stadium redevelopment funded by Fidesz since Orbán's return to power in 2010. It will host the 2026 Champions League final. Viktor Orbán will almost certainly be there. For him, as for the communists he loathed, football is the most potent of political weapons.

What would the man himself have thought of all these tributes? Ferenc Puskás was diagnosed with Alzheimer's Disease in 2000. He died six years later at the age of seventy-nine, before Orbán took control of Hungarian politics. In 1996, British journalist Ann McElvoy travelled to Budapest to interview the Galloping Major for the fortieth anniversary of the Hungarian Revolution. She found him reticent, unwilling or perhaps unable – the signs of Alzheimer's were there – to discuss the events of 1956. One comment, though, cut through the evasions: 'I didn't care about politics. I cared about football. I still don't care about politics. Then, ideology ruled, now money does. What's the difference? As long as people still like football'.[5]

If money ruled football after the fall of communism, as Puskás grumbled, it certainly didn't replace politics. The two were deeply intertwined in post-Cold War Europe, as the story of Orbán's Hungary illustrates. Francis Fukuyama's 'end of history' – the post-1991 'universalization' of Western democracy as 'the final form of human government' – proved illusory.[6] So did the end of football history. Communism's collapse accelerated the remaking of football in capitalism's triumphant image, all deregulated markets and freedom of movement. Any history of the 1990s can chart the highlights, or lowlights, of the game's arrival in the neo-liberal age. The creation of the English Premier League. The European Cup's rebranding as the Champions League. All-seater stadiums. The opening of television markets to cable and satellite companies. The Bosman Ruling. Sepp Blatter becoming FIFA President. The uncontested ascendancy of capitalism transformed football and politics, not only in its self-proclaimed heartland, Europe, but wherever the game was played, as players, no longer constrained by Cold War or colonial borders, migrated in vast numbers, often from the Global South to the Global North.

After the Cold War, football's popularity and profitability mushroomed. But the game's wealth, as befitted the times, was distributed unequally, creating a chasm between the haves and have nots. From post-colonial Africa, where the UN Commission for Human Rights warned in 1999 of a modern-day 'slave trade' in footballers, to democratic Brazil, the world's biggest exporter of players, the new era brought great opportunities and wealth for a select few, but homesickness, poverty and racism for many more. Some of the inequalities played out along Cold War lines. Eastern European clubs once challenged West European sides for UEFA's biggest prizes, the peak of communist success coinciding, ironically enough, with the period (c. 1985–1991) when communism fell apart. Since 1992, no ex-communist team has come close to winning the Champions League. Only three former Soviet clubs, CSKA Moscow, Zenit St. Petersburg and Shakhtar Donetsk, have won the Europa League. Dynamo Berlin, Lutz Eigendorf's feared old team, finished 2024/25 eighth in the Regionalliga Nordost, Germany's fourth tier. Steaua Bucharest and 'eternal derby' rivals Dinamo, our 1988 protagonists, haven't fallen this far, with Steaua (now FCSB) continuing to pick up league titles since the fall of Ceauşescu. But neither has made inroads in Europe, where teams from the 'big five' leagues in England, France, Germany, Italy and Spain rule. The same is true for Red Star Belgrade (FK Crvena Zvezda), whose 1991 win over Marseille marked the last time an Eastern European team won the European Cup.

Red Star's victory feels poignant because it occurred on the cusp of two intersecting moments of history: the final collapse of communism in Eastern Europe and the radical transformation of European football into the commercialised, TV-led product that we know today. It was a last hurrah for the Socialist Federal Republic of Yugoslavia, which descended in 1991 into a series of conflicts that would span the decade. Red Star's starting line-up in Bari on 29 May included players from five of the country's six republics – four Serbs, two Montenegrins, two Macedonians, one Croat and one Bosnian – as well as Romanian defender Miodrag Belodedici, who we last encountered in Chapter 9, helping Steaua Bucharest win the 1986 European Cup. Victory on penalties, after a turgid game in which Ljupko Petrović's side displayed little of the brilliance that lit up their 4–3 aggregate win over Bayern

Munich in the semi-final, sparked joy across the republic, from Ljubljana in the north to Skopje in the south: 'that May evening everyone was united under a single red and white flag!' But there was a Serbian nationalist core to the celebrations, as President Slobodan Milošević, a self-confessed football neophyte, got the obligatory photo ops with a Red Star shirt and the returning heroes. Before summer was over, Croatia had declared independence from the Serb-dominated Federal Republic. A civil war began, one that made Milošević's regime an international pariah. In May 1992, shortly after UN sanctions were imposed, Yugoslavia was kicked out of that year's European Championship, replaced at the last minute by Denmark, who went on to win it. Before resigning as national team manager, a tearful Ivica Osim, whose wife and kids were trapped in his native Sarajevo, said his country didn't deserve to play in the Euros: 'Everyone is shooting, barricades are everywhere ... How can you play football in this situation?'[7]

The Yugoslav Wars strike a discordant note in the success story of European football in the 1990s. The end of the Cold War, evidently, didn't make football a politics-free zone. Quite the opposite. Look at Euro '92. Look at China's mobilisation of women's football. Look at the nexus of hooliganism and paramilitarism in Yugoslavia, where Red Star ultras were prominent in the Serb Volunteer Guard that ethnically cleansed Croatia and Bosnia-Herzegovina. Look at the ever-murkier process of bidding for World Cups. The large sums of money flowing into the game made it more politically important than ever. Football in the Cold War was sometimes a tool of hard power, a reflection of a state's coercive capabilities. More often, it was about soft power, 'the ability to get what you want through attraction'.[8] To persuade, to distract from the violence and unpopularity of regimes, to build friendships across ideological divides. Football after the Cold War became increasingly about hard power, a central element of statehood, notably in Qatar, host of the 2022 World Cup, whose authoritarian government placed football 'at the heart of its foreign policy and economic development'.[9]

The afterlives of the legends in our Cold War story varied. Some, like Ferenc Puskás and Konstantin Beskov, were winding down long coaching careers when communism collapsed. Puskás' eclectic CV, which peaked when he led Panathinaikos to the 1971 European Cup final, closed in 1993 with a four-game spell as Hungary coach. Beskov's final gig was in 1994–95, when he returned to coach Dynamo Moscow, the team for whom he'd scored five goals on the 1945 tour that kicked off football's Cold War. Both men died in 2006, four years after Puskás' nemesis, Fritz Walter, passed away. Walter's hometown club, FC Kaiserslautern, the team Lutz Eigendorf joined after defecting from East Germany in 1979, had renamed their iconic hilltop stadium, the Betzenberg, for Germany's first World Cup-winning captain in 1985. But Walter didn't live long enough to see the Fritz-Walter-Stadion host five World Cup matches in 2006. His coaching career, like the man himself, was modest – a few years at local club SV Alsenborn, then a quiet life running a cinema and a laundrette with his wife in Kaiserslautern.

A quiet life wasn't in the script for the man who lifted Germany's second World Cup in 1974. Franz Beckenbauer coached Germany to a third World Cup in 1990 (Spain's coach for this tournament was, less successfully, Luis Suárez), before embarking on a controversial career as a football administrator, the highlight of which was heading Germany's bid for the 2006 World Cup. Beckenbauer died in 2024, a year after Suárez. Both were feted as giants of the game, as was Eusébio, the greatest African footballer of all time. After he died of a heart attack in Lisbon in 2014, Portugal declared three days of national mourning.

Not all our icons left behind such powerful impressions. The world has largely forgotten the Cold War exploits of Jürgen Sparwasser and Carlos Caszely, those very different heroes of '74. Both men are alive at the time of writing, as is another star of the 1966 World Cup, North Korea's Pak Do Ik. His story, as we saw in Chapter 5, remains shrouded in the mysteries of a secretive dictatorship. Punishment for blowing a three-goal lead over Portugal at Goodison Park, then, much later, rehabilitation on Kim Jong Il's orders.

Outside Middlesborough and Liverpool, Pak Do Ik's legend might be fading, even in North Korea, where the only permitted superstar is Kim Jong Il's successor as Supreme Leader, his son Kim Jong Un. Helmut Duckadam's descent into obscurity happened almost immediately after his penalty shoot-out brilliance won Steaua Bucharest the 1986 European Cup. But, like Pak Do Ik, he remained a beloved figure, a man who put his country on the football map. When Duckadam died in 2025, Steaua fans unveiled a tifo during a Europa League game against

Manchester United. Under an image of their smiling keeper holding the European Cup, it read: 'Legends never die'.

Some of our cast didn't see out the Cold War. Lev Yashin died of stomach cancer in March 1990, just as ex-KGB officer Vladimir Putin began his political career in St. Petersburg. Twenty-eight years later, the now Russian President identified Yashin, Maradona and Pelé as his favourite footballers. Putin was speaking before the 2018 World Cup in Russia, the latest sports spectacle hosted by an authoritarian regime looking to score political points. 'You know', he said in 2010, after FIFA controversially awarded Russia the tournament, 'a great many cliches survive since the Cold War. They roam Europe like so many flies, buzzing above one's head to frighten people. Things are really quite different'.[10] After the 2018 tournament, FIFA President Gianni Infantino – never one to miss a chance to pander to powerful leaders – called it 'the best World Cup ever'. Putin claimed that 'myths and stereotypes have been dispelled'.[11] All the talk of a new Cold War, or a second Cold War? Nothing to see here.

Even in 2018, it required high levels of cognitive dissonance to buy what Infantino and Putin were selling. Talk about a new Cold War might have been inaccurate – Russia was weaker than the Soviet Union and the bipolar world wasn't coming back anytime soon – but military clashes were already destabilising Russia's Western neighbour, Ukraine. In February 2014, fresh from the sportswashing and doping triumph that was the Sochi Winter Olympics, the Putin regime invaded and annexed the Crimea, an ethnically majority Russian territory granted to Ukraine in 1954. A couple of months later, Russia provoked and supported a war by pro-Russian separatists in eastern Ukraine, who created the breakaway Donetsk and Lugansk People's Republics within Ukraine's Donetsk and Luhansk regions. All this reflected long-standing Kremlin views that Russians and Ukrainians were 'one people', that, in the words of Putin's ideologue, Vladislav Surkov, 'there is no Ukraine'.[12]

On 24 February 2022, Russia launched a full-scale invasion of Ukraine, starting (or, rather, escalating) a war that shows no sign of ending. Four days later, FIFA and UEFA issued a joint statement banning Russian teams from all international competition 'until further notice'. Men's World Cup qualifiers. The upcoming Women's Euros. Europa League ties scheduled for March. Less than four years after hosting the football world, Russia was shoved outside the FIFA family. UEFA ended its sponsorship deal with Russian gas company Gazprom. The 2022 Champions League final was moved from St. Petersburg's Gazprom Arena to Paris.

Despite international support, football in Ukraine has struggled since the invasion. And, sometimes, since long before it. Shakhtar Donetsk, the country's most successful post-communist club, haven't played in their home city since war began there in 2014. Hamburg and Gelsenkirchen. Warsaw and Lviv. Kharkiv and Kyiv. Shakhtar have become an itinerant club, competing, often successfully, with no fixed abode. Six league titles since 2014 are testament to that. Darijo Srna, Shakhtar's Croatian sporting director, lived through the Yugoslav Wars, as well as the events of 2014 and 2022. 'You can't mix sport and politics', he said in 2023. 'But this time you have to ... we lost our home because of [Russia]'.[13]

Since the invasion, Russian bombs have damaged or destroyed seventy-seven football stadiums in Ukraine, like Kharkiv's Sonyachny Stadium, parts of which went on display in Germany in 2024. Many footballers were among the 487 Ukrainian athletes killed in the conflict (as of 2024), with others since joining the death toll, like former Kolos Kovalivka player Mykyta Kalin, killed in a combat mission in the Kharkiv region in 2025. Unsurprisingly, teams in the Ukrainian Premier League (UPL) have struggled financially and the country's biggest clubs, Shakhtar and Dynamo Kyiv, have struggled in Europe. But 1,700 tickets are sold for games in the capital, despite the air raid warnings. A full UPL season returned in 2024/25.

Football continues in Russia's absence, even in war-torn Ukraine. And it continues to expand. Bigger World Cups (forty-eight teams from 2026). An extended FIFA World Club Cup, squeezed into an already bloated calendar. Bulkier Champions League group stages, with the 'Swiss system' – a thirty-six-team 'league' where each club plays eight different opponents and 144 matches are required to eliminate just twelve participants – introduced in 2024. Ongoing growth in women's football, a welcome development that nonetheless brings challenges in everything from finances to player workload. Some critics feel that football, or men's football at least, is in danger of consuming itself. The venality, political bootlicking, dangerously high temperatures and content for content's sake that characterised the 2025 Club World Cup in the USA, Gianni Infantino's project to create a FIFA money-spinner on par with UEFA's Champions League, is the latest evidence for the prosecution. Many though would admit, whether happily or grudgingly, that post-Cold War football has been a huge success. The game is more popular, more lucrative and more international than ever, with higher technical standards and far better access to playing opportunities for the half of the world's population ignored by FIFA et al. until the 1990s.

Yet perhaps something is lost in the saturation TV coverage, the performative super-fans (including many politicians) and ever larger, carbon-footprinted Sports Mega Events. What's lost is the sense of stepping into the unknown typical of Cold War football encounters, from White Hart Lane in 1945 to Tianhe Stadium in 1991. And, paradoxically, a sense of stability, once the uneasy by-product of a divided world of Mutually Assured Destruction. Football remains as political as it was in the Cold War. Given the money involved, the stakes are probably higher in 2025 than in 1985, when football was at its hooligan-driven nadir, or 1955, when UEFA's 'Europe of football' was born. Whether it's war (in the former Yugoslavia and former Soviet Union), sportswashing or athlete activism (among women footballers in Spain, the USA and elsewhere), football reflects and shapes all kinds of political discussions in the twenty-first century – in good and bad ways.

Nobody should mourn the loss of a football world of borders, walls and armed soldiers. Just ask today's Palestinian or Ukrainian footballers. But perhaps we can regret, just a little, the loss of the unfamiliar. The players and teams who played each other, who made rivalries, friendships and history, through the wind and the rain – not to mention the fog and the heat – of football's Cold War.

NOTES

Introduction

1. Alan McDougall, *The People's Game: Football, State and Society in East Germany* (Cambridge: Cambridge University Press, 2014), pp. 123–124.
2. Authors' telephone conversation with Peter Jones, Wrexham AFC historian, 3 September 2021; Jonathan Grieve and Richard Williams, 'From Russia with love …', *The Leader*, 9 January 2018, p. 8; 'The incredible story of 1.FC Magdeburg & Wrexham AFC': www.youtube.com/watch?v=czuU8M32n2A.
3. 'What's taking the knee and why is it important?', *BBC News*, 21 November 2022: www.bbc.co.uk/news/explainers-53098516; 'Luis Rubiales: The kiss that shook Spanish and global football', *BBC Sport*, 23 September 2023: www.bbc.co.uk/sport/football/66645961; 'FIFA's Saudi Arabia World Cup host pick sparks "sports-washing" accusations by rights groups', *France 24*, 11 December 2024: www.france24.com/en/sport/20241211-fifa-s-saudi-arabia-world-cup-host-pick-sparks-sportswashing-accusations-by-rights-groups.
4. Iain Adams, 'A game for Christmas? The Argylls, Saxons and football on the Western Front, December 1914', *International Journal of the History of Sport* 32, no. 11–12 (2015): 1395–1415; Andy Dougan, *Dynamo: Defending the Honour of Kiev* (London: Fourth Estate, 2001); Vincent Cable, 'The football war and the Central American common market', *International Affairs* 45, no. 4 (1969): 658–671; Peter Hough, '"Make goals not war": The contribution of international football to world peace', *International Journal of the History of Sport* 25, no. 10 (2008): 1291.
5. David Caute, *The Dancer Defects: The Struggle for Cultural Supremacy during the Cold War* (Oxford: Oxford University Press, 2003); Nicholas J. Cull, 'Reading, viewing, and tuning into the Cold War', in Melvyn P. Leffler and Odd Arne Westad (eds.), *The Cambridge History of the Cold War, Volume II: Crises and Détente* (Cambridge: Cambridge University Press, 2010), pp. 438–459.
6. McDougall, *The People's Game*, p. 229.

1 The Fog of War: Arsenal vs. Dynamo Moscow, London, November 1945

1. George Orwell, 'The sporting spirit', *Tribune*, 14 December 1945: 10–11.
2. George Orwell, 'You and the atom bomb', *Tribune*, 19 October 1945: 7–8.

3. 'Fog turned Dynamo game into a farce', *Daily Worker*, 22 November 1945: 4; 'Russians win in the fog', *Western Morning News*, 22 November 1945: 5.

4. Roy Peskett in *Daily Mail*, 22 November 1945, cited in Ronald Kowalski and Dilwyn Porter, 'Political football: Moscow Dynamo in Britain, 1945', *International Journal of the History of Sport* 14, no. 2 (1997): 111.

5. 'The Workers' Sports Movement', pamphlet, 1927, MSS.292/807.12/5, Trades Union Congress Collection, Warwick University, UK: https://cdm21047.con tentdm.oclc.org/digital/collection/russian/id/1673; Anton Rippon, *Gas Masks for Goal Posts* (Stroud: Sutton, 2005), p. 210.

6. Robert Edelman, *Spartak Moscow: A History of the People's Team in the Workers' State* (Ithaca, NY: Cornell University Press, 2009), pp. 78–93; Stephen G. Jones, *Workers at Play: A Social and Economic History of Leisure, 1918–1939* (London: Routledge, 2019), pp. 183–187; Peter J. Beck, *Scoring for Britain: International Football and International Politics, 1900–1939* (London: Frank Cass, 1999), pp. 1–2, 173–212.

7. Tony Shaw, 'The British popular press and the early Cold War', *History* 83, no. 269 (1998): 66–85.

8. 'A Report of the Visit of the Dynamo FC, Moscow, November 1945', 14 January 1946, Minutes of Council 1943–1946, Football Association, London, The National Football Museum, Preston, UK; Kowalski and Porter, 'Political football': 103.

9. Peter Beck, 'Britain and the Cold War's "Cultural Olympics": Responding to the political drive of Soviet sport, 1945–58', *Contemporary British History* 19, no. 2 (2005): 170–171; Frank Roberts to Foreign Office, 31 October 1945, FO371/47857/N14898 and Foreign Office to Stanley Rous, 9 November 1945, FO371/47858/N15510, The National Archives, London, UK.

10. Robert Edelman, *Serious Fun: A History of Spectator Sports in the USSR* (Oxford: Oxford University Press, 1993), pp. 87–88, 91; Edelman, *Spartak Moscow*, p. 138; Kowalski and Porter, 'Political football': 104.

11. Edelman, *Spartak Moscow*, pp. 17, 118; Kowalski and Porter, 'Political football': 107.

12. Stanley Rous, *Football Worlds: A Lifetime in Sports* (London: Faber, 1976), pp. 119–120; David Downing, *Passovotchka: Moscow Dynamo in Britain, 1945* (London: Bloomsbury, 1999), pp. 33–37.

13. 'Report of the Visit of the Dynamo FC, Moscow, November 1945'; Stanley Matthews, *Feet First* (London: Ewen and Dale, 1952), p. 103; Downing, *Passovotchka*, pp. 37–46.

14. Downing, *Passovotchka*, pp. 59–60; Jonathan Wilson, *Inverting the Pyramid: The History of Football Tactics* (London: Weidenfeld and Nicolson, 2018), pp. 104–110; 'Talking sport with Harold Palmer', *Evening Standard*, 7 November 1945: 7.

15. 'Dynamo crowd break into houses', *Daily Mirror*, 14 November 1945: 1.

16. 'Dynamo crowd break into houses'; Harold Palmer, 'Dynamos will meet full FA XI before going home', *Evening Standard*, 14 November 1945: 7; Downing, *Passovotchka*, pp. 96–100.

17. 'Dynamo team win by 10 goals to one', *Sunday Dispatch*, 18 November 1945: 5; 'Dynamo "miners" get set for test No. 2 today', *Daily Mirror*, 17 November 1945: 4; 'Grease stops enthusiasts', *Liverpool Echo*, 17 November 1945: 4; Downing, *Passovotchka*, pp. 139, 144.

18. 'Dynamos knocked sparks out of Welsh dragons', *People*, 18 November 1945: 6; Frank Coles, 'Matthews to play against the Dynamos', *Daily Telegraph*, 10 November 1945: 3; Downing, *Passovotchka*, pp. 145–149.

19. Wilson, *Inverting the Pyramid*, pp. 53–72.

20. George Allison, *Allison Calling* (London: Staples, 1948), pp. 223–224.

21. Matthews, *Feet First*, pp. 105–106; 'Matthews in Arsenal XI', *Grimsby Evening Telegraph*, 19 November 1945: 4; 'Many players borrowed', *Western Morning News*, 20 November 1945: 5.

22. 'Dynamo surprise: "We meet an English team"', *Daily Herald*, 21 November 1945: 4; 'Not Arsenal, but England', *Manchester Guardian*, 21 November 1945: 5.

23. See, in particular: https://tinyurl.com/fkkxz2cw and www.youtube.com/watch?v=6TMDCgvpe38.

24. Edelman, *Serious Fun*, p. 87.

25. 'Nine hour wait for Dynamo's match', *Grimsby Evening Telegraph*, 21 November 1945: 4; Downing, *Passovotchka*, p. 168.

26. 'Dynamos in a fog', British Movietone, 26 November 1945, AP Archive: www.youtube.com/watch?v=CE5tUCv5438.

27. Cliff Bastin, *Cliff Bastin Remembers* (London: Ettrick, 1950), p. 167; 'Dynamo's first minute goal against Arsenal', *Grimsby Evening Telegraph*, 21 November 1945: 4; 'Moscow crows: We beat an all-England side', *Daily Record*, 22 November 1945: 1.

28. 'Dynamo's first minute goal against Arsenal'; 'Russian victory in the fog', *Birmingham Post*, 22 November 1945: 1; Bastin, *Cliff Bastin Remembers*, pp. 167–168, 171.

29. 'Dynamos' narrow victory', *Evening Sentinel*, 21 November 1945: 4; 'Dynamos score right from kick-off', *Birmingham Mail*, 21 November 1945: 1; 'Russians win in the fog', *Western Morning News*, 22 November 1945: 5; Bastin, *Cliff Bastin Remembers*, p. 168.

30. Downing, *Passovotchka*, p. 175.

31. Allison, *Allison Calling*, pp. 228–229; Bastin, *Cliff Bastin Remembers*, p. 169; Brian Glanville, *Arsenal* (London: Convoy, 1952), pp. 98–99.

32. Bastin, *Cliff Bastin Remembers*, pp. 169–170.

33. Bernard Joy, *Forward, Arsenal!* (London: Phoenix House, 1952), p. 131; 'Invisible men in an unseen game', *Liverpool Daily Post*, 22 November 1945: 3.

34. Allison, *Allison Calling*, pp. 229–232; 'The Dynamos refused', *Evening Sentinel*, 21 November 1945: 4; Bastin, *Cliff Bastin Remembers*, p. 169; Downing, *Passovotchka*, pp. 180–181.

35. 'Invisible men in an unseen game'; 'Arsenal were not fairly treated', *Daily Record*, 22 November 1945: 7; Bastin, *Cliff Bastin Remembers*, pp. 170–171.

36. Downing, *Passovotchka*, pp. 183–184; Kowalski and Porter, 'Political football': 112; 'Fog turned Dynamo game into a farce', *Daily Worker*, 22 November 1945: 4.

37. Kowalski and Porter, 'Political football': 112, 115; 'Most fantastic match in football history', *Birmingham Gazette*, 22 November 1945: 3; Foot in House of Commons, 22 November 1945: https://hansard.parliament.uk/commons/1945-11-22/debates/f87bd39e-98a4-46bb-ae46-c572ec5e2987/OralAnswersToQuestions.

38. 'Rooke replies to Dynamo', *Newcastle Journal and North Mail*, 24 November 1945: 4; 'Arsenal prepare answer to Moscow "rough play" charge', *Daily Mirror*, 24 November 1945: 4; Downing, *Passovotchka*, pp. 192–193.

39. 'Regrettable incidents in the Dynamo match', *Birmingham Gazette*, 29 November 1945: 3; Kowalski and Porter, 'Political football': 113; Downing, *Passovotchka*, p. 232.

40. Peter J. Beck, '"War minus the shooting": George Orwell on international sport and the Olympics', *Sport in History* 33, no. 1 (2013): 81–88.

41. Sinyavsky's articles in *Soviet Weekly*, 29 November 1945: 1; *Soviet Weekly*, 6 December 1945: 1; *Soviet Weekly*, 13 December 1945: 2; Edelman, *Serious Fun*, pp. 91, 101–102.

42. Frank Roberts, *Dealing with Dictators* (London: Weidenfeld and Nicolson, 1991), p. 103; Odinnadtsat molchalivykh muzhchin (2022) – IMDb.

43. Shaw, 'British popular press': 76–85.

44. Strip cartoon from Soviet magazine *Krokodil* by Rice I. Semyonova in *Russia Today*, March 1946: 8; Robert Edelman, 'Stalin and his soccer soldiers', *History Today* 43, no. 2 (1993): 46–51.

45. Allison, *Allison Calling*, pp. 224, 233; Kowalski and Porter, 'Political football': 117–118.

46. Nick Barnett, 'Football's cultural side helped Britain wage the last Cold War', *The Conversation*, 14 June 2018: https://theconversation.com/footballs-cultural-side-helped-britain-wage-the-last-cold-war-96681; footage highlights and reports: https://afchistory.wordpress.com/2012/10/05/arsenal-thrashed-in-moscow-on-this-day-5th-october-1954/; 'Arsenal run down in Dynamoland!', *Daily Herald*, 6 October 1954: 8.

2 A Miracle and a Revolution: West Germany vs. Hungary, Bern, July 1954

1. Jonathan Wilson, *Behind the Curtain: Travels in Eastern European Football* (London: Orion, 2006), p. 69.

2. Lőrinc Szabó, 'Vereség után' ['After a Defeat'] (1954): https://konyvtar.dia.hu/html/muvek/SZABOL/szabol00154/szabol01225/szabol01225.html.

3. Nils Havemann, *Samstags um Halb 4: Die Geschichte der Fußballbundesliga* (Munich: Siedler, 2013), pp. 30–31.

4. 'England lose record to great Hungarian XI', *The Times*, 26 November 1953: 12; www.youtube.com/watch?v=Ech4_f6tCek.

5. Quoted in Downing, *Passovotchka*, p. 239.

6. Quoted in Jonathan Wilson, *The Names Heard Long Ago: How the Golden Age of Hungarian Soccer Shaped the Modern Game* (New York: Bold Type, 2019), p. 318.

7. Wilson, *The Names Heard Long Ago*, p. 172.

8. Rogan Taylor, 'Father of modern football', *The Guardian*, 17 February 2002: www.theguardian.com/football/2002/feb/17/sport.comment.

9. 'England lose record to great Hungarian XI', *The Times*, 26 November 1953: 12.

10. Wilson, *The Names Heard Long Ago*, pp. 311–312.

11. 'Ungarn-Oesterreich mit unseren Augen', *Die Neue Fußballwoche* 21, 27 May 1953: 3–4.

12. David Goldblatt, *The Ball Is Round: A Global History of Football* (London: Penguin, 2007), p. 344.

13. Buzánsky quoted in Wilson, *Behind the Curtain*, p. 78; 'Curtain down on England supremacy', *Liverpool Echo*, 26 November 1953: 8.

14. Quoted in Wilson, *Behind the Curtain*, p. 79.

15. 'Hungarian football gains a new triumph', *The Times*, 24 May 1954: 2; Winterbottom quoted in 'Hungarian rhapsody', *Liverpool Daily Post*, 24 May 1954: 1.

16. Quoted in Nils Havemann, *Fussball unterm Hakenkreuz* (Frankfurt/Main: Campus Verlag, 2005), p. 203.

17. Quoted in Havemann, *Fussball unterm Hakenkreuz*, p. 10.

18. Fritz Walter, *11 Rote Jäger – Nationalspieler im Kriege* (Munich: Copress, 1959), p. 74.

19. Stiftung der Parteien und Massenorganisationen, Bundesarchiv (SAPMO-BArch), DY 12/281, Protokoll der Arbeitstagung der Fußball-Übungsleiter am 24./25.11.50 im Casino Heinz-Steyer-Stadion Dresden, 27 November 1950.

20. '16 Länder um Kampf um den Titel', *Die Neue Fußballwoche* 24, 15 June 1954: 8; Herberger quoted in Ulrich Hesse-Lichtenberger, *Tor! The Story of German Football* (London: WSC Books, 2002), p. 118.

21. Goldblatt, *The Ball Is Round*, p. 350.

22. 'Hungary trounce Koreans', *Birmingham Gazette*, 18 June 1954: 8.

23. 'Das ist die beste Mannschaft der Welt!', *Die Neue Fußballwoche* 25, 22 June 1954: 3; Eckel quoted in Daniel Harris, 'The most important soccer game ever played', *The Ringer*, 13 July 2018: www.theringer.com/soccer/2018/7/13/17568582/world-cup-most-important-game-1954-final-hungary-west-germany.

24. Hesse-Lichtenberger, *Tor!*, p. 123; Wilson, *The Names Heard Long Ago*, p. 344.

25. 'Germans in semi-finals', *Birmingham Gazette*, 28 June 1954: 6; 'Cajkowski-Vukas nur vor der Pause feldbeherrschend', *Die Neue Fußballwoche* 26, 29 June 1954: 4.

26. Quoted in Roman Horak, 'Germany versus Austria: Football, urbanism and national identity', in Alan Tomlinson and Christopher Young (eds.), *German Football: History, Culture, Society* (Abingdon: Routledge, 2006), p. 30. The Battle of Königgratz (Sadowa) in July 1866 decided the Austro-Prussian War in Prussia's favour.

27. 'Erst die Abwehr, dann der Angriff', *Die Neue Fußballwoche* 27, 6 July 1954: 6; 'Germany in World Cup final', *Liverpool Echo*, 1 July 1954: 3.

28. Gerd von der Lippe and Malcolm MacLean, 'Brawling in Berne: Mediated transnational moral panics in the 1954 Football World Cup', *International Review for the Sociology of Sport* 43, no. 1 (2008): 78–79, 86.

29. 'Das war Fußballkunst in Reinkultur', *Die Neue Fußballwoche* 27, 6 July 1954: 5; 'Germany in World Cup final', *Liverpool Echo*, 1 July 1954: 3.

30. 'German soccer rise due to Pools', *Daily Herald*, 3 July 1954: 5.

31. Quoted in Hesse-Lichtenberger, *Tor!*, p. 127.

32. Quoted in Harris, 'The most important soccer game'.

33. www.youtube.com/watch?v=og1RAWvnpAo.

34. Hesse-Lichtenberger, *Tor!*, p. 14.

35. 'It's not Hungary's after all', *Daily Herald*, 5 July 1954: 8.

36. 'World Cup for Germany', *The Guardian*, 5 July 1954: 4.

37. 'World Cup for Germany', *The Guardian*, 5 July 1954: 4; 'It's not Hungary's after all', *Daily Herald*, 5 July 1954: 8.

38. Fritz Walter, *3:2. Das Spiel ist aus! Deutschland ist Weltmeister!* (Munich: Copress, 2004), p. 188.

39. 'Germans beat Hungary', *Daily Telegraph*, 5 July 1954: 4; Puskás quoted in Wilson, *The Names Heard Long Ago*, p. 344; Günter Grass, *My Century* trans. Michael Henry Heim (New York: Harcourt, 1999), p. 140.

40. Szepesi quoted in György Majtényi, 'Demonstration against the power: The soc(cer)ialist revolution of Hungary, July 4–6, 1954', *International Journal of the History of Sport* 38, no. 6 (2021): 594.

41. Arthur Heinrich, 'The 1954 soccer World Cup and the Federal Republic of Germany's self-discovery', *American Behavioral Scientist* 46, no. 11 (2003): 1495.

42. Walter, *3:2*, p. 202.

43. Majtényi, 'Demonstration against the power': 595–598; Harris, 'The most important soccer game'.

44. Fest and Beckenbauer quoted in Janek Speight, 'The miracle of Bern: West Germany's 1954 World Cup win', Deutsche Welle (DW), 21 March 2020: www.dw.com/en/the-miracle-of-bern-west-germanys-run-to-1954-world-cup-win/a-52870532.

45. Rudolf Oswald, 'Das "Wunder von Bern" und die deutsche Fußball-Volksgemeinschaft 1954', in Johannes Paulmann (ed.), *Auswärtige Repräsentationen: Deutsche Kulturdiplomatie nach 1945* (Cologne: Böhlau, 2005), pp. 88–101.

46. Oswald, 'Das "Wunder von Bern"', pp. 91, 93.

47. Christian Becker and Wolfgang Buss, 'Das "Wunder von Bern" und die DDR', *Deutschland Archiv* 37, no. 3 (2004): 394; Oswald, 'Das "Wunder von Bern"', p. 95.

48. Becker and Buss, 'Das "Wunder von Bern" und die DDR': 393, 395.

49. Oswald, 'Das "Wunder von Bern"', p. 96.

50. Franz-Josef Brüggemeier, 'Das Wunder von Bern: The 1954 football World Cup, the German nation and popular histories', in Sylvia Paletschek (ed.), *Popular Historiographies in the 19th and 20th Centuries: Cultural Meanings, Social Practices* (Oxford and New York: Berghahn, 2011), p. 192.

51. *Süddeutsche Zeitung*, 3 July 2004, quoted in Brüggemeier, 'Das Wunder von Bern', p. 189.

52. Quoted in Péter Fodor, 'Erasing, rewriting, and propaganda in the Hungarian sports films of the 1950s', *The Hungarian Historical Review* 6, no. 2 (2017): 346.

53. Wilson, *Behind the Curtain*, pp. 84, 86–87.

54. Quoted in Majtényi, 'Demonstration against the power': 599.

55. 'Mighty Magyars end a legend', *Daily Mirror*, 16 July 1966: 14.

56. Quoted in Wilson, *Behind the Curtain*, p. 84.

57. Billy Liddell, *My Soccer Story* (London: Stanley Paul, 1960), pp. 79–80.

58. 'Ferenc Puskas: Footballer and idealist', *The Guardian*, 29 October 1956: 1.

59. FIFA Archive, Information to national associations about the transfer of Hungarian refugee footballers, 17 July 1957.

60. Wilson, *Behind the Curtain*, p. 87.

61. Quoted in Goldblatt, *The Ball Is Round*, p. 407.

62. Quoted in Harris, 'The most important soccer game'.

63. Quoted in Stephen F. Kelly, *Bill Shankly: It's Much More Important Than That. A Biography* (London: Virgin, 1996), p. 76.

3 Football Beats God: Ireland vs. Yugoslavia, Dublin, October 1955

1. Garry Doyle, 'Twenty years of drama in Irish football, chapter 2: Saipan – paradise lost', *The 42*, 12 May 2020: www.the42.ie/irish-football-series-garry-doyle-saipan-5090915-May2020/; Paul Rouse, *Sport and Ireland: A History* (Oxford: Oxford University Press, 2015), p. 335.

2. Kelly Grovier, 'Is football the universal religion?' *BBC Culture*, 13 July 2018: www.bbc.com/culture/article/20180713-is-football-the-universal-religion.

3. See, for instance, Ryan Ferguson, 'Tranmere, Tito and a random tour of Yugoslavia', blog, 17 October 2019: https://ryanferguson.co.uk/blogs/planet-prentonia/tranmere-tito-and-a-random-tour-of-yugoslavia.

4. 'Tito and Yugoslav football', *BBC Sporting Witness*, 10 May 2015: www.bbc.co.uk/sounds/play/po2qk8l7.

5. Richard Mills, *The Politics of Football in Yugoslavia: Sport, Nationalism and the State* (London: I. B. Tauris, 2018).

6. Richard Mills, 'Cold War football: Soviet defence and Yugoslav attack following the Tito–Stalin split of 1948', *Europe-Asia Studies* 68, no. 10 (2016): 1736–1758.

7. Mills, *The Politics of Football in Yugoslavia*, p. 107.

8. Ibid., pp. 107–114, 134–135; Pierre Lanfranchi and Matthew Taylor, *Moving with the Ball: The Migration of Professional Footballers* (London: Berg, 2001), pp. 116–120.

9. Enda Delaney, 'Anti-communism in mid-twentieth-century Ireland', *English Historical Review* 126, no. 521 (2011): 878–903; Eunan O'Halpin, *Defending Ireland: The Irish State and Its Enemies since 1922* (Oxford: Oxford University Press, 1999), pp. 280–282.

10. Paul Rouse, 'The politics of culture and sport in Ireland: A history of the GAA ban on foreign games, 1884–1971', *International Journal of the History of Sport* 10, no. 3 (1990): 333–360; John Giles, *A Football Man: The Autobiography* (London: Hodder and Stoughton, 2010), p. 42.

11. Robert Redmond, 'The sliding history of the league of Ireland', *These Football Times*, 12 February 2016: https://thesefootballtimes.co/2016/02/12/the-declining-history-of-the-league-of-ireland/; *Green Is the Colour*, Episode 2, RTE television documentary series, 2012: www.dailymotion.com/video/xr4x2l.

12. Carey, John Joseph ('Johnny', 'Jackie'), *Dictionary of Irish Biography*: www.dib.ie/biography/carey-john-joseph-johnny-jackie-a1473; W. P. M., 'Godwin's saves helped in historic win', *Irish Independent*, 22 September 1949: 8; David Gorman, 'A wonderful Irish triumph', *Irish Times*, 4 September 2024: https://tinyurl.com/3jk32s94.

13. Wickham, Joseph Ignatius ('Joe'), *Dictionary of Irish Biography*: www.dib.ie/biography/wickham-joseph-ignatius-joe-a9765.

14. John Cooney, *John Charles McQuaid: Ruler of Catholic Ireland* (Dublin: O'Brien Press, 1999), pp. 80–82, 172, 243.

15. Ibid., pp. 210, 218–220, 226–230; Frank J. Coppa, 'Pope Pius XII and the Cold War: The post-war confrontation between Catholicism and Communism', in Dianne Kirby (ed.), *Religion and the Cold War* (Basingstoke: Palgrave Macmillan, 2013), pp. 50–66.

16. Klaus Buchenau, 'What went wrong? Church–state relations in socialist Yugoslavia', *Nationalities Papers* 33, no. 4 (2005): 547–567; Aidan O'Malley, 'An easy conscience', *Dublin Review of Books*, March 2018: https://drb.ie/articles/an-easy-conscience/.

17. Football Association of Ireland International Affairs Committee Minutes, 26 November and 15 December 1954, Archives of the Football Association of Ireland, University College Dublin, Ireland.

18. Joe Wickham to Archbishop McQuaid, 17 January 1952, XXII/48/1, Papers of Archbishop John Charles McQuaid, Archdiocese of Dublin Archive (ADA), Dublin, Ireland.

19. 'Footballers from Yugoslavia', *Irish Independent*, 29 August 1955: 8; 'Yugoslavia football visitors', *Irish Press*, 17 October 1955: 11.

20. 'Yugoslavs come tonight', *Irish Press*, 17 October 1955: 7, 11; 'Archbishop objects to Yugoslav visit', *Irish Times*, 17 October 1955: 1.

21. Cooney, *John Charles McQuaid*, pp. 310–311.

22. 'Archbishop objects to Yugoslav visit'.

23. 'Archbishop objects to Yugoslav visit'; John A. Murphy, 'The strange ways of a "control freak"', *Irish Independent*, 21 November 1999: www.independent.ie/woman/celeb-news/article521486.ece.

24. 'Broadcast ban on Eire–Yugoslavia football match', *Belfast Newsletter*, 18 October 1955: 5; 'Irish team's trainer withdraws', *Irish Times*, 19 October 1955: 1; Conor McCabe, 'Catholics, communists and hat-tricks', *Beyond the Last Man*, 15 September 2016: https://beyondthelastman.com/2016/09/15/catholics-communists-hat-tricks-the-ireland-v-yugoslavia-soccer-international-of-1955/.

25. 'Archbishop objects to Yugoslav visit'; 'No R.E. broadcasts for international match', *Irish Times*, 18 October 1955: 1; 'Man parades with flag at Dublin soccer ground', *Limerick Leader*, 19 October 1955: 1.

26. Eamon Dunphy, *The Rocky Road* (London: Penguin, 2014), pp. 41–43; Cooney, *John Charles McQuaid*, p. 314.

27. 'Yugoslav ambassador regrets "intolerance"', *Irish Times*, 18 October 1955: 1; 'Man parades with flag at Dublin soccer ground'.

28. W. P. Murphy, 'Can Republic soccer team hold Yugoslavia today?', *Irish Independent*, 19 October 1955: 17; *Green Is the Colour*.

29. Jonathan Wilson, 'Meet Yugoslavia's ballerina Beara, once the best keeper in the world', *The Guardian*, 5 August 2008: www.theguardian.com/football/2008/aug/05/europeanfootball.

30. Daniela Rogulj, 'Remembering Hajduk legend Bernard Vukas 35 years after his death', *Total Croatia News*, 4 April 2018: www.total-croatia-news.com/sport/27186-remembering-hajduk-legend-bernard-vukas-35-years-after-his-death.

31. Stephen McGarrigle, *The Complete Who's Who of Irish International Football: 1945–1996* (Edinburgh: Mainstream, 1996), pp. 66–67; 'Martin, Con', *Irish Dictionary of Biography*: www.dib.ie/biography/martin-con-a10068.

32. Lynda Slattery, 'Two bishops and a football: Ireland and the Balkans in the 1940s and 50s', *History Ireland* 15, no. 5 (2007): 41–43; 'Man parades with flag at Dublin soccer ground'; Cooney, *John Charles McQuaid*, p. 312.

33. 'Yugoslavija–Irska 4:1', *Slobodna Dalmacija*, 20 October 1955: 3.

34. 'There was no band at Dalymount', *Evening Herald*, 19 October 1955: 1; 'Crowd of 21,400 sees Yugoslavia beat Irish team', *Irish Times*, 20 October 1955: 1.

35. Cooney, *John Charles McQuaid*, p. 312.

36. Sean Piondar, 'Yugoslavia – a great team!', *Irish Press*, 20 October 1955: 10; Frank Johnstone, 'Heaviest home defeat since 1949', *Irish Times*, 20 October 1955: 2.

37. Cooney, *John Charles McQuaid*, p. 313; McQuaid to Alberto Levame, 9 November 1955, XXII/48/9/2, ADA.

38. Cooney, *John Charles McQuaid*, pp. 313–314.

39. Miro Mrsic to McQuaid, 21 October 1955, XXII/48/7/1; P. J. Kilroy to McQuaid, 26 October 1955, XXII/48/8/1; Fr Tom Ryan to Chris Mangan, 7 December 1955, XXII/48/11/1, ADA; Cooney, *John Charles McQuaid*, p. 313.

40. McQuaid to Fr George Finnegan, XXII/48/13, 21 February 1956; Finnegan to McQuaid, 26 February 1956, XXII/48/14/(1); McQuaid to Finnegan, 26 October 1956, XXII/48/16; Finnegan to McQuaid, 28 October 1956, XXII/48/17/(1) & (2); Interview with Fr George Finnegan, 13 October 1957, XXII/48/21; Diocesan Soccer Committee's General Report, September 1958, XXII/48/22/2/(1) & (2), ADA.

41. Cooney, *John Charles McQuaid*, pp. 314–315; McCabe, 'Catholics, communists and hat-tricks'; Rouse, *Sport and Ireland*, pp. 295–296.

42. K. J. Kenealy, 'Yugoslav "stars" complete masters', *Evening Herald*, 20 October 1955: 9; Piondar, 'Yugoslavia – a great team!'.

43. Rouse, *Sport and Ireland*, p. 295; W. P. Murphy, 'Ringstead's great goal earned Ireland 2–2 draw with Spain', *Irish Independent*, 28 November 1955, p. 11.

44. Carey, John Joseph ('Johnny', 'Jackie'), *Dictionary of Irish Biography*; Peter Byrne, *Green Is the Colour: The Story of Irish Football* (London: Carlton Books, 2012), pp. 231–244.

45. '"Yugoslavs teams need a rest"', *Irish Press*, 18 October 1955: 10.

46. Lanfranchi and Taylor, *Moving with the Ball*, pp. 116–120.

47. James Horncastle, 'Paying tribute to the miracle man who made Sampdoria', *Eurosport*, 7 May 2015: www.eurosport.co.uk/football/paying-tribute-to-the-miracle-man-who-made-sampdoria_sto4717583/story.shtml.

48. Stephen Dodd, 'Moving the goalposts', *Sunday Independent*, 6 June 1999, p. 11; Bill Pierce, 'Keane leads Republic's conquest', *Birmingham Post*, 2 September 1999: 35.

49. Michael Walker, 'Irish cash in on season of Given take', *The Guardian*, 12 November 2001: 36.

4 Settling Old Scores: Spain vs. Soviet Union, Madrid, June 1964

1. Quoted in Jimmy Burns, *La Roja: A Journey through Spanish Football* (London: Simon & Schuster, 2012), p. 200.
2. Quoted in Duncan Shaw, 'The political instrumentalisation of professional football in Francoist Spain, 1939–1975', PhD thesis, University of London (1988), p. 269.
3. Quoted in Alejandro Quiroga, *Football and National Identities in Spain: The Strange Death of Don Quixote* (Basingstoke: Palgrave Macmillan, 2013), p. 39.
4. Quoted in Shaw, 'The political instrumentalisation of professional football', p. 270.
5. Miguel Delaney, 'Spain evokes memories of one of the most politicised football matches ever', *The Independent*, 29 June 2018: https://tinyurl.com/bdh9bsr5.
6. Jim O'Brien, 'In the shadow of the state: The national team and the politics of national identity in Spain', in Brenda Elsey and Stanislao G. Pugliese (eds.), *Football and the Boundaries of History: Critical Studies in Soccer* (New York: Palgrave Macmillan, 2017), p. 77.
7. Quoted in Alejandro Quiroga, 'Spanish fury: Football and national identities under Franco', *European History Quarterly* 45, no. 3 (2015): 517.
8. Burns, *La Roja*, p. 61.
9. Quoted in Quiroga, *Football and National Identities in Spain*, p. 40.
10. An unnamed Francoist officer quoted in Burns, *La Roja*, p. 130.
11. Quoted in Burns, *La Roja*, p. 116.
12. Quoted in Edelman, *Serious Fun*, p. 63.
13. Starostin quoted in Edelman, *Spartak Moscow*, p. 104. The photo is on p. 109.
14. Quoted in Jonathan Wilson, 'The Soviet tactical revolution has its roots in a 1930s Basque team', *The Guardian*, 26 June 2008: www.theguardian.com/football/2008/jun/26/russia.euro20081.
15. 'Real Madrid once more show their omnipotence', *The Guardian*, 19 May 1960: 4.
16. Delaney, 'Spain evokes memories'.
17. Quoted in Shaw, 'The political instrumentalisation of professional football', p. 266.
18. 'Spanish footballers not for Moscow', *The Times*, 26 May 1960: 13; Saporta quoted in Shaw, 'The political instrumentalisation of professional football', p. 266.
19. Quoted in Shaw, 'The political instrumentalisation of professional football', p. 265.
20. Quoted in Shaw, 'The political instrumentalisation of professional football', p. 266; Michael Cox, 'How the Soviet Union won Euro 1960: A "WM" formation, Franco's Spain withdrawal and Lev Yashin', *The Athletic*, 23 October 2023: www.nytimes.com/athletic/4981388/2023/10/23/how-soviet-union-won-euro-1960/.
21. *Daily Telegraph* quoted in Juan Antonio Simón and Julian Rieck, 'Football, propaganda and international relations under Francoism: The 1960 and 1964 European Nations' Cup and their impact on the international press', *International Journal of the History of Sport* 39, no. 5 (2022): 475; Pereda quoted in Burns, *La Roja*, p. 189.
22. Quoted in Paul Preston, *Franco* (London: HarperCollins, 1993), p. 776.
23. Quoted in Burns, *La Roja*, p. 193.
24. Quoted in Shaw, 'The political instrumentalisation of professional football', p. 116.
25. Jenifer Parks, *The Olympic Games, the Soviet Sports Bureaucracy, and the Cold War: Red Sport, Red Tape* (Lanham, MD: Lexington Books, 2017), pp. 40, 43.
26. Juan Antonio Simón, 'Football, diplomacy, and international relations during Francoism, 1937–1975', in Heather Dichter (ed.), *Soccer Diplomacy: International Relations since 1914* (Lexington: The University Press of Kentucky, 2020), p. 63.
27. Juan Antonio Simón, *Football and International Relations under Francoism, 1937–1975* (Abingdon: Routledge, 2025), p. 107.
28. Simón and Rieck, 'Football, propaganda and international relations': 478.

29. Philippe Vonnard, *Creating a United Europe of Football: The Formation of UEFA (1949–1961)* (Cham: Springer, 2020), p. 1.

30. Simón and Rieck, 'Football, propaganda and international relations': 479.

31. 'This was a great day for the English', *Liverpool Daily Post*, 24 October 1963: 12.

32. Edelman, *Spartak Moscow*, p. 168.

33. Quoted in Edelman, *Serious Fun*, p. 133.

34. Simón and Rieck, 'Football, propaganda and international relations': 480, 483.

35. Michael Cox, 'How Spain won Euro 1964: Unheralded manager, Franco's approval and Luis Suarez', *The Athletic*, 5 November 2023: www.nytimes.com/athletic/5028409/2023/11/05/euro-1964-spain/.

36. Quoted in 'Spain too good for Eire', *Leicester Mercury*, 12 March 1964: 30.

37. 'Hosts Spain edge Hungary to reach EURO 1964 final', uefa.com, 2 October 2003: www.uefa.com/uefaeuro/history/news/0253-0d7b30679e5d-024cb42f103e-1000-hosts-spain-edge-hungary-to-reach-euro-1964-final/.

38. 'Russia and Spain clash in final', *Evening Chronicle*, 18 June 1964: 20.

39. Quoted in Burns, *La Roja*, p. 200.

40. Simón and Rieck, 'Football, propaganda and international relations': 480.

41. 'Franco sees Spain win by a late goal', *Liverpool Daily Post*, 22 June 1964: 12; Suárez quoted in 'Marcelino heads Spain to EURO 1964 final win against USSR', uefa.com, 2 October 2003: https://tinyurl.com/5df3ccuk.

42. Burns, *La Roja*, p. 201; O'Brien, 'In the shadow of the state', p. 81.

43. Cox, 'How Spain won Euro 1964'.

44. Daniel Gómez, *La Patria Del Gol: Futbol y política en el Estado Español* (Irun: Alberdania, 2007), p. 88.

45. Quoted in Delaney, 'Spain evokes memories'.

46. Both quoted in Shaw, 'The political instrumentalisation of professional football', p. 269.

47. Both quoted in Cox, 'How Spain won Euro 1964'.

48. Quoted in Quiroga, *Football and National Identities in Spain*, p. 39.

49. Ferreira quoted in Simon Kuper, *Football against the Enemy* (London: Orion, 1994), p. 179.

50. Mikhail Yokhin, 'Pep idol: The anti-Lobanovsky who inspired a generation – inside and outside Russia', *FourFourTwo*, 19 November 2013: www.fourfourtwo.com/features/pep-idol-anti-lobanovsky-who-inspired-generation-inside-and-outside-russia.

51. Burns, *La Roja*, p. 203.

52. Quoted in Burns, *La Roja*, p. 204.

53. Mandeep Sanghera, 'Euro 1964: A forgotten Spanish triumph', BBC Sport, 12 May 2012: www.bbc.co.uk/sport/football/17451950.

54. Shaw, 'The political instrumentalisation of professional football', p. 295.

55. Quoted in Simón and Rieck, 'Football, propaganda and international relations': 481.

5 Eusébio and the 'Mystery Men of the East': North Korea vs. Portugal, Liverpool, July 1966

1. Henry Holloway, 'Shocking fate of North Korea's doomed 1966 World Cup squad revealed', *Daily Star*, 27 June 2018: www.dailystar.co.uk/news/world-news/world-cup-north-korea-1966-16863773; Kang Chol-hwan and Pierre Rigoulot, *The Aquariums of Pyongyang: Ten Years in the North Korean Gulag* (New York: Basic Books, 2011), p. 78.

2. Simon J. Rofe and Alan Tomlinson, 'The untold story of FIFA's diplomacy and the 1966 World Cup: North Korea, Africa and Sir Stanley Rous', *International History Review* 42, no. 3 (2020): 505–525.

3. Fabio Chisari, 'When football went global: Televising the 1966 World Cup', *Historical Social Research* 31, no. 1 (2006): 42–54.

4. John Hughson, *England and the 1966 World Cup: A Cultural History* (Manchester: Manchester University Press, 2016), pp. 5, 11, 165; Wesley Britton, *Beyond Bond: Spies in Fiction and Film* (Westport, CT: Praeger, 2005), p. 107.

5. Udo Merkel, 'Bigger than Beijing 2008: Politics, propaganda and physical culture in Pyongyang', *International Journal of the History of Sport* 27, nos. 14–15 (2010): 2470–2471; Benjamin R. Young, 'Not there for the nutmeg: North Korean advisors in Grenada and Pyongyang's internationalism, 1979–1983', *Cross-Currents: East Asian History and Culture Review* 27 (2018): 116.

6. Jong Sung Lee, 'Football in North and South Korea c. 1910–2002: Diffusion and Development', PhD thesis, De Montfort University, Leicester (2012), pp. 131–132.

7. Lee, 'Football in North and South Korea', pp. 274, 120–123.

8. Guy Podoler, 'Nation, state and football: The Korean case', *International Journal of the History of Sport* 25, no. 1 (2008): 10.

9. Martin Polley, 'The diplomatic background to the 1966 football World Cup', *Sport Historian* 18, no. 2 (1988): 1–18.

10. Frank Keating, 'Blair banks on polls and goals', *The Guardian*, 15 June 2000: E7.

11. 'Spielpartner der Nationalelf: WM-Endrunden-Teilnehmer Chile und die KVDR', *Die Neue Fußballwoche* 24, 14 June 1966: 5.

12. Geoffrey Green, 'A glorious occasion for British sport', *F.A. News* no. 15, 12 July 1966: 468–470; Tosh Warwick, 'The FIFA World Cup, international friendship and the "mystery men of the east": When Middlesbrough fell in love with North Korea', *North Korea Review* 15, no. 1 (2019): 56; Kevin Mitchell, 'Brian Glanville was fearless, witty and hovered in the press box like Banquo's ghost', *The Guardian*, 17 May 2025: www.theguardian.com/football/2025/may/17/brian-glanville-fearless-witty-vitriolic-football-journalist.

13. 'Korea will get a cheer', *The Guardian*, 5 July 1966: 1; Jim White, 'Koreans revel in return of the underdogs', *The Guardian*, 18 October 2002: 35.

14. Tony Mason, 'England 1966: Traditional and modern?' in Alan Tomlinson and Christopher Young (eds.), *National Identity and Global Sports Events* (Albany: State University of New York Press, 2006), p. 90.

15. Interview with Pak Do Ik, *The Game of Their Lives*, film directed by Daniel Gordon, released 2002; Louise Taylor, 'How little stars from North Korea were taken to a town's heart', *The Guardian*, 6 September 2010: 5.

16. Warwick, 'The FIFA World Cup': 57; 'North v. south: A tale of two Koreas', *Sky News*, 7 June 2018: https://news.sky.com/story/north-v-south-a-tale-of-two-koreas-11347485.

17. Lee, 'Football in North and South Korea', p. 137; Gordon, *The Game of Their Lives*.

18. Gordon, *The Game of Their Lives*; 'North Korea: The secret heroes of the 1966 World Cup', *Sky History*: www.history.co.uk/article/north-korea-the-secret-heroes-of-the-1966-world-cup.

19. Hughson, *England and the 1966 World Cup*, pp. 46–47.

20. Lee, 'Football in North and South Korea', p. 145; John Foot, *Calcio: A History of Italian Football* (London: Harper Perennial, 2008), pp. 488–494.

21. Tom Gallagher, *Salazar: The Dictator Who Refused to Die* (London: Hurst, 2020).

22. Odd Arne Westad, *The Global Cold War* (Cambridge: Cambridge University Press, 2007).

23. Todd Cleveland, *Following the Ball: The Migration of African Soccer Players across the Portuguese Colonial Empire, 1949–1975* (Athens: Ohio University Press, 2017), pp. 178–179; Gallagher, *The Dictator*, pp. 209–227.

24. Cleveland, *Following the Ball*, pp. 2–4, 44–45, 181–182, 203–204.

25. Ibid., pp. 86–87; Goldblatt, *The Ball Is Round*, pp. 421–426.

26. Cleveland, *Following the Ball*, pp. 4, 89, 163–164, 187; Lanfranchi and Taylor, *Moving with the Ball*, pp. 178–181.

27. Jonathan Wilson, *Anatomy of England* (London: Orion, 2010), p. 117.

28. Gordon, *The Game of Their Lives*; Taylor, 'How little stars'.

29. Hughson, *England and the 1966 World Cup*, pp. 46–47.

30. Eric Todd, 'Koreans overcome only after a splendid fight', *The Guardian*, 25 July 1966: 10.

31. 'Eusebio scores four for Portugal in 1966 World Cup', www.bbc.co.uk/sport/av/football/25604175; Hughson, *England and the 1966 World Cup*, pp. 46–47.

32. Wilson, *Anatomy of England*, pp. 115–116, 133; John Brewin, 'Eusebio's tears and Charlton's genius: 1966 and England's "other" World Cup semi-final', *Eurosport*, 8 June 2018: https://tinyurl.com/4be3hehd.

33. Cleveland, *Following the Ball*, p. 185; Westad, *The Global Cold War*, pp. 208–218.

34. Cleveland, *Following the Ball*, pp. 184–185.

35. Gallagher, *The Dictator*, pp. 249–254; Cleveland, *Following the Ball*, pp. 186, 198–200.

36. Cleveland, *Following the Ball*, pp. 209–210, 187; Lanfranchi and Taylor, *Moving with the Ball*, pp. 178–181.

37. Gordon, *The Game of Their Lives*; Lee, 'Football in North and South Korea', pp. 144–148.

38. Lee, 'Football in North and South Korea', pp. 162–164; 'Pak Do Ik first to carry Olympic torch in Pyongyang', *North Korean Economy Watch*, 28 April 2008: www.nkeconwatch.com/2008/04/28/pak-do-ik-to-carry-olympic-flame/.

39. Lee, 'Football in North and South Korea', pp. 150–161, 169–172, 201–247.

40. Jason Wood and Neville Gabie, 'The football ground and visual culture: Recapturing place, memory and meaning at Ayresome Park', *International History of the Journal of Sport* 28, no. 8–9 (2011): 1195.

41. Warwick, 'The FIFA World Cup': 61–63; 'Ball signed by 1966 North Korea team', *Evening Gazette*, 8 August 2014: 14; Eric Paylor, 'World Cup will be poorer without Teesside fans' adopted country', *Evening Gazette*, 5 June 2018: 56–57.

42. Warwick, 'The FIFA World Cup': 63.

43. Ibid.: 63–66; Jeremy Armstrong and Ned Kelly, 'Come on you reds', *Daily Mirror*, 24 September 2010: 24–25.

6 The Game of Shame: Chile vs. Soviet Union, Santiago, November 1973

1. See footage here: https://the18.com/soccer-entertainment/fifa-intercontinental-play offs-throwback-chile-vs-soviet-union-1973.

2. Westad, *The Global Cold War*, pp. 340–363.

3. Goldblatt, *The Ball Is Round*, pp. 391–392; CIA Memorandum, 'The New Order in Brazil', 1971, p. 4: www.cia.gov/readingroom/docs/CIA-RDP79R00967A0004000 20007-9.pdf; CIA's National Intelligence Survey, 'Brazil September 1973', pp. 17–18: www.cia.gov/readingroom/docs/CIA-RDP01-00707R000200080016-0.pdf.

4. Roger Kittleson, *The Country of Sport: Soccer and the Making of Modern Brazil* (Berkeley: University of California Press, 2014), pp. 85–87, 103–104; Victor Andrade De Melo and Mauricio Drumond, 'The military in Brazilian sport', in

Michael L. Butterworth (ed.), *Sport and Militarism* (New York: Routledge, 2017), pp. 185–186; Goldblatt, *The Ball Is Round*, pp. 391–392.

5. Kittleson, *The Country of Sport*, pp. 97–98.

6. Westad, *The Global Cold War*, p. 356.

7. 'Chile's Coup at 50', *National Security Archive*, 2023: https://nsarchive.gwu.edu/briefing-book/chile/2023-09-08/chiles-coup-50-countdown-toward-coup.

8. Carmen Luz Parot's documentary *Estadio Nacional* (2003): https://tinyurl.com/28bcm3cm; David Wood, 'General Pinochet's long shadow still hangs over Chile's national stadium', *The Conversation*, 19 December 2016: https://theconversation.com/general-pinochets-long-shadow-still-hangs-over-chiles-national-stadium-70305; 'O Chile aberto aos capitais', *A Voz de Timor*, 28 September 1973: 10; '10,000 wait to be bombed', *Times Colonist*, 3 October 1973: 3.

9. Carl Worswick, 'Playing under Pinochet: How Chile's stars of the 1970s feared for their lives', *The Guardian*, 9 September 2015: www.theguardian.com/football/2015/sep/09/chile-military-coup-general-pinochet-leonardo-veliz; Brenda Elsey, *Citizens and Sportsmen: Fútbol and Politics in 20th-Century Chile* (Austin: University of Texas Press, 2011), p. 244.

10. Diego Antonio Vilches Parra, 'The Pinochet's team: The soccer national team and the coup d'état of September 11, 1973', *International Journal of the History of Sport* 39, no. 15 (2022): 1648.

11. Jonathan Wilson, 'Peru, Pele and Grimsby: Henry Kissinger and his curious football links', *The Guardian*, 30 November 2023: www.theguardian.com/football/2023/nov/30/henry-kissinger-football-peru-pele-grimsby-catenaccio; Patrick J. Haney, 'Soccer fields and submarines in Cuba: The politics of problem definition', *Naval War College Review* 50, no. 4 (1997): 67–84; CIA file on excerpts from 'The Soviet elite's daily life', article in *Der Spiegel* (Hamburg), 24 May 1971: www.cia.gov/readingroom/docs/CIA-RDP79-01194A000300060001-7.pdf; Kissinger memorandum to the White House, 'Meeting with Pele', 28 June 1975: www.cia.gov/readingroom/docs/LOC-HAK-74-5-2-2.pdf.

12. Brenda Elsey, '"Because we have nothing": The 1962 World Cup and Cold War politics in Chile', in Dichter (ed.), *Soccer Diplomacy*, pp. 108–109.

13. Michelle D. Paranzino, 'From détente to revolution: Soviet solidarity with Chile after Allende, 1973–79', *International History Review* 44, no. 1 (2022): 6; Mikhail Prozumenshikov, 'Action in the era of stagnation: Leonid Brezhnev and the Soviet Olympic dream', in Robert Edelman and Christopher Young (eds.), *The Whole World is Watching: Sport in the Cold War* (Stanford, CA: Stanford University Press, 2020), pp. 82–83; 'Ford and Brezhnev: Jests amid the snow', *New York Times*, 24 November 1974: 26: www.nytimes.com/1974/11/24/archives/ford-and-brezhnev-jests-amid-the-snow-brezhnev-plays-left-side.html.

14. Worswick, 'Playing under Pinochet'; Francisco Fluxa to Helmut Käser, *FIFA News*, November 1973: 465–466.

15. Worswick, 'Playing under Pinochet'; match reports in *Soviet Sport*, 27 September 1973: 3 and *Football-Hockey*, 30 September 1973: 8.

16. Parra, 'Pinochet's team': 1650–1651.

17. Agenda for FIFA World Cup Organising Committee meeting, Frankfurt, 5 January 1974: 3, FIFA Museum Library, Zurich, Switzerland.

18. See, for instance, Adam Leventhal, 'Chile's walkover against the USSR 50 years on: "The military junta used us"', *The Athletic*, 21 November 2023: https://theathletic.com/5073149/2023/11/21/chile-ussr-fifa-pinochet-50/; Gareth Thomas, 'An open goal for fascism', *The Football History Boys*, 18 September 2021: www.thefootballhistoryboys.com/2021/03/an-open-goal-for-fascism-1973-chile-vs.html.

19. Radoslav A. Yordanov, 'Warsaw Pact countries' involvement in Chile from Frei to Pinochet, 1964–1973', *Journal of Cold War Studies* 21, no. 3 (2019): 80–81.

20. *FIFA News*, November 1973: 461; *Soviet Sport*, 20 October 1973: 4; 'Pinochet, the Cold War, and the most pathetic match ever played', *Bosbobet*, undated: www .footandball.net/pinochet-the-cold-war-and-the-most-pathetic-match-ever-played/.

21. Rofe and Tomlinson, 'The untold story of FIFA's diplomacy': 515–518.

22. Käser and d'Almeida Santiago visit report, dated 26 October 1973, FIFA Museum Library, Zurich, Switzerland.

23. Goldblatt, *The Ball Is Round*, pp. 609–610; John Sugden and Alan Tomlinson, 'Global power struggles in world football: FIFA and UEFA, 1954–74, and their legacy', *International Journal of the History of Sport* 14, no. 2 (1997): 13–14.

24. *FIFA News*, November 1973: 462–463; *Football-Hockey*, 13 November 1973: 5.

25. For the hundreds of letters and newspaper clippings FIFA received and compiled during this controversy, see FIFA's Chile–Soviet Union protest file, FIFA Museum Library, Zurich, Switzerland.

26. *FIFA News*, November 1973: 463–467.

27. Victor Lusinschi, 'Soviet Union kicked out of World Cup in soccer', *New York Times*, 13 November 1973: 55; 'Cancel Russian ban, say East Germans', *Evening Standard*, 13 November 1973, unpaged, in FIFA's Chile–Soviet Union protest file, FIFA Museum Library, Zurich, Switzerland; Agenda for FIFA World Cup organising committee meeting, Frankfurt, 5 January 1974, FIFA Museum Library, Zurich, Switzerland.

28. Worswick, 'Playing under Pinochet'.

29. Worswick, 'Playing under Pinochet'; footage here: https://the18.com/soccer-enter tainment/fifa-intercontinental-playoffs-throwback-chile-vs-soviet-union-1973.

30. Parra, 'Pinochet's team': 1654–1655.

31. 'Now Rous is accused', *Cambridge Evening News*, 21 November 1973: 10; 'Russians' bitter attack on Rous', *The Guardian*, 22 November 1973: 31.

32. *Soviet Sport*, 21 November 1973: 4; *FIFA News*, December 1973: 480.

33. Sugden and Tomlinson, 'Global power struggles in world football': 14–15; cartoons in *Süddeutsche Zeitung* and *Die Presse*, both dated 11 November 1973, FIFA's Chile–Soviet Union protest file, FIFA Museum Library, Zurich, Switzerland; Harry Fuchs, Zurich Police, to Helmut Käser, 23 November 1973, protest file, FIFA Museum Library, Zurich, Switzerland.

34. Minutes of FIFA World Cup organising committee meeting, Frankfurt, 5 January 1974, FIFA Museum Library, Zurich, Switzerland.

35. *Football-Hockey*, 13 January 1974: 12; Rous, *Football Worlds*, pp. 198–203; Sugden and Tomlinson, 'Global power struggles in world football': 19–24.

36. Elsey, *Citizens and Sportsmen*, pp. 245–246; Thomas, 'An open goal for fascism'; Dan Williamson, 'Carlos Caszely: The Colo-Colo legend who fought in open rebellion against Augusto Pinochet', *These Football Times*, 20 November 2017: https:// thesefootballtimes.co/2017/11/22/carlos-caszely-the-colo-colo-legend-who-fought-in-open-rebellion-against-augusto-pinochet/.

37. David Winner, 'But was this the beautiful game's ugliest moment?' *FT.com*, 21 June 2008: https://web.archive.org/web/20100611233444/http:/www.ft.com/cms/s/0/e6347c16-3f2a-11dd-8fd9-0000779fd2ac.html.

38. Rut Diamint, 'Truth, justice and declassification: Secret archives show US helped Argentine military wage "dirty war" that killed 30,000', *The Conversation*, 10 May 2019: https://theconversation.com/truth-justice-and-declassification-secret-archives-show-us-helped-argentine-military-wage-dirty-war-that-killed-30-000-115611.

39. Lívia Magalhães, '40 years after victory: Disputing memories over the 1978 World Cup in Argentina', *Soccer and Society* 21, no. 8 (2020): 904–917; Felix A. Jiménez Botta, '"Yes to football, no to torture!" The politics of the 1978 football World Cup in West Germany', *Sport in Society* 20, no. 10 (2016): 3; Paul Doyle, 'Kidnappers made Cruyff miss World Cup', *The Guardian*, 16 April 2008: www.theguardian.com/football/2008/apr/16/newsstory.sport15.

40. Goldblatt, *The Ball Is Round*, pp. 612–613; Adriana Novoa and Robert Koch, 'Argentina's national style: Maradona, Peronism, and metaphysical football', *Journal of Sport and Social Issues*, no. 47 (2022): 158–181.

41. Jonathan Wilson, *Angels with Dirty Faces: The Footballing History of Argentina* (London: Orion, 2016), pp. 288–297; Will Hersey, 'Remembering Argentina 1978: The dirtiest World Cup of all time', *Esquire*, 14 June 2018: www.esquire.com/uk/culture/a21454856/argentina-1978-world-cup/; 'Argentina's 1978 World Cup win against Peru was fixed in a brutal political deal, former senator says', *Yahoo Sports*, 11 February 2012: https://sports.yahoo.com/news/argentinas-1978-world-cup-win-052800565-sow.html.

42. Winner, 'But was this the beautiful game's ugliest moment?'.

7 Us against Us, or Us against Them? West Germany vs. East Germany, Hamburg, June 1974

1. SAPMO-BArch, DY 30/IV 2/2.039/251, Gesamtbericht über die Teilnahme der Altherrmannschaft des 1. FCM am Hallenturnier des 1. FC Saarbrücken in der Zeit vom 8–10.1.1988: 188–192.

2. Elke Wittich (ed.), *Wo waren Sie, als das Sparwasser-Tor fiel?* (Hamburg: Konkret Literatur Verlag, 1998), p. 126; Thomas Blees, *90 Minuten Klassenkampf: Das Länderspiel BRD-DDR 1974* (Frankfurt/Main: Fischer Taschenbuch Verlag, 1999), p. 113.

3. 'Nun intensiv auf Endrunde vorbereiten!' *Die Neue Fußballwoche* 2, 8 January 1974: 3–4.

4. Quoted in Kay Schiller, 'The 1974 World Cup in West Germany: A non-event?', in Stefan Rinke and Kay Schiller (eds.), *The FIFA World Cup 1930–2010: Politics, Commerce, Spectacle and Identities* (Göttingen: Wallstein Verlag, 2014), p. 230.

5. Josie McLellan, *Love in the Time of Communism: Intimacy and Sexuality in the GDR* (Cambridge: Cambridge University Press, 2011), p. 28.

6. Jutta Braun and René Wiese, 'DDR-Fußball und gesamtdeutsche Identität im Kalten Krieg', *Historische Sozialforschung* 30, no. 4 (2005): 203.

7. Mary Fulbrook, *The People's State: East German Society from Hitler to Honecker* (New Haven, CT: Yale University Press, 2005), pp. 241–242.

8. Hanns Leske, *Erich Mielke, die Stasi und das runde Leder: Der Einfluß der SED und des Ministeriums für Staatssicherheit auf dem Fußballsport in der DDR* (Göttingen: Verlag die Werkstatt, 2004), pp. 402–408; Stefan Wolle, *Die heile Welt der Diktatur: Alltag und Herrschaft in der DDR 1971–1989* (Bonn: Bundeszentrale für politische Bildung, 1998), pp. 166–167; Kay Schiller, *WM 74: Als der Fußball modern wurde* (Berlin: Rotbuch Verlag, 2014), p. 148.

9. McDougall, *The People's Game*, pp. 88–89.

10. Quoted in Michael Horn and Gottfried Weise, *Das große Lexikon des DDR-Fußballs* (Berlin: Schwarzkopf & Schwarzkopf, 2004), pp. 16, 72.

11. Quoted in Hesse-Lichtenberger, *Tor!*, p. 189.

12. Annett Gröschner, *Sieben Tränen muß ein Club-Fan weinen: 1. FC Magdeburg – eine Fußballegende* (Leipzig: Gustav Kiepenhauer, 1999), p. 89; Wittich (ed.), *Wo waren Sie*, p. 125.

13. Hesse-Lichtenberger, *Tor!*, pp. 189–191; Schiller, *WM 74*, pp. 152–172.

14. Hanns Leske, *Enzyklopädie des DDR-Fußballs* (Göttingen: Verlag die Werkstatt, 2007), p. 419.

15. Judge for yourself: www.youtube.com/watch?v=eBuIMowtBq4.

16. Quoted in Schiller, *WM 74*, p. 188.

17. 'Streich's Traumtor sicherte erste WM Punkte', *Die Neue Fußballwoche* 25, 18 June 1974: 4.

18. www.youtube.com/watch?v=3mr-5YUVvjY.

19. Quoted in Wittich (ed.), *Wo waren Sie*, p. 18.

20. Brandenburgisches Landeshauptarchiv (BLHA), Rep 730 Nr. 4736, Für die Schulung zu den 10. Fußballweltmeisterschaften vom 13. Jun bis 7. Juli in der BRD, n.d.; Landeshauptarchiv Sachsen-Anhalt, Abteilung Merseburg (LHASA, MER), SED Bezirksleitung-Halle, IV/C-2/16/557, Maßnahmeplan für die Auswahl und politische Vorbereitung von Touristen zur Teilnahme an der Fußballweltmeisterschaft 1974, 13 February 1974; Plan für die Vorbereitung der Touristendelegation am 11.6.1974 im PI Halle-Kröllwitz, 29 May 1974; BLHA, Rep 931 Calau Nr. 379, Information über Stimmung und Meinungen zur Fußballweltmeisterschaft, 21 June 1974.

21. Hesse-Lichtenberger, *Tor!*, p. 192.

22. Buschner quoted in Wittich (ed.), *Wo waren Sie*, p. 96; 'Freude über den Erfolg, aber sachliche Wertung', *Die Neue Fußballwoche* 26, 25 June 1974: 5.

23. Horn and Weise, *Das große Lexikon*, p. 64.

24. Kuper, *Football against the Enemy*, p. 21.

25. Olaf S., interview with the authors, Berlin, 29 May 2011; Dassler quoted in Markus Hesselmann and Robert Ide, 'A tale of two Germanys: Football culture and national identity in the German Democratic Republic', in Tomlinson and Young (eds.), *German Football*, p. 44.

26. Thomas Brussig, *Leben bis Männer* (Frankfurt/Main: Fischer Taschenbuch Verlag, 2001), pp. 35–37.

27. Wittich (ed.), *Wo waren Sie*, p. 115; Frank Leonhard, interview with the authors, Berlin, 25 May 2011.

28. Schiller, *WM 74*, p. 138.

29. Hesse-Lichtenberger, *Tor!*, p. 194.

30. Quoted in Schiller, *WM 74*, p. 142.

31. 'Den Weltmeister zwar aus dem Rhythmus gebracht … ', *Die Neue Fußballwoche* 27, 2 July 1974: 10.

32. 'Nach frühem Rückstand zu vorsichtig!', *Die Neue Fußballwoche* 27, 2 July 1974: 4–5.

33. SAPMO-BArch, DY 12/1243, Schlussfolgerungen für die weitere Arbeit im DFV der DDR im Ergebnis der Einschäztung des Abschneidens der Weltmeisterschaft 1974, 25 November 1974: 96–97.

34. Manfred Ewald, *Ich war der Sport* (Berlin: Elefanten Press, 1994), p. 66; Archivgut des Deutschen Fußballverbandes der DDR (DFV), I/2, Günter Schneider, 'Dokumentation über 45 Jahre Fußball in der SBZ/DDR' (unpublished, 1996).

35. Quoted in Hesse-Lichtenberger, *Tor!*, p. 197.

36. On 'Re-Enactment', see Michael Wagg, *The Turning Season: DDR-Oberliga Revisited* (Chichester: Pitch, 2021), pp. 5–9; Donald Mahoney, 'At the Olympiastadion', *LRB Blog*, 28 May 2018: www.lrb.co.uk/blog/2018/may/at-the-olympiastadion.

37. Sparwasser quoted in Wittich (ed.), *Wo waren Sie*, p. 126; Hoffmann quoted in Leske, *Enzyklopädie*, p. 419.

38. Elke Wittich and Martin Krauss, 'Wo ist der Sparwasser? Die beliebtesten Leserfragen zum Sportteil der "Jungle World"', jungle.world, 6 June 2017: https:// jungle.world/artikel/2017/23/wo-ist-der-sparwasser.
39. Wittich (ed.), *Wo waren Sie*, p. 37, 90.
40. Wittich and Krauss, 'Wo ist der Sparwasser?'; Wittich (ed.), *Wo waren Sie*, p. 115.
41. Klaus Hansen in Wittich (ed.), *Wo waren Sie*, p. 67.
42. Veit Spiegel in Wittich (ed.), *Wo waren Sie*, p. 51.

8 Leopards on Trial: Zaire vs. Yugoslavia, Gelsenkirchen, June 1974

1. Scott Newman, '5 of the most bizarre moments in World Cup history', *Sportskeeda*, 4 June 2018: www.sportskeeda.com/football/5-of-the-most-bizarre-moments-in-world-cup-history; 'The World Cup's most iconic players: Mwepu Ilunga, Zaire's defender of free kicks in 1974', *TalkSPORT*, 13 April 2018: https://tinyurl.com/mast3v6d; 'Zaire 1974 World Cup': https://zaire1974.blogspot.com/.
2. Westad, *The Global Cold War*, pp. 136–143.
3. Ibid., pp. 140–143; Michael G. Schatzberg, *Mobutu or Chaos? The United States and Zaire, 1960–1990* (Lanham, MD: University Press of America, 1991).
4. Thomas M. Callaghy, *The State–Society Struggle: Zaire in Comparative Perspective* (New York: Columbia University Press, 1984); Georges Nzongola-Ntalaja, *The Congo from Leopold to Kabila: A People's History* (New York: Zed Books, 2007); Westad, *The Global Cold War*, pp. 226–227.
5. Conor Heffernan, '"In Zaire, we do not consider sport as a mere amusement": Mobutu, sport and Zairian identity, 1965–74', *Sporting Traditions* 1, no. 2 (2014): 1–14; Lewis A. Erenberg, *The Rumble in the Jungle: Muhammad Ali and George Foreman on the Global Stage* (Chicago: University of Chicago Press, 2019).
6. Goldblatt, *The Ball Is Round*, pp. 479–510.
7. Heffernan, '"In Zaire"', pp. 1–4; Paul Dietschy, 'Football imagery and colonial legacy: Zaire's disastrous campaign during the 1974 World Cup', *Soccer and Society* 13, no. 2 (2012): 226.
8. Heffernan, '"In Zaire"', p. 6; Leopards player Adelard Mayanga, cited in Ian Hawkey, *Feet of the Chameleon* (London: Portico, 2010), p. 81.
9. Hawkey, *Chameleon*, pp. 81–83; Heffernan, '"In Zaire"', pp. 3–4; Dietschy, 'Football imagery', p. 229; Tshimpumpu wa Tshimpumpu, 'Zaire qualifies for final tournament of the World Cup', *FIFA News*, No. 28, January 1974: 17. 'Africa's no. 1 – but they're outsiders', *Grimsby Evening Telegraph*, 22 May 1974: 15.
10. Robert Niebuhr, *The Search for a Cold War Legitimacy: Foreign Policy and Tito's Yugoslavia* (Leiden: Brill, 2018); Richard Burton, 'The longest days', *Harper's Magazine*, October 2012: https://harpers.org/archive/2012/10/the-longest-days/.
11. Gerard McCann, 'The sixties and red Africa', *The Conversation*, 21 April 2016: https://theconversation.com/the-sixties-and-red-africa-the-decade-of-searching-for-african-utopias-57906.
12. Richard Mills, 'Scoring for the non-aligned movement: Yugoslavia, football and the third world', *History Workshop*, 25 June 2018: www.historyworkshop.org.uk/sport/scoring-for-the-non-aligned-movement-yugoslavia-football-and-the-third-world/; Richard Mills, *The Politics of Football in Yugoslavia*, p. 160.
13. Jonathan Wilson, 'Puff goes magic Dragan's reputation', *The Guardian*, 12 February 2008: www.theguardian.com/football/2008/feb/12/europeanfootball.sport1.

14. Mills, *The Politics of Football,* pp. 155–156; Donald Saunders, 'West Germany and Italy best bets for world cup final', *Daily Telegraph,* 13 June 1974: 33; Mills, 'Scoring'.

15. David Lacey, 'Putting the viewer in the picture', *The Guardian,* 11 June 1974: 28.

16. Archie Macpherson, *Flower of Scotland: A Scottish Football Odyssey* (Newbury: Highdown, 2005), pp. 62–63; James Sandersen, 'Scots to wing in', *Daily Mirror,* 14 June 1974: 30.

17. David Lacey, 'Scots suffer more qualms', *The Guardian,* 15 June 1974: 25; Jim Kernaghan, 'Scotland unhappy with win', *Toronto Star,* 15 June 1974: 7.

18. Interview with Facchetti, *Shoot,* 16 March 1974: 37; John Hennessy, 'A wandering star never far from home', *The Times,* 16 March 1974: 7; Dietschy, 'Football imagery': 232.

19. Dietschy, 'Football imagery': 226; Hawkey, *Chameleon,* p. 83.

20. Mayanga, cited in Hawkey, *Chameleon,* p. 84.

21. Schatzberg, *Mobutu or Chaos?* pp. 35–38.

22. Ndaye Mulamba, cited in Claire Raynaud, *La Mort M'attendra* (Paris: Calmann-Lévy, 2010), pp. 130–131.

23. Tubilandu Ndimbi and Mwepu Ilunga, interviewed in *Entre La Coupe et L'Élection,* documentary by Monique Mbeka Phoba and Guy Kabeya Muya, 2008; Mayanga, cited in Hawkey, *Chameleon,* p. 84.

24. 'Odlična' Igra – Rekordna Pobjeda', *Slobodna Dalmacija,* 19 June 1974: 8.

25. Faouzi Mahjoub, 'Le Zaire: Une faillite signée Vidinic', *Miroir du Football* 223, 1 August 1974: 5.

26. Hawkey, *Chameleon,* p. 85.

27. Dietschy, 'Football imagery': 226; 'The dark story of Zaire's 9-nil defeat in the 1974 World Cup', *Sky History:* www.history.co.uk/article/the-dark-story-of-zaires-9-nil-defeat-in-the-1974-world-cup.

28. Bernard Joy, 'Tension could be the big killer', *Evening Standard,* 13 June 1974: 55; 'Big wages don't guarantee success', *Evening Standard,* 24 June 1974: 51.

29. 'Odlična' Igra – Rekordna Pobjeda'.

30. Paul Wilcox, 'Scots unchanged for vital game', *The Guardian,* 22 June 1974: 22.

31. Hugh McIlvanney, 'The week that Scotland were out of this world', *The Observer,* 23 June 1974: 24.

32. 'Would change qualifying system', *Hamilton Spectator,* 21 June 1974: 21; 'Nine-goal romp sets finals alight', *Liverpool Echo,* 19 June 1974: 26.

33. Mark Dummett, '1974: Zaire's show of shame', *BBC Sport Online,* 22 May 2002: http://news.bbc.co.uk/sport3/worldcup2002/hi/history/newsid_1993000/1993333.stm; Mayanga, cited in Hawkey, *Chameleon,* p. 86.

34. Mayanga, cited in Hawkey, *Chameleon,* p. 86.

35. Mafu Kibonge, interviewed in *Entre La Coupe et L'Élection.*

36. 'Zaire's infamous World Cup free-kick moment', *Sporting Witness,* BBC Sounds, 1 December 2022: www.bbc.co.uk/sounds/play/w3ct36gj.

37. Donald Saunders, 'Eastern Europe make major drive for honours', *Daily Telegraph,* 24 June 1974: 26.

38. Alfred Green, 'Day the news hit town', *Liverpool Echo,* 13 July 1974: 16.

39. Mills, *The Politics of Football,* pp. 160–161, 290–291; Neven Andjelic, 'The rise and fall of Yugoslavia: Politics and football in the service of nation(s)', *Sudosteuropa* 62, no. 2 (2014): 115; Branko Oblak, cited in Wilson, *Behind the Curtain,* p. 129.

40. Dietschy, 'Football imagery': 235–236.

41. Mayanga, cited in Hawkey, *Chameleon,* p. 87; Leopards player Mantantu Kidumu, cited in Wim Vos, 'De meest bizarre deelname ooit aan een WK: Drie tovenaars om

de ploeg te begeleiden en "babyvlees" op het menu', *Het Nieuwsblad, Mobile*, 13 July 2018: www.nieuwsblad.be/cnt/dmf20180620_03571505; Dietschy, 'Football imagery': 236.

42. Geoffrey Greene, 'Brazilian wall between East and West Europe', *Globe and Mail*, 22 June 1974: 6; 'UEFA president urges changes in qualifying', *Globe and Mail*, 21 June 1974: 30; Goldblatt, *The Ball Is Round*, pp. 874–898.

43. Goldblatt, *The Ball Is Round*, pp. 509–510, 887–888.

44. Ekofa Mbungu, interviewed in *Entre La Coupe et L'Élection*; Paul Doyle, 'Ndaye Mulamba is living like a pauper 44 years after red-card farce', *The Guardian*, 18 March 2018: www.theguardian.com/football/blog/2018/mar/18/football-pierre-ndaye-mulamba-zaire-1974-world-cup; Ed Aarons, 'Former Zaire defender Mwepu Ilunga dies aged 66 after long illness', *The Guardian*, 8 May 2015: www.theguardian.com/football/2015/may/08/zaire-mwepu-ilunga-free-kick-world-cup-1974.

9 'A Crazy Day, a Show of Power': Steaua Bucharest vs. Dinamo Bucharest, Bucharest, June 1988

1. Quoted in Wilson, *Behind the Curtain*, p. 204.

2. https://cuparomaniei.frf.ro/stiri/istoric/.

3. For Version 1, see Wilson, *Behind the Curtain*, pp. 203–204; for Version 2, see Florin Poenaru, 'Power at play: Soccer stadiums and popular culture in 1980s Romania', in Catherine M. Giustino, Catherine J. Plum and Alexander Vari (eds.), *Socialist Escapes: Breaking Away from Ideology and Everyday Routine in Eastern Europe, 1945–1989* (New York and Oxford: Berghahn, 2013), pp. 232–233; for Version 3 (the 'true story'), see 'Povestea adevărată şi în imagini a gesturilor halucinante ale lui Andone la adresa publicului din Ghencea şi a lui Valentin Ceauşescu în '89!', *Orange Sport*, 7 October 2012: https://tinyurl.com/4eetxrz7.

4. Quoted in Rob Gloster, 'Awfully tough to beat a Ceausescu team', *Los Angeles Times*, 1 April 1990: www.latimes.com/archives/la-xpm-1990-04-01-sp-883-story.html.

5. Quoted in Gloster, 'Awfully tough'.

6. On this relationship, see Stejărel Olaru, *Nadia Comăneci and the Secret Police: A Cold War Escape* trans. by Alistair Ian Blyth (London: Bloomsbury Academic, 2023), pp. 218–219.

7. All quoted in Wilson, *Behind the Curtain*, p. 205.

8. Quoted in Robert Adam, 'Football and authoritarianism in twentieth century Romania: Between propaganda and subversion', *Soccer & Society* 21, no. 6 (2020): 660.

9. On dissident football TV viewers ('rooters'), see László Péter, *Forbidden Football in Ceausescu's Romania* (Cham: Palgrave Macmillan, 2018).

10. Quoted in Thore Haugstad, 'Tainted gold: Nicolae Ceauşescu and the curious high point of Romanian club football', *The Blizzard* no. 41 (2021): 97.

11. 'Only Steaua stand between El Tel and the inevitable', *The Guardian*, 7 May 1986: 28.

12. 'Steaua leave Venables on the spot', *The Guardian*, 8 May 1986: 28; 'Steaua shoot Barcelona out on penalties', *Daily Telegraph*, 8 May 1986: 34.

13. Duckadam quoted in Haugstad, 'Tainted gold': 96; Jenei quoted in 'The quiet heroes', *The Guardian*, 9 May 1986: 28.

14. Quoted in Haugstad, 'Tainted gold': 96.

15. Poenaru, 'Power at play', p. 239; Adam, 'Football and authoritarianism': 662.

16. Quoted in Haugstad, 'Tainted gold': 96.

17. Péter, *Forbidden Football*, p. 117.

18. 'Milan's Dutch double treat', *The Guardian*, 25 May 1989: 16.

19. Adam, 'Football and authoritarianism': 663–664.

20. See c. 23:20–23:39 here: www.youtube.com/watch?v=IH8GadJLKHg.

21. Quoted in Wilson, *Behind the Curtain*, p. 203.

22. Quoted in 'Povestea adevărată'.

23. 'Gloucester Gym Club travels to Romania', *Gloucester Leader*, May 1989: 5.

24. Dave Hewitson and Dave Hardman, *Places I Remember: Liverpool FC European Adventures as Told by the Fans* (Liverpool: 80s Casuals, 2014), pp. 80–81.

25. Quoted in Olaru, *Nadia Comăneci and the Secret Police*, p. 14.

26. Simona Petracovschi and Jessica W. Chin, 'Sport and defection from Romania during the Cold War', *Journal of Sport and Social Issues* 45, no. 6 (2020): 511.

27. Both quoted in Mihnea Lazăr, 'The inside story of why the entire Romania '98 team bleached their hair', *Vice Magazine*, 18 June 2024: www.vice.com/en/article/the-inside-story-of-why-the-entire-romania-98-team-bleached-their-hair/.

28. Florin Faje, 'Managing *Furia Latina*: The making of a Romanian football system and style of play', *Nationalities Papers* 44, no. 6 (2016): 911.

29. Bogdan Popa and Pompiliu-Nicolae Constantin, 'Football economy in Romania: Breaking away from socialism, facing capitalism', in Dariusz Wojtaszyn, Daniel Fitzpatrick and Roland Benedikter (eds.), *The Political Economy of European Football: Perspectives from Central and Eastern Europe* (London & New York: Routledge, 2025), p. 97.

30. 'The battle for Steaua Bucharest – an Eastern European giant at war with itself', *BBC Sport*, 20 January 2022: www.bbc.com/sport/football/59974018.

31. Popa and Constantin, 'Football economy in Romania', p. 94.

32. Wilson, *Behind the Curtain*, pp. 185–190.

33. Alan McDougall, '"Eulogy to theft": Berliner FC Dynamo, East German football, and the end of East German communism', in Edelman and Young (eds.), *The Whole World Was Watching*, p. 124.

34. Poenaru, 'Power at play', p. 233.

10 A New Era: China vs. Norway, Guangzhou, November 1991

1. 'The golden phoenix spreads its wings and wants to fly thousands of miles', *People's Daily*, 17 November 1991: 4.

2. Andrei S. Markovits and Steven L. Hellerman, 'Women's soccer in the United States: Yet another American "exceptionalism"', *Soccer & Society*, 4, nos. 2–3 (2003): 14.

3. Quoted in Lindsay Parks Pieper, *Sex Testing: Gender Policing in Women's Sports* (Champaign: University of Illinois Press, 2016), p. 89.

4. 'The golden phoenix': 4; Fan Hong and J. A. Mangan, 'Will the "Iron Roses" bloom forever? Women's football in China: Changes and challenges', in Hong and Mangan (eds.), *Soccer, Women, Sexual Liberation: Kicking Off a New Era* (London: Frank Cass, 2004), p. 55.

5. Wille quoted in Katie Wright and Sophie Hartley, 'The speech that changed the course of women's football', *BBC Sport*, 31 October 2024: www.bbc.com/sport/football/articles/ce9gz57dlr3o; Blatter quoted in Bente Ovedie Skogvang, 'Scandinavian women's football: The importance of male and female pioneers in the development of the sport', *Sport in History* 39, no. 2 (2019): 216.

6. Quoted in 'Blooming roses', *South China Morning Post*, 14 September 2000: 89.

7. Both quoted in Hong and Mangan, 'Will the "Iron Roses" bloom forever?', p. 60.

8. Quoted in Hong and Mangan, 'Will the "Iron Roses" bloom forever?', p. 54.

9. 'China stake claim for women's World Cup', *South China Morning Post*, 14 June 1988: 25.

10. The lower figure came from the Chinese government, the higher one from Amnesty International.

11. 'Giant strides in "lily-foot" land', *South China Morning Post*, 26 November 1991: 24.

12. Kari Fasting, 'Small country – big results: Women's football in Norway', in Hong and Mangan (eds.), *Soccer, Women, Sexual Liberation*, p. 157.

13. Fasting, 'Small country', p. 158; Bente Ovedie Skogvang, 'Breaking barriers in Norwegian women's football', in Mihaly Szerovay, Arto Nevala and Hannu Itkonen (eds.), *Football in the Nordic Countries: Practices, Equality and Influence* (Abingdon: Routledge, 2023), p. 153.

14. Eivind Å. Skille, 'Biggest but smallest: Female football and the case of Norway', *Soccer & Society* 9, no. 4 (2008): 521.

15. Skogvang, 'Breaking barriers', p. 154; Skogvang, 'Scandinavian women's football': 216.

16. Jo Inge Bekkevold, 'Norges relasjon med Kina i 70 år: Småstatsidealisme og realisme i møte med en stormakt', *Internasjonal Politikk* 70, no. 1 (2021): 75–77.

17. Rich Laverty, 'The untold stories of the 1991 Women's World Cup', *Women's Football Chronicles* (19 July 2023): https://richlaverty.substack.com/p/the-inside-untold-stories-of-the.

18. Laverty, 'The untold stories of the 1991 Women's World Cup'; 'Women's World Championship kicks off: Chinese girls defeat Norwegian team', *People's Daily*, 17 November 1991: 4.

19. Quoted in Laverty, 'The untold stories'.

20. Quoted in Laverty, 'The untold stories'.

21. 'Women's World Championship kicks off': 4.

22. Quoted in Laverty, 'The untold stories'.

23. Quoted in 'Giant strides in "lily-foot" land': 24.

24. Clemente A. Lisi, *The U.S. Women's Soccer Team: An American Success Story* (Lanham, MD: Scarecrow, 2010), p. 11.

25. Quoted in Jean Williams, *A Beautiful Game: International Perspectives on Women's Football* (Oxford: Berg, 2007), p. 84.

26. Quoted in Barry Glendenning, 'Women's World Cup game-changing moments No 3: China in 1991', *The Guardian*, 18 June 2019: www.theguardian.com/football/2019/jun/18/womens-world-cup-game-changing-moments-no-3-china-in-1991.

27. Quoted in 'US women find the formula', *The Guardian*, 29 November 1991: 20.

28. *FIFA Women's World Cup China '91 – Technical Report & Statistics* (Zurich: FIFA, 1991), pp. 67, 80, 86; Havelange quoted in Marcus Chu, *Sporting Events in China as Economic Development, National Image, and Political Ambition* (Cham: Springer, 2021), p. 18.

29. 'Fans flocking to the sisters of skill', *South China Morning Post*, 22 November 1991: 34.

30. All quoted in Laverty, 'The untold stories'.

31. 'Fans flocking to the sisters of skill': 34.

32. 'Germans prepare to test United States resolve', *Daily Telegraph*, 27 November 1991: 40; 'Giant strides in "lily-foot" land': 24.

33. Quote from unnamed USSF official in 'US women reach world soccer final', *San Bernardino County Sun*, 28 November 1991: C3.

34. Akers-Stahl quoted in Lisi, *The U.S. Women's Soccer Team*, p. 2; Glendenning, 'Women's World Cup'.

35. Laverty, 'The untold stories'.

36. 'Pride on line in World Cup final', *South China Morning Post*, 11 July 1999: 6.

37. Hamm quoted in Lisi, *The U.S. Women's Soccer Team*, p. 19; Clinton quoted in 'US women rule world', *South China Morning Post*, 12 July 1999: 27.

38. Quoted in Glendenning, 'Women's World Cup'.

39. Espeseth quoted in 'Golden goal sinks golden girls', *Daily Telegraph*, 29 September 2000: 41; 'Riise: Coaching Norway at a World Cup was always in my dreams', FIFA.com, 8 April 2023: https://tinyurl.com/mwb93d45.

40. DeCicco quoted in 'US women rule world': 27; Daniel Storey, 'How China's Steel Roses lost their crown as queens of Asia due to years of underfunding', *The i Paper*, 31 July 2023: https://tinyurl.com/mwrvv74r.

41. Quoted in Hun Chan Wong, 'China nearly won the Women's World Cup in 1999: Now it's aiming for the top again', *Wall Street Journal*, 25 July 2023: www.wsj.com/sports/soccer/china-womens-world-cup-e84a0cb8?st=xdtsbmg38984q61.

42. Quoted in Aihua Zhao, Peter Horton and Liu Liu, 'Women's football in the People's Republic of China: Retrospect and prospect', *International Journal of the History of Sport* 29, no. 17 (2012): 2377.

43. Both quoted in Nick Marsh, 'China's dream of becoming a football superpower lies in tatters', *BBC News*, 26 March 2025: www.bbc.com/news/articles/ce8vp2e7p64o.

44. Quoted in Wong, 'China nearly won the Women's World Cup'.

45. 'Giant strides in "lily-foot" land': 24.

46. Quoted in 'Giant strides in "lily-foot" land': 24.

Epilogue

1. David Goldblatt, *The Age of Football: The Global Game in the Twenty-First Century* (London: Picador, 2019), p. 267.

2. Quoted in David Goldblatt and Daniel Nolan, 'Viktor Orbán's reckless football obsession', *The Guardian*, 11 January 2018: www.theguardian.com/news/2018/jan/11/viktor-orban-hungary-prime-minister-reckless-football-obsession.

3. Quoted in Goldblatt, *The Age of Football*, p. 268.

4. 'Puskás Museum opens with Viktor Orbán speech', *Hungarian Conservative*, 29 November 2024: www.hungarianconservative.com/articles/current/viktor-orban-puskas-arena-museum-opening-legacy/.

5. Quoted in Ann McElvoy, 'Nightmare of the golden team', *The Spectator*, 2 November 1996: 23.

6. Francis Fukyama, 'The end of history?', *The National Interest* no. 16 (1989): 16.

7. *Tempo* (Serbian sports magazine) and Osim quoted in Mills, *The Politics of Football in Yugoslavia*, pp. 254, 290.

8. Joseph S. Nye Jr., *Soft Power: The Means to Success in World Politics* (New York: PublicAffairs, 2004), p. x.

9. David Goldblatt, 'How to get on TV', *London Review of Books* 44 no. 22 (17 November 2022): 7.

10. Quoted in Goldblatt, *The Age of Football*, p. 520.

11. Infantino quoted in 'Infantino says 2018 World Cup is the best-ever', reuters.com, 13 July 2018: www.reuters.com/article/sports/-infantino-says-2018-world-cup-is-the-best-ever-idUSKBN1K31M9/; Putin quoted in 'FIFA president says World Cup has changed perception of Russia', reuters.com, 14 July 2018: www.reuters.com/article/sports/fifa-president-says-world-cup-has-changed-perception-of-russia-idUSKBN1K40ZI/.

12. Quoted in Björn Alexander Düben, '"There is no Ukraine": Fact-checking the Kremlin's version of Ukrainian history', LSE Blog, 1 July 2020: https://blogs.lse.ac.uk/lseih/2020/07/01/there-is-no-ukraine-fact-checking-the-kremlins-version-of-ukrainian-history/.
13. Quoted in Andy Brassell, *We Play On: Shakhtar Donetsk's Fight for Ukraine, Football and Freedom* (London: Robinson, 2023), p. 1.

FIGURES

ACKNOWLEDGEMENTS

We would like to thank the following archivists, scholars, journalists, friends and family: Dave Bannerman, Norbert Bauer, Peter Beck, John Bell, Joe Brewin, Heather Dichter, Noelle Dowling, Robert Edelman, Brenda Elsey, Andrew Glennerster, Ifan Hughes, James Hulse, Alex Jackson, Wojciech Janich, Peter Jones, Pete Kind, Maria Lau, Chris Lee, György Majtényi, Kate Manning, Simon Martin, Dave McDougall, Ciara Meehan, Richard Mills, Chris Moran, Tom Morren, Pete Niesen, Ray Ryan, Ilia Sannikov, Michael Schmalholz, Mark Shaw, Norman Smith, Thomas Spielhofer, June Venables, Pete Venables, Haoqian Yu.

Tony dedicates the book to Shirley and Isaac.

Alan dedicates the book to Erika, Sophie and Lotte.

WORKS CITED

Archives

Africa Museum, Tervuren, Belgium

Archives of the Football Association of Ireland, University College Dublin, Ireland

Archivgut des Deutschen Fußballverbandes der DDR (DFV), Berlin, Germany

Brandenburgisches Landeshauptarchiv (BLHA), Potsdam, Germany

FIFA Museum Library, Zurich, Switzerland

Football Association, England, The National Football Museum Research Centre, Preston, UK

Foreign Office, The National Archives, London, UK

Landeshauptarchiv Sachsen-Anhalt, Abteilung Merseburg (LHASA, MER), Merseburg, Germany

Papers of Archbishop John Charles McQuaid, Archdiocese of Dublin Archive, Dublin, Ireland

Stiftung der Parteien und Massenorganisationen, Bundesarchiv (SAPMO-BArch), Berlin, Germany

Trades Union Congress Collection, Warwick University, UK

Newspapers and Magazines

A Voz de Timor
Belfast Newsletter
Birmingham Gazette
Birmingham Post

Cambridge Evening News
Daily Herald
Daily Mirror
Daily Record
Daily Star
Daily Telegraph
Daily Worker
Die Neue Fußballwoche
Die Presse
Esquire
Evening Chronicle
Evening Gazette
Evening Herald
Evening Sentinel
Evening Standard
Football-Hockey
FourFourTwo
Globe and Mail
Grimsby Evening Telegraph
Hamilton Spectator
Het Nieuwsblad
Irish Independent
Irish Press
Irish Times
Leicester Mercury
Limerick Leader
Liverpool Daily Post
Liverpool Echo
London Review of Books
Los Angeles Times
Manchester Guardian
Miroir du Football
Newcastle Journal and North Mail
New York Times
People
People's Daily
Russia Today
San Bernardino County Sun
Shoot
Slobodna Dalmacija
South China Morning Post
Soviet Sport

Soviet Weekly
Sports Illustrated
Süddeutsche Zeitung
Sunday Dispatch
Sunday Independent
Times Colonist
Toronto Star
Tribune
The Athletic
The Blizzard
The Guardian
The i Paper
The Independent
The Observer
The Times
Wall Street Journal
Western Morning News

Select Bibliography

Allison, George. *Allison Calling*. London: Staples, 1948.

Ball, Phil. *White Storm: 100 Years of Real Madrid*. Edinburgh: Mainstream, 2002.

Bastin, Cliff. *Cliff Bastin Remembers*. London: Ettrick, 1950.

Beck, Peter J. *Scoring for Britain: International Football and International Politics, 1900–1939*. London: Frank Cass, 1999.

Blees, Thomas. *90 Minuten Klassenkampf: Das Länderspiel BRD DDR 1974*. Frankfurt/Main: Fischer Taschenbuch Verlag, 1999.

Bolchover, David. *The Greatest Comeback: From Genocide to Football Glory*. London: Biteback, 2018.

Brassell, Andy. *We Play On: Shakhtar Donetsk's Fight for Ukraine, Football and Freedom*. London: Robinson, 2023.

Brüggemeier, Franz-Josef. 'Das Wunder von Bern: The 1954 football World Cup, the German nation and popular histories', in *Popular Historiographies in the 19th and 20th Centuries: Cultural Meanings, Social Practices*, edited by Sylvia Paletschek, pp. 188–200. Berghahn: Oxford and New York, 2011.

Brussig, Thomas. *Leben bis Männer*. Frankfurt/Main: Fischer Taschenbuch Verlag, 2001.

Burns, Jimmy. *La Roja: A Journey through Spanish Football*. London: Simon & Schuster, 2012.

Butterworth, Michael L., ed. *Sport and Militarism*. New York: Routledge, 2017.

Caute, David. *The Dancer Defects: The Struggle for Cultural Supremacy during the Cold War*. Oxford: Oxford University Press, 2003.

Chu, Marcus. *Sporting Events in China as Economic Development, National Image, and Political Ambition*. Cham: Springer, 2021.

Cleveland, Todd. *Following the Ball: The Migration of African Soccer Players across the Portuguese Colonial Empire, 1949–1975*. Athens: Ohio University Press, 2017.

Cooney, John. *John Charles McQuaid: Ruler of Catholic Ireland*. Dublin: O'Brien Press, 1999.

Dichter, Heather, ed. *Soccer Diplomacy: International Relations and Football Diplomacy since 1914*. Lexington: University of Kentucky Press, 2020.

Dougan, Andy. *Dynamo: Defending the Honour of Kiev*. London: Fourth Estate, 2001.

Downing, David. *Passovotchka: Moscow Dynamo in Britain, 1945*. London: Bloomsbury, 1999.

Dunphy, Eamon. *The Rocky Road*. London: Penguin, 2014.

Edelman, Robert. *Serious Fun: A History of Spectator Sport in the USSR*. Oxford: Oxford University Press, 1993.

Edelman, Robert. *Spartak Moscow: A History of the People's Team in the Workers' State*. Ithaca, NY: Cornell University Press, 2009.

Edelman, Robert and Christopher Young, eds. *The Whole World Was Watching: Sport in the Cold War*. Stanford, CA: Stanford University Press, 2020.

Elsey, Brenda. *Citizens and Sportsmen: Futbol and Politics in 20th-Century Chile*. Austin: University of Texas Press, 2011.

Erenberg, Lewis A. *The Rumble in the Jungle: Muhammad Ali and George Foreman on the Global Stage*. Chicago: University of Chicago Press, 2019.

Ewald, Manfred. *Ich war der Sport*. Berlin: Elefanten Press, 1994.

Faje, Florin. 'Romania', in *The Palgrave International Handbook of Football and Politics*, edited by Jean-Michel De Waele, Suzan Gibril, Ekaterina Gloriozova and Ramón Spaaij, pp. 245–264. Cham: Palgrave Macmillan, 2018.

Foot, John. *Calcio: A History of Italian Football*. London: Harper Perennial, 2008.

Gallagher, Tom. *Salazar: The Dictator Who Refused to Die*. London: Hurst, 2020.

Giles, John. *A Football Man: The Autobiography*. London: Hodder and Stoughton, 2010.

Glanville, Brian. *Arsenal*. London: Convoy, 1952.

Goldblatt, David. *The Ball Is Round: A Global History of Football*. London: Penguin, 2007.

Goldblatt, David. *The Age of Football: The Global Game in the Twenty-First Century*. London: Picador, 2019.

Grass, Günter. *My Century*. Trans. Michael Henry Heim. New York: Harcourt, 1999.

Gröschner, Annett. *Sieben Tränen muß ein Club-Fan weinen: 1. FC Magdeburg – eine Fußballegende*. Leipzig: Gustav Kiepenhauer, 1999.

Havemann, Nils. *Fussball unterm Hakenkreuz*. Frankfurt/Main: Campus Verlag, 2005.

Havemann, Nils. *Samstags um Halb 4: Die Geschichte der Fußballbundesliga*. Munich: Siedler, 2013.

Hawkey, Ian. *Feet of the Chameleon*. London: Portico, 2010.

Hesse-Lichtenberger, Ulrich. *Tor! The Story of German Football*. London: WSC Books, 2002.

Hong, Fan and J. A. Mangan, eds. *Soccer, Women, Sexual Liberation: Kicking Off a New Era*. London: Frank Cass, 2004.

Horn, Michael and Gottfried Weise. *Das große Lexikon des DDR-Fußballs*. Berlin: Schwarzkopf & Schwarzkopf, 2004.

Hughson, John. *England and the 1966 World Cup: A Cultural History*. Manchester: Manchester University Press, 2016.

Jones, Stephen G. *Workers at Play: A Social and Economic History of Leisure, 1918–1939*. London: Routledge, 2019.

Joy, Bernard. *Forward, Arsenal!* London: Phoenix House, 1952.

Kittleson, Roger. *The Country of Sport: Soccer and the Making of Modern Brazil*. Berkeley: University of California Press, 2014.

Kuper, Simon. *Football against the Enemy*. London: Orion, 1994.

Lanfranchi, Pierre and Matthew Taylor. *Moving with the Ball: The Migration of Professional Footballers*. London: Berg, 2001.

Leffler, Melvyn P. and Odd Arne Westad, eds. *The Cambridge History of the Cold War, Volume II: Crises and Détente*. Cambridge: Cambridge University Press, 2010.

Leske, Hanns. *Erich Mielke, die Stasi und das runde Leder: Der Einfluß der SED und des Ministeriums für Staatssicherheit auf dem Fußballsport in der DDR*. Göttingen: Verlag die Werkstatt, 2004.

Leske, Hanns. *Enzyklopädie des DDR-Fußballs*. Göttingen: Verlag die Werkstatt, 2007.

Lisi, Clemente A. *The U.S. Women's Soccer Team: An American Success Story*. Lanham, MD: Scarecrow, 2010.

Macpherson, Archie. *Flower of Scotland: A Scottish Football Odyssey*. Newbury: Highdown, 2005.

Matthews, Stanley. *Feet First*. London: Ewen and Dale, 1952.

McDougall, Alan. *The People's Game: Football, State and Society in East Germany*. Cambridge: Cambridge University Press, 2014.

Mills, Richard. *The Politics of Football in Yugoslavia: Sport, Nationalism and the State*. London: I. B. Tauris, 2018.

Niebuhr, Robert. *The Search for a Cold War Legitimacy: Foreign Policy and Tito's Yugoslavia*. Leiden: Brill, 2018.

Nzongola-Ntalaja, Georges. *The Congo from Leopold to Kabila: A People's History*. New York: Zed Books, 2007.

O'Brien, Jim. 'In the shadow of the state: The national team and the politics of national identity in Spain', in *Football and the Boundaries of History: Critical Studies in Soccer*, edited by Brenda Elsey and Stanislao G. Pugliese, pp. 73–97. New York: Palgrave Macmillan, 2017.

O'Halpin, Eunan. *Defending Ireland: The Irish State and Its Enemies since 1922*. Oxford: Oxford University Press, 1999.

Olaru, Stejărel. *Nadia Comăneci and the Secret Police: A Cold War Escape*. Trans. Alistair Ian Blyth. London: Bloomsbury Academic, 2023.

Oswald, Rudolf. 'Das "Wunder von Bern" und die deutsche Fußball-Volksgemeinschaft 1954', in *Auswärtige Repräsentationen: Deutsche Kulturdiplomatie nach 1945*, edited by Johannes Paulmann, pp. 87–103. Cologne: Böhlau, 2005.

Parks, Jenifer. *The Olympic Games, the Soviet Sports Bureaucracy, and the Cold War: Red Sport, Red Tape*. Lanham, MD: Lexington Books, 2017.

Péter, László. *Forbidden Football in Ceausescu's Romania*. Cham: Palgrave Macmillan, 2018.

Pieper, Lindsay Parks. *Sex Testing: Gender Policing in Women's Sports*. Champaign: University of Illinois Press, 2016.

Poenaru, Florin. 'Power at play: Soccer stadiums and popular culture in 1980s Romania', in *Socialist Escapes: Breaking Away from Ideology and Everyday Routine in Eastern Europe, 1945–1989*, edited by Catherine M. Giustino, Catherine J. Plum and Alexander Vari, pp. 232–251. New York and Oxford: Berghahn, 2013.

Popa, Bogdan and Pompiliu-Nicolae Constantin. 'Football economy in Romania: Breaking away from socialism, facing capitalism', in *The Political Economy of European Football: Perspectives from Central and Eastern Europe*, edited by Dariusz Wojtaszyn, Daniel Fitzpatrick and Roland Benedikter, pp. 94–108. London & New York: Routledge, 2025.

Quiroga, Alejandro. *Football and National Identities in Spain: The Strange Death of Don Quixote*. Basingstoke: Palgrave Macmillan, 2013.

Rinke, Stefan and Kay Schiller, eds. *The FIFA World Cup 1930–2010: Politics, Commerce, Spectacle and Identities*. Göttingen: Wallstein Verlag, 2014.

Rous, Stanley. *Football Worlds: A Lifetime in Sports*. London: Faber, 1976.

Rouse, Paul. *Sport and Ireland: A History*. Oxford: Oxford University Press, 2015.

Schatzberg, Michael G. *Mobutu or Chaos? The United States and Zaire, 1960–1990*. Lanham, MD: University Press of America, 1991.

Schiller, Kay. *WM 74: Als der Fußball modern wurde*. Berlin: Rotbuch Verlag, 2014.

Simón, Juan Antonio. *Football and International Relations under Francoism, 1937–1975*. Abingdon: Routledge, 2025.

Skogvang, Bente Ovedie. 'Breaking barriers in Norwegian women's football', in *Football in the Nordic Countries: Practices, Equality and Influence*, edited by Mihaly Szerovay, Arto Nevala and Hannu Itkonen, pp. 150–162. Abingdon: Routledge, 2023.

Tomlinson, Alan and Christopher Young, eds. *German Football: History, Culture, Society*. London: Routledge, 2006.

Tomlinson, Alan and Christopher Young, eds. *National Identity and Global Sports Events*. Albany: State University of New York Press, 2006.

Vonnard, Philippe. *Creating a United Europe of Football: The Formation of UEFA (1949–1961)*. Cham: Springer, 2020.

Wagg, Michael. *The Turning Season: DDR-Oberliga Revisited*. Chichester: Pitch, 2021.

Walter, Fritz. *11 Rote Jäger – Nationalspieler im Kriege*. Munich: Copress, 1959.

Walter, Fritz. *3:2. Das Spiel ist aus! Deutschland ist Weltmeister!* Munich: Copress, 2004.

Westad, Odd Arne. *The Global Cold War*. Cambridge: Cambridge University Press, 2007.

Westad, Odd Arne. *The Cold War: A World History*. London: Penguin, 2017.

Williams, Jean. *A Beautiful Game: International Perspectives on Women's Football*. Oxford: Berg, 2007.

Wilson, Jonathan. *Behind the Curtain: Travels in Eastern European Football*. London: Orion, 2006.

Wilson, Jonathan. *Anatomy of England*. London: Orion, 2010.

Wilson, Jonathan. *Angels with Dirty Faces: The Footballing History of Argentina*. London: Orion, 2016.

Wilson, Jonathan. *Inverting the Pyramid: The History of Football Tactics*. London: Weidenfeld and Nicolson, 2018.

Wilson, Jonathan. *The Names Heard Long Ago: How the Golden Age of Hungarian Soccer Shaped the Modern Game*. New York: Bold Type, 2019.

Wittich, Elke, ed. *Wo waren Sie, als das Sparwasser-Tor fiel?* Hamburg: Konkret Literatur Verlag, 1998.

Wrack, Suzanne. *A Woman's Game: The Rise, Fall, and Rise Again of Women's Football*. London: Guardian Faber, 2022.

INDEX

Page numbers in *italics* refer to content in figures.

Printed by Integrated Books International,
United States of America